PageMaker® 4

An Active–Learning Approach

for Macintosh and PC versions of PageMaker 4

Tony Waters

Tony Waters is a Lecturer in Computing at The Sheffield College. As well as commercial experience in desk top publishing and computing he has taught IT and DTP skills at a variety of levels.

DP PUBLICATIONS LIMITED
Aldine Place
142 / 144 Uxbridge Road
London W12 8AW
1993

Acknowledgements

My thanks to the following:

Annie Ostapenko and Di Burgess for their time and patience while trying out this book. Their comments, criticisms and wit were invaluable.
Paul Delmar and Charlie Varley for their assistance with the PC graphics.
Technicians at The Sheffield College, Mawse, Dermot and Richard.
My students for their questions and insights.

Acknowledgements to Terry and Helen for teaching me most of what I know about the value of education.

ISBN 1 85805 065 0

A complete list of trademarks appears in Appendix 2.

Typeset by the author using PageMaker

Printed by The Guernsey Press Co. Ltd, Braye Road, Vale, Guernsey

Preface

Who should use this book

This book is aimed at students on a wide variety of courses who want to know how to use Macintosh or PC versions of PageMaker 4 (4.0, 4.1 and 4.2). The learning material requires minimal, if any, input by lecturers and can be used for student self–instruction. It makes no assumption about publishing knowledge, but teaches PageMaker techniques and their applications in easy to understand language. Where publishing jargon is used the meaning is explained in layperson's terms. All students can successfully use this book — from those needing only a grasp of the basics of desk top publishing with PageMaker to those needing to utilise PageMaker's advanced facilities. New features are progressively introduced in the context of practical activities and examples.

What this book is not

It is not the purpose of this book to cover all the facilities offered by PageMaker 4 and explain them in detail. To do this would take a document much larger than this one and would call for a different approach to the methods used in the following pages. This book is not an installation guide — it assumes you have a standard version of PageMaker 4 fully installed on your computer. Neither is it a training guide in using the Macintosh operating system or Windows for the PC. There are many good, easy to follow books available for these purposes. This book is also not a reference manual for PageMaker (although it can be used to refer back on activities previously completed as an aid to learning).

What this book is

The function of this book is to cover the essentials of desk top publishing with PageMaker 4 and to get the student producing high quality, professional documents. This book is designed to give students the skills and knowledge to:

- produce single and multiple–page documents
- combine text and graphics on a page
- add repeating items to a document (like headers, footers and page numbers)
- draw boxes and lines
- use pre–defined styles to speed up production
- use advanced techniques of document production to improve presentation
- set up contents and index pages automatically

The structure of this book

This book is divided into three main sections:

Section 1 covers the basics of creating a single–page document including setting up a page, adding 'guides' to help line up elements on a page, and placing text, lines and boxes onto a page.

Section 2 moves on to producing multiple–page documents and introduces further PageMaker techniques including adding graphics and using 'master pages' for repeating items.

Section 3 looks at applying pre–defined 'styles' to text and many of the advanced techniques used in document production. This section also deals with automatically setting up a contents page and an index.

How to use this book

This book uses activity–based learning or 'learning by doing'. Each activity is designed to be followed methodically so be careful not to jump between activities or omit activities as each one builds on previously gained skills and knowledge.

An activity consists of three main parts:

Objectives — which state what the activity is designed to help you achieve. You can think of each objective as being prefixed by the words 'After this activity I should be able to ...'.

Introduction — which explains what the activity will do and supplies any background information you may need.

Guided activity — is a step–by–step set of instructions to be followed which help achieve the stated objectives of the activity.

In addition there may be an...

Independent activity — to give more practice in the area you have just covered. These should not be missed out as the following 'Guided activity' may depend on completion of the previous 'Independent activity'.

The activities are grouped into chapters which serve to perform a general function. For example, the first chapter in section 1 deals with setting up a single–page document and consists of seven activities which facilitate this.

At the end of each chapter there is an **End of chapter summary** highlighting the main techniques covered followed by a list of common problems and their solutions under the title **Trouble–shooting**.

At the end of each section there are a number of **Additional exercises** to consolidate the material covered in that section. These are optional and may be omitted if the student feels confident with the material covered.

Terminology

There are a number of techniques used in this book to make following the material easier.

• some of the text in the 'Guided activities' is in bold — **this indicates something you should actually do (like pressing a key or moving the mouse)**. The plain text around it explains why you are doing it and what happens when you have done it.

• a word in square brackets (like [File]) refers to one of the options on the menu bar at the top of the PageMaker screen.

• the letters 'PC' above a word indicates that PC users of PageMaker should take note of the text below (enclosed by lines). For example,

PageMaker starts a document on the page shown in the 'Start page #' box ('#' is an abbreviation for 'number'). In this case we want to begin on the first page.
Move the pointer so that it is just after the number in this box[PC] (see (a) below) **and 'click' the mouse button.**
There should now be a flashing vertical line, the 'cursor', after the number (see (b) below).

PC users will find that the pointer changes to a 'I' — the text tool — as it moves over the box

Macintosh users can ignore the text enclosed by lines.

• where a separate description is needed for PC and Macintosh users the activity is split into part A (for Macintosh users) and part B (for PC users). This will be made clear when it arises.

• when a full explanation of desk top publishing jargon is needed a box like the one shown below is included. These do not form part of the main activities but serve to give the reader an understanding of some common terminology as it arises.

Orientation

A pages orientation can either be 'Tall' (also known as 'Portrait') or 'Wide' (also known as 'Landscape').

Tall or Portrait

Wide or Landscape

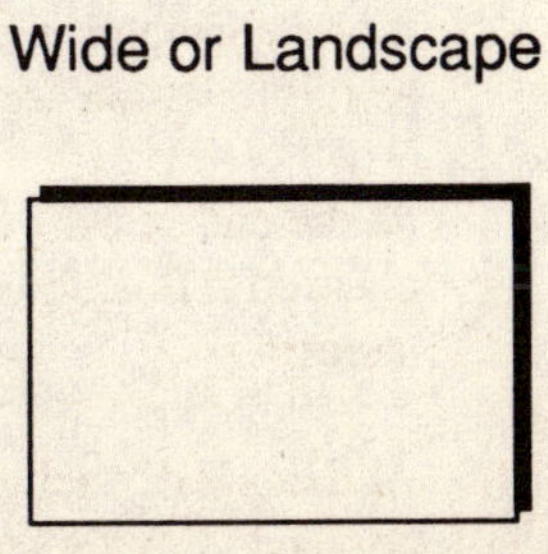

Differences between Macintosh and PC versions of PageMaker 4

Essentially, for the person using the package, there are few differences between Macintosh and PC versions of PageMaker 4. The discrepancies which do occur are mainly to do with file handling — Macintosh and PC computers use a different system of operating and as such handle files in a different way. Once you are familiar with one of these versions of PageMaker 4 it is likely that you will have little, if any, trouble using the other.

The dialogue boxes in Macintosh and PC versions of PageMaker differ in very slight ways. Throughout this book it is generally Macintosh screens which are used for diagrams — because the different versions differ in small ways only it is anticipated that PC users will have no problems with this.

And finally

PageMaker is a powerful and versatile desk top publisher. This versatility can sometimes cause problems to the learner (and to the author trying to explain how it all works!) The crux of these problems is that, because of the versatility of the package, there may be slight differences between PageMaker 4 on one computer and PageMaker 4 on another computer. For example, PageMaker may allow you to use a particular type of lettering (or 'font') on one computer and not have it available on another computer. The same 'font' may also be called by different names on different machines or its name may be abbreviated. Try not to be too put off by this. Every care has been taken to foresee such potential problems but, should the unexpected happen, patience and a little common sense should see you through.

As a final note, the greatest aid to learning is the desire to discover — so be willing to experiment! If you are unsure about a particular explanation or function use the knowledge you have already attained to try a few things out. If all goes wrong you can always start again.

Free lecturers' supplement

A disc is available containing all the files needed to create the documents shown in the following pages. The disc is free for lecturers who wish to adopt this book as a course text and can be obtained by writing to the publishers, stating which format (Macintosh or PC) is required.

Contents

Preface iii

Getting started x

Section 1 1

Chapter 1 — Preparing a single–page document 5

Using the menus —Macintosh 6
Using the menus —PC 8
Setting up a page 11
Setting up the PageMaker window 14
Adding column guides 16
Additional guides 17
Saving a document —Macintosh 19
Saving a document —PC 21
Leaving PageMaker 22
Opening a document —Macintosh 23
Opening a document —PC 24
End of chapter summary 26
Trouble-shooting 26

Chapter 2 — Entering text 27

Entering text on a word processor 28
Using the Story editor 28
End of chapter summary 30
Trouble-shooting 30

Chapter 3 — Working with blocks of text 31

Placing text into columns 32
Changing the page view 35
Removing text blocks 37
Flowing text across columns 38
Moving guides 41
Moving text blocks 42
Changing the length of text blocks 43
Changing the text of a story 45
Abandoning a document 49
PageMaker shortcuts 49
End of chapter summary 50
Trouble–shooting 50

Chapter 4 — Working with small pieces of text 51

Entering small pieces of text 52
Moving text onto a page 54
Centring text 56
Changing text 58
End of chapter summary 60
Trouble–shooting 60

Chapter 5 — Lines and boxes 61

Adding a line 62
Moving and stretching a line 63
Adding a box 64
Changing the shape of a box 65
Printing a document 66
End of chapter summary 68
Trouble–shooting 68

Additional exercises 69

Section 2 79

Chapter 1 — Preparing a multiple–page document 83

Setting up pages 84
Adding repeating guides 87
Additional guides 89
Adding 'headers' and 'footers' 91
Page numbers 93
'Hiding' master page items 95
End of chapter summary 96
Trouble–shooting 96

Chapter 2 — Working with graphics 97

Where to get graphics from 98
Adding and 'cropping' a graphic 99
Moving and 'scaling' a graphic 103
End of chapter summary 106
Trouble–shooting 106

Chapter 3 — Ways with text 107

Changing text in text blocks 108
Changing 'leading' 110
'Tracking' and 'Width' 111
Special effects with 'Width' 113
End of chapter summary 116
Trouble–shooting 116

Chapter 4 — Working with paragraphs 117

Type specifications 118
Paragraph specifications 120
Indents and Tabs 121
Hyphenation 122
End of chapter summary 124
Trouble–shooting 124

Additional exercises 125

Section 3 133

Chapter 1 — Pre–defined styles 137

Using pre–defined styles 138
Adding new styles 139
Changing an existing style 142
Removing styles 143
Working with 'tags' 144
End of chapter summary 145
Trouble-shooting 145

Chapter 2 — Advanced techniques 147

Rotating text 148
Moving column guides 150
Drop capitals 152
Text wrap 155
Layers 158
Selecting multiple–items 160
End of chapter summary 164
Trouble–shooting 164

Chapter 3 — Creating a table of contents 165

Including items in a table of contents 166
Creating a table of contents 167
End of chapter summary 170
Trouble–shooting 170

Chapter 4 — Creating a simple index 171

Creating an index entry 172
Creating an index 173
End of chapter summary 174
Trouble–shooting 174

Additional exercises 175

Appendices 189

Index 195

Getting started

It is assumed that the student is familiar enough with the environment they are working in to start PageMaker. For completeness a brief summary of the process is included below.

Macintosh users

If the PageMaker program was held in a folder called 'PageMaker 4.0' on the hard disc then to start PageMaker you would:

- Click twice in quick succession (double–click) on the 'hard disc' icon
- Locate the folder 'PageMaker 4.0' in the window which appears and double–click on this
- Locate the file 'PageMaker' in this new window and double–click to start the application

PC users

If the PageMaker program was held in a window (assuming PageMaker is being run under 'Windows') named 'Aldus' then to start PageMaker you would:

- Start 'Windows' and locate the window 'Aldus' (within the 'Program Manager' window)
- If this window is not already 'open' then click twice in quick succession (double–click) to open it
- Locate the 'PageMaker' icon and double–click to start the application

Section 1

- preparing a single–page document
- entering text
- working with blocks of text
- working with small pieces of text
- lines and boxes

Introduction to section 1

In this first section we will be covering many of the basic functions of PageMaker and also creating our first sample document. The creation of this document is broken down into a number of stages — covered by the chapters shown below.

Chapter 1 — Preparing a single–page document

This chapter shows you how to specify the page attributes (size, way up, etc.) and add 'guides' to help place text accurately onto a page.

Chapter 2 — Entering text

The main text in the examples in this book should be typed in using a word processor or PageMaker's own 'built in' word processor. This chapter leads you through the process of entering such text.

Chapter 3 — Working with blocks of text

This chapter explains how to position the text prepared in chapter 2 onto a page and how to move it from one place to another.

Chapter 4 — Working with small pieces of text

Shows how you can type smaller pieces of text directly into PageMaker and add them to the page.

Chapter 5 — Lines and boxes

Covers adding lines and boxes to documents to improve their presentation.

Documents created in this section

In this section you will be creating the A4 sized notice shown below, advertising a forthcoming talk on desk top publishing.

You are invited to a talk on

The impact of desk top publishing on the 'person in the street'

A talk by Professor C Package on the impact of desk top publishing on the process of creating documents. The talk begins with a look at the history of publishing and the major dramatic changes in these processes. Questions will be welcomed from the audience in the second part of the talk which consists of a discussion on how publishing will change in the future.

Professor Package is a well known figure in desk top publishing having written a number of books on the subject - amoung them being 'Desk top publishing for children' and 'Life, the universe, and desk top publishing'.

Future events are planned to continue from this talk where visitors will get the opportunity for 'hands on' experience of some of the more well known desk top publishing packages. Anyone interested in participating in these events should write to the address shown below. Book early to avoid disappointment.

Start time : 7.30pm
Finish time : 9.30pm
on 1st April
at
The Community Centre
45 Publishing Road
Topsmoor
Sheffield

Chapter 1

Preparing a single–page document

- using the menus
- setting up a page
- setting up the PageMaker window
- adding column guides
- additional guides
- saving a document
- leaving PageMaker
- opening a document

Introduction to chapter 1

The earliest stages of document production are often the most important. To get good, high quality documents it is well worth doing a little preparation in advance. This chapter goes through the stages of preparing a single–page document for the addition of text and graphics.

Activity 1a

Using the menus — Macintosh

Objectives

1. To use the PageMaker menus

Introduction

In this first activity we will see how to select items from the PageMaker menus. PC users of PageMaker can skip this and go straight to activity 1b.

Guided activity

1. Once PageMaker has been fully started (see 'Getting started') the screen should have a row of seven words along the very top — the 'menu bar'. Each of these words holds a hidden menu. **Using the mouse, move the pointer over the first of these words, [File], and hold down the mouse button.**
A menu should appear under the word [File] giving a list of different options (figure 1a.1a). Don't worry if these seem fairly meaningless at the moment — we will deal with each one as it arises. Some of the options are in light text — this means they are not currently available for selection. If the menu does not stay on the screen it means the mouse button has been released or the pointer is no longer over the word [File]. Just point again and keep the button held down.
You have just displayed the contents of the [File] menu.

2. **With the mouse button still held down, move to the menu option 'Page setup'.**
Notice how this word becomes 'highlighted' (turns to page coloured text on a text coloured background) as you move to it (figure 1a.1b).

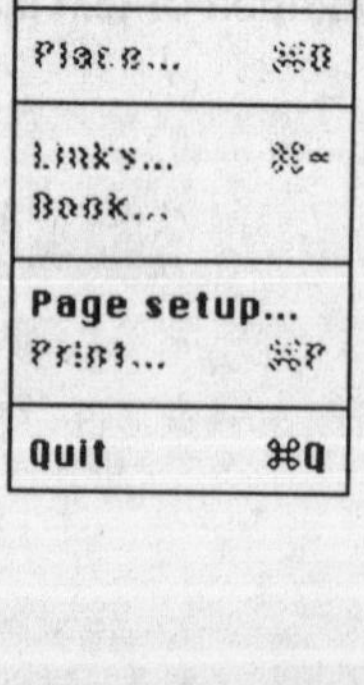

Figure 1a.1a

Figure 1a.1b

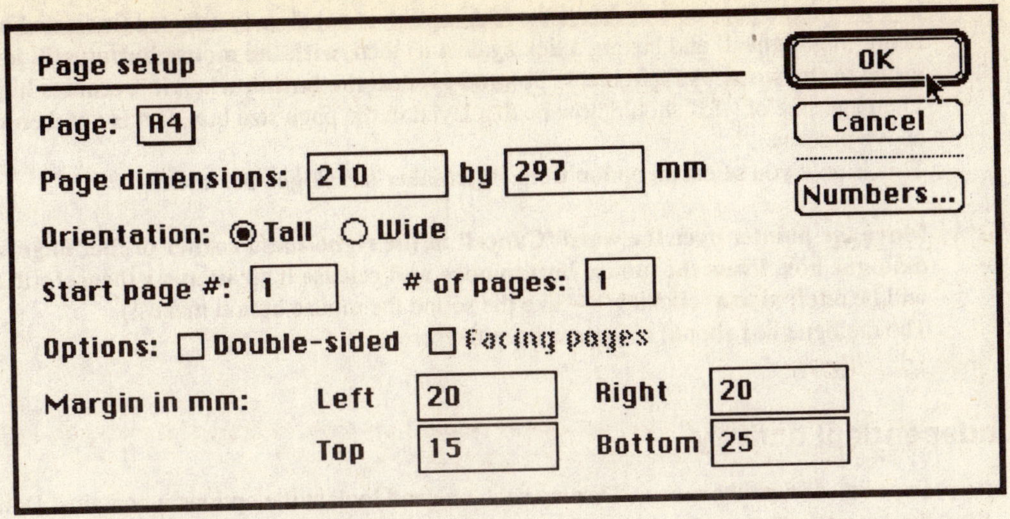

Figure 1a.2

3. **With the pointer still over the 'Page setup' option, release the mouse button.**
This is how you select an option from a PageMaker menu. You have just selected the 'Page setup' option from the [File] menu.
The 'Page setup' option tells PageMaker you want to describe some details about the page you will be using. PageMaker brings a 'Page setup' box for you to tell it these details. This box should now have appeared on your screen (figure 1a.2).
The box before you is known as a 'dialogue box'. PageMaker often displays dialogue boxes to get detailed information on various things.

4. Near the top of the dialogue box is the word 'Page' with the current page size in a box next to it. The box holding the current page size has a 'shadow' behind it. This indicates there is a hidden menu here.
Move the pointer over the small box next to the words 'Page' and, with the pointer located in the middle of this box, hold down the mouse button.
Another menu should appear giving a list of standard page sizes (figure 1a.3a). This is one of PageMaker's 'dialogue box' menus.

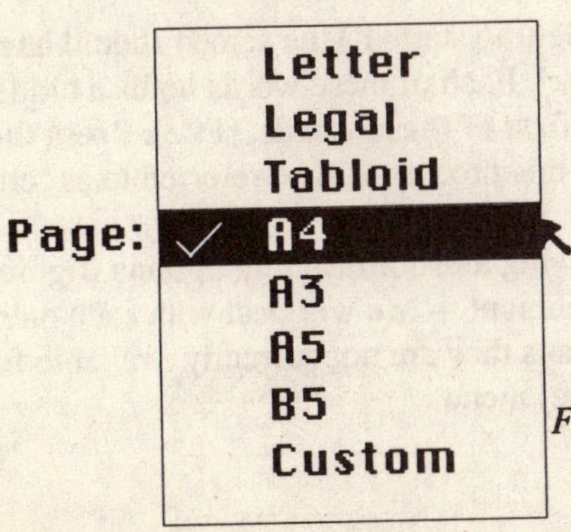

Figure 1a.3a

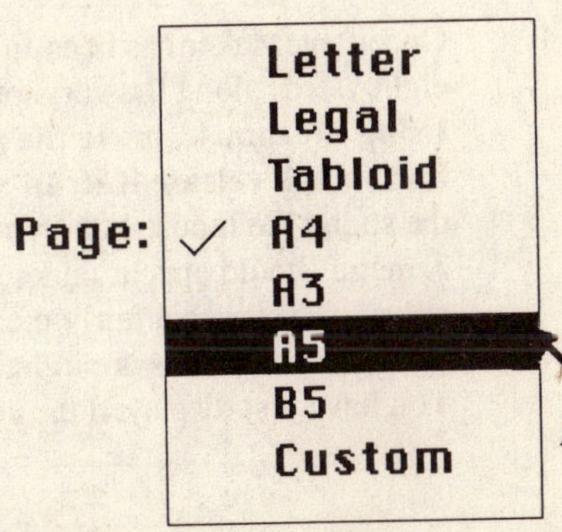

Figure 1a.3b

5. Say we want a page size of A5. If the 'A5' option is not already selected (indicated by that option being 'highlighted' and having a tick against it) then, **with the mouse button still held down, move to the word 'A5'** (figure 1a.3b) **and release the button when it becomes highlighted.** The page size of 'A5' should now be displayed in the page size box. If it is not then repeat the above process.
This is how you select an option from PageMaker's dialogue box menus.

6. **Move the pointer over the word 'Cancel' in the right–hand corner of the 'Page setup' dialogue box. Press the mouse button once and release it strait away** (henceforth this process will be referred to a 'clicking' — like the sound the mouse button makes!)
The dialogue box should disappear from the screen.

Independent activity

1. Experiment with the menus. Display each one and look at the options it contains. Don't worry if they seem fairly meaningless at the moment — they will become more meaningful as you progress through this book.

Activity 1 b

Using the menus — PC

Objectives

1. To use the PageMaker menus

Introduction

In this first exercise we will see how to select items from the menus. Macintosh users should skip this activity.

Guided activity

1. Once PageMaker has been fully started (see 'Getting started') the screen should have a row of eight words along the very top — the 'menu bar'. Each of these words holds a hidden menu. **Using the mouse, move the pointer over the first of these words, [File]. Press the mouse button and release it strait away** (henceforth this process will be referred to as 'clicking' — like the sound the mouse button makes!)
A menu should appear under the word [File] giving a list of different options (figure 1b.1a). Don't worry if these seem fairly meaningless at the moment — we will deal with each one as it arises. Some of the options are in light text — this means they are not currently available for selection. You have just displayed the contents of the [File] menu.

2. **Move away from the menu, over the space below or at the side of it, and 'click' the mouse button.**
The menu should disappear.

3. **Display the [File] menu again** (move the pointer over the word [File] and click the mouse button).

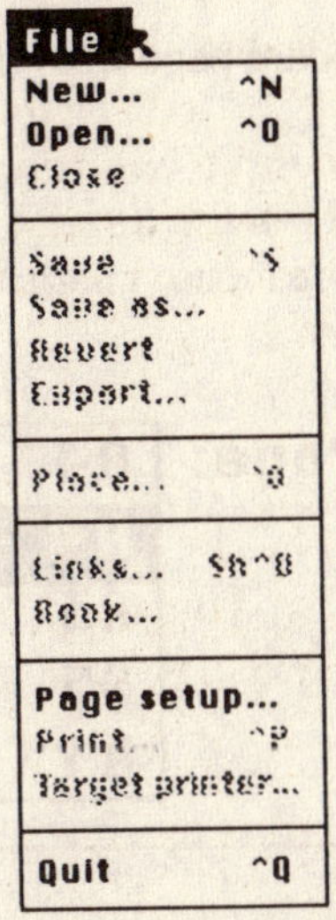

Figure 1b.1a

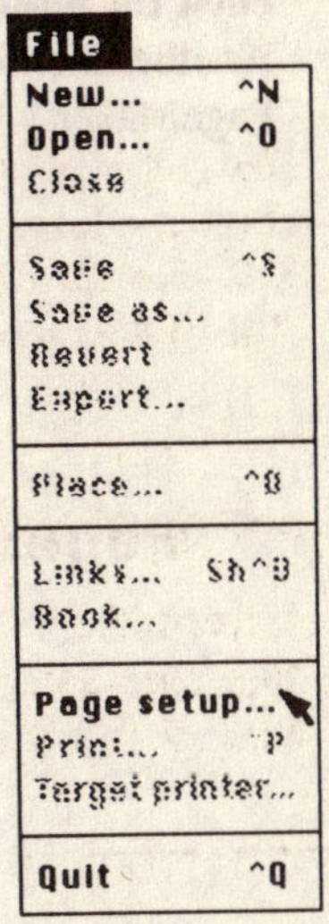

Figure 1b.1b

4. **Move the pointer over the menu option 'Page setup' and click the mouse button** (figure 1b.1b).
This is how you select an option from a PageMaker menu. You have just selected the 'Page setup' option from the [File] menu.
The 'Page setup' option tells PageMaker you want to describe some details about the page you will be using. PageMaker brings a 'Page setup' box for you to tell it these details. This box should now have appeared on your screen (figure 1b.2).
The box before you is known as a 'dialogue box'. PageMaker often displays dialogue boxes to get detailed information on various things.

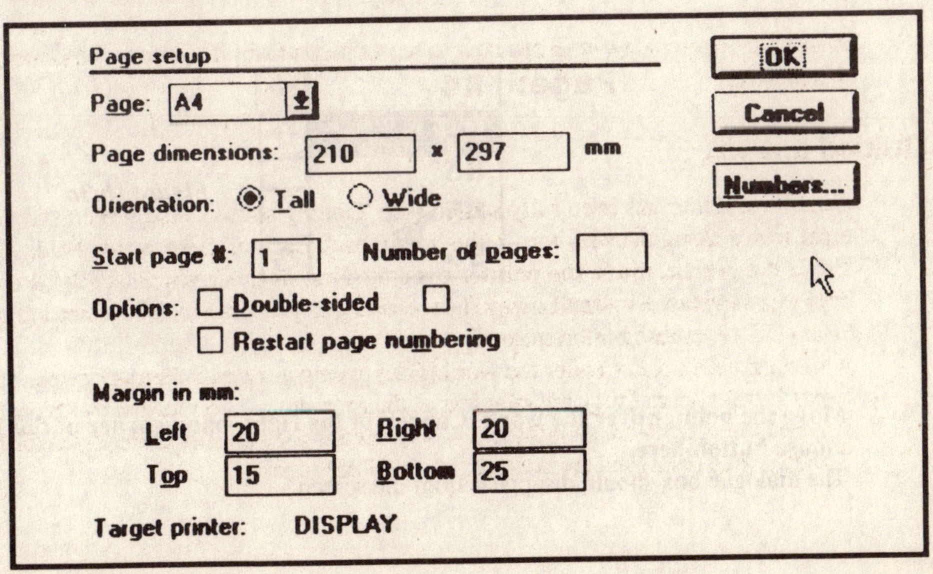

Figure 1b.2

5. Near the top of the dialogue box is the word 'Page' with the current page size in a box next to it. At the side of the box holding the current page size there is a downward pointing arrow. This indicates there is a hidden menu here.
Move the pointer over the downward pointing arrow next to the page size (figure 1b.3a) **and click the mouse button.**
Another menu should appear giving a list of standard page sizes (figure 1b.3b). This is one of PageMaker's 'dialogue box' menus.

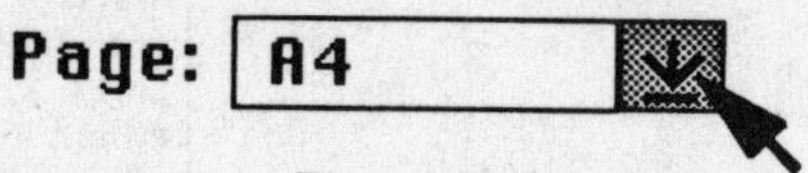

Figure 1b.3a

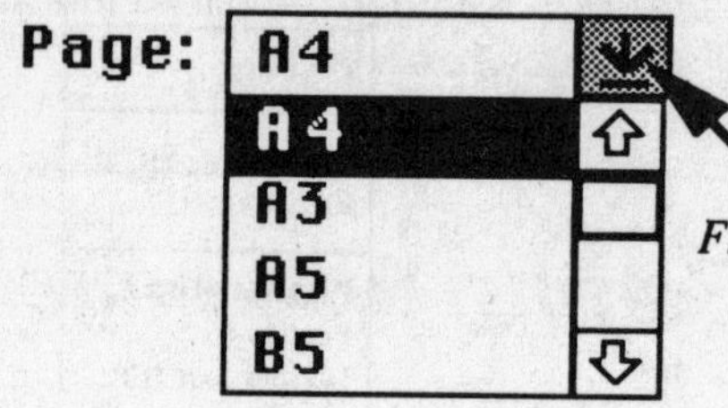

Figure 1b.3b

6. Say we want a page size of A5. If the 'A5' option is not already selected (indicated by that option being 'highlighted') then, **move over the word 'A5'** (figure 1b.3c) **and click the mouse button.**
The page size of 'A5' should now be displayed in the page size box. If it is not then repeat the above process.
This is how you select an option from PageMaker's dialogue box menus.

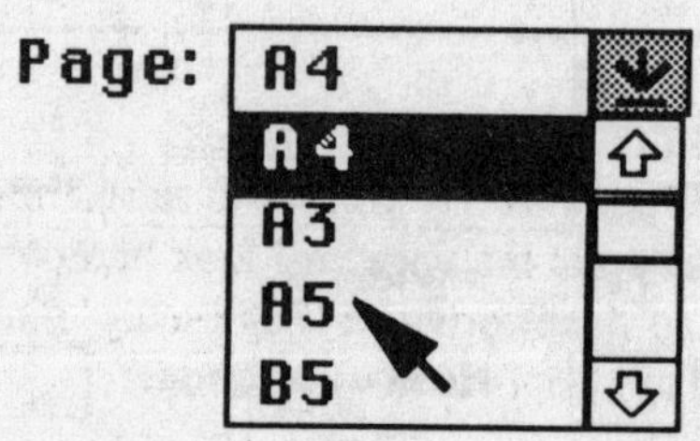

Figure 1b.3c

7. **Move the pointer over the word 'Cancel' in the right–hand corner of this box. Click the mouse button here.**
The dialogue box should disappear from the screen.

Independent activity

1. When Making a new page PageMaker works with a particular printer in mind. PC users need to ensure PageMaker is targeted to the correct printer before they start to lay out their documents. Display the [File] menu and select the 'Target printer' option. When the dialogue box appears select the printer you will be using by clicking over its name and then clicking over 'OK'. PageMaker may then ask you to confirm that you wish to recompose the publication for a different printer. Click over 'OK' again.

2. Experiment with the menus. Display each one and look at the options it contains. Don't worry if they seem fairly meaningless at the moment — they will become more meaningful as you progress through this book.

Activity 2

Setting up a page

Objectives

1. To start a new page
2. To tell PageMaker how a page should look

Introduction

The first step in preparing a document is to tell PageMaker some details about the page itself. PageMaker needs to know the size of the page, which way up it will be, etc.. This activity takes you through the process of using the 'Page setup' box to give these details.

Guided Activity

1. **Select the 'New' option from the [File] menu.**
   The 'New' option tells PageMaker you want to start a new page. Before it can do this it needs to know some details about what the page will look like (what size it will be, which way up, etc.). To get this information PageMaker brings a 'Page setup' dialogue box for you to fill in (figure 1a.2 / 1b.2). This should have now appeared.

2. We want a page size of A4. If the 'A4' option is not already selected then **select the 'A4' option from the hidden menu in the 'Page' box.**
   The page size of 'A4' should now be displayed in the 'Page' box. The 'Page dimensions' boxes, showing the dimensions of the page, should automatically contain the appropriate values for an A4 piece of paper.

3. PageMaker needs to know the orientation of the page, or, which way up the page should be. This is sometimes called portrait or landscape but PageMaker refers to it as ‘Tall’ or ‘Wide’.
Move the pointer so that it points just inside the small circle next to the ‘Tall’ option. Click the mouse button here.
If the black selection dot was not already in the ‘Tall’ circle then it should be now. A dot here indicates that a ‘tall’ or ‘portrait’ orientation is wanted.

4. PageMaker starts a document on the page shown in the ‘Start page #’ box (‘#’ is an abbreviation for ‘number’). In this case we want to begin on the first page.
Move the pointer so that it is just after the number in this box[PC] (see (a) below) **and ‘click’ the mouse button.**
There should now be a flashing vertical line, the ‘cursor’, after the number (see (b) below).

PC users will find that the pointer changes to a ‘ ’ — the text tool — as it moves over the box

---

(a)  (b) 

5. With the cursor inside the box **press the delete left key until the number it contains has been erased** (see (c) below). **Type in the new number, ‘1’** (see (d) below).

(c)  (d) 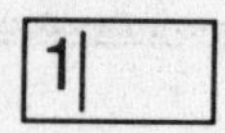

6. **If the ‘Number of pages’ box does not contain ‘1’** (since we want a single–page document) **then change this in the same way.**

7. A PageMaker document can be thought of as having a single side or two (double) sides, depending on how we want to use it. The first document we are producing uses only one side so, for simplicity, tell PageMaker you do not want a ‘Double–sided’ document. A cross in the small box next to the words ‘Double–sided’ indicates that two–sided pages are required, so, if this box contains a cross **move the pointer so that it points inside the ‘Double–sided’ box and click the mouse button.**
The box is now empty indicating it is not selected. The ‘Facing pages’ option next to ‘Double sided’ should now be grey or a different colour (indicating it cannot be selected) — this will be dealt with in a later chapter.

8. The four small boxes in the bottom of the dialogue box hold the page margin settings. **Move the pointer to just after the number in the ‘Left’ box and click the mouse button.**
The cursor should appear next to the number.

9. **Press the delete key until the number in the ‘Left’ box is erased.**
The measurements in this example are in millimetres. If the ‘Page setup’ box does not specify ‘Margins in mm’ then PageMaker is using a different system of measurement. We will change this in a later activity. For now, put ‘m’ after each of the following numbers to tell PageMaker they are in millimetres.

10. **Type in the number '20' instead** (or '20m' if PageMaker is not working in millimetres) **— don't** press the RETURN key!

11. **Repeat the above process for the 'Right', 'Top' and 'Bottom' boxes making their values '20', '15' and '25' respectively.**

12. The 'Page setup' dialogue box should now be ready.
Move the pointer over the word 'OK' in the top right–hand corner of the box. Click the mouse button here to tell PageMaker you are happy with the details.
A blank page should now appear.

Independent Activity

1. If you need to change any of the details in the 'Page setup' dialogue box it can be recalled by selecting the 'Page setup' option from the [File] menu.
Select this option and change the bottom margin to '20' mm.

Orientation

A page's orientation can either be 'tall' (also known as 'portrait') or 'wide' (also known as 'landscape').

Tall or Portrait

Wide or Landscape

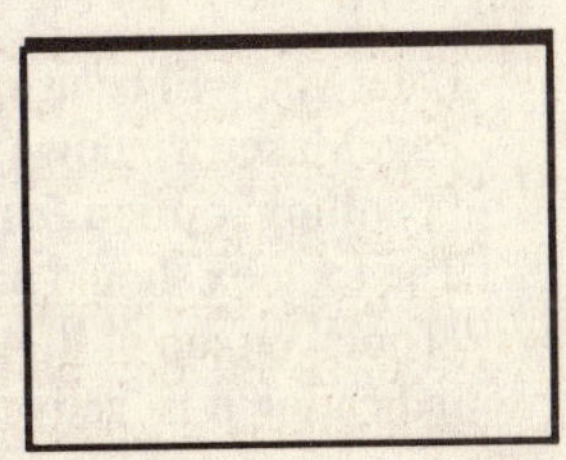

Activity 3

Setting up the PageMaker window

Objectives

1. To see the different elements PageMaker can have on its window
2. To add or remove these elements as required
3. To move around the desktop

Introduction

Because of the flexibility of PageMaker the window may contain many elements which we may or may not want on the screen at one time — depending on what we are doing. The screen should now consist of the menu bar at the top and the PageMaker 'window' beneath. This activity introduces you to the different elements the window may contain and the process of adding them to and removing them from the window as required.

Guided activity

1. **Display the [Options] menu.** When the menu appears look if there is a tick against the 'Guides' option. A tick here indicates that the guides are showing or 'active'.

2. If there is no tick against the 'Guides' option then **select this option.**
   If the guides were switched off they should now appear (in the form of dotted lines), showing the margins set in the 'Page setup' box. There is now a tick against the 'Guides' option — indicating it is 'active'.

3. Later you will be using the 'toolbox'. Make sure it is already displayed somewhere in the PageMaker window (figure 3.1). **If the toolbox is not in the PageMaker window then select the 'Toolbox' option from the [Window] menu** (in the usual way).
   The toolbox should now be somewhere in the PageMaker window with the word 'Toolbox' or 'Tools' on top of it. Again, there is now a tick against this option in the [Windows] menu — indicating it is 'active'.

4. It is helpful to be able to move around the desktop. This can be done using the 'scroll bars' (figure 3.1). Make sure they are switched on by checking there is a tick against this option in the [Window] menu. **If they are not then select this option.**

5. **Point inside the arrow box at the right–hand end of the horizontal scroll bar** (located at the bottom of the screen) **and click the mouse button.**
   The page should move slightly left as your view moves right across the desktop.

6. **Point in the arrow box at the left–hand end of the horizontal scroll bar and click the mouse button.**
   The page should move slightly right as your view moves left along the desktop.

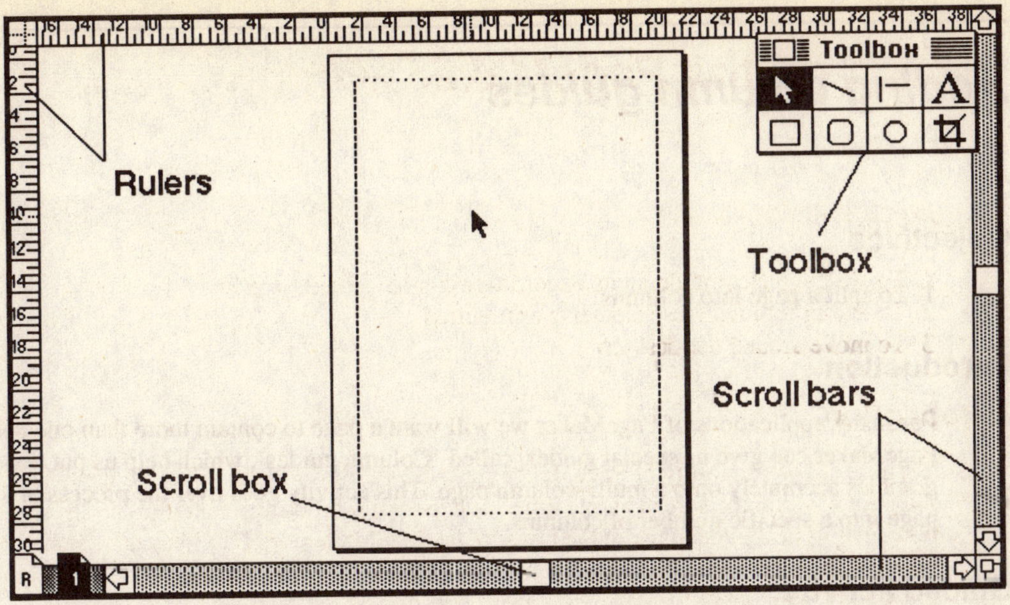

Figure 3.1

7. Do the same with the vertical scroll bar (located at the right–hand side of the screen). **Click inside the arrow boxes at the top and bottom of the scroll bar to move your view up and down the desktop.**

8. Make sure there are no unwanted elements on the window. Check that the 'Style pallet' option in the [Window] menu does not have a tick against it. **If it does then select this option** to make the 'Style palette' inactive.

9. **Repeat this process to ensure the 'Colour palette' is not selected.**

Independent activity

1. Practice switching the different PageMaker elements off and on. Make sure the window is left with the 'Scroll bars', 'Guides' and 'Toolbox' switched on. The other elements should be off.

2. The toolbox can sometimes get in the way of what you are doing. Practice moving it around the window. Hold down the mouse button with the pointer on the word 'Tools' or 'Toolbox' at the top of the toolbox. Keep it held down as you move the pointer, the toolbox should follow as long as the mouse button is depressed.

Activity 4

Adding column guides

Objectives

1. To split a page into columns

Introduction

For many applications of PageMaker we will want a page to contain more than one column. PageMaker can give us special guides, called 'Column guides', which help us put text and graphics accurately onto a multi–column page. This activity goes over the process of splitting up a page into a specific number of columns.

Guided activity

1. **Select the 'Column guides' option from the [Options] menu.**
   A dialogue box entitled 'Column guides' should appear on your screen (figure 4.1).

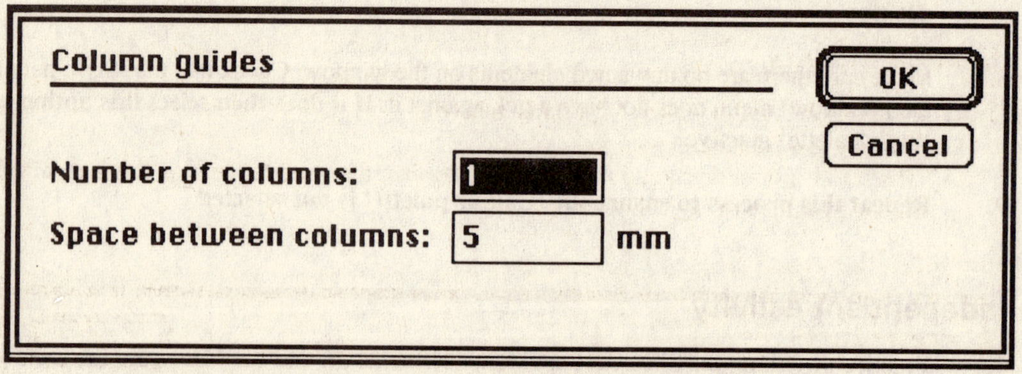

Figure 4.1

2. For this document we want to have two columns. **Move the pointer to just after the number in the 'Number of columns' box and click the mouse button.**
   The flashing cursor should appear in this box.

3. **Use the delete key to erase the number currently in this box. Type in the number '2' instead.**

4. We normally put space between the columns. If they are touching then the text in them will also touch and make the document difficult to read.
   Set the 'Space between columns' to 5mm in the usual way (just like before, put '5m' if you are not working in millimetres.)

5. **Click on the 'OK' box to tell PageMaker you have finished.**
   The page should now reappear. It should contain two columns of equal width.

Independent activity

1. Change the number of columns to 4. Then go back and select 2 columns, 5mm apart again.

Activity 5

Additional guides

Objectives

1. To add rulers to a page
2. To set measurements to a specific system
3. To get additional guides from the rulers

Introduction

In addition to the margin and column guides PageMaker allows the addition of further guides to assist when placing items onto a page. There are additional horizontal and vertical guides. In this activity we will try and place an additional guide onto the page.

Guided activity

1. First check that the 'Rulers' option is 'active'.
   Display the [Options] menu.
   The [Options] menu should appear. A tick against the word 'Rulers' in this menu indicates that the rulers are active or 'switched on'.

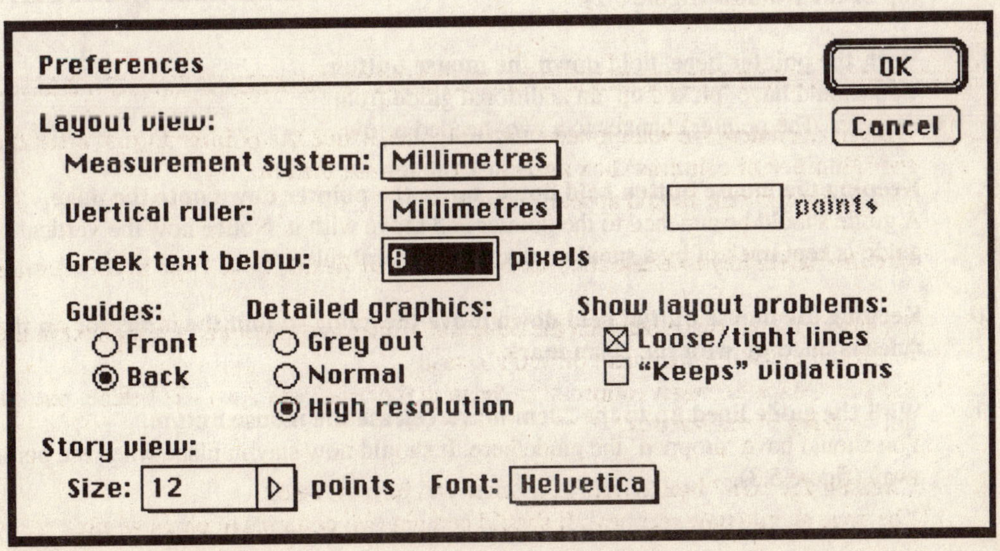

Figure 5.1

2. If 'Rulers' has no tick against it then **select this option from the menu.**
If the PageMaker window did not already have rulers then it should have them now (figure 3.1). They are used to measure elements on a page and to get additional guides.
In most of the examples in this book we will be measuring in centimetres and millimetres. Let's check that PageMaker is set to measure in this system.

3. **Select the 'Preferences' option from the [Edit] menu.**
A dialogue box entitled 'Preferences' should appear (figure 5.1).

4. If the box next to the words 'Measurement system' does not contain 'Millimetres' then **display the hidden menu it contains.**
A menu should appear giving a list of different systems of measurement.
Select the 'Millimetres' option in this menu.
The selection 'Millimetres' should now be in the 'Measurement system' box.

5. If the box next to the word 'Vertical ruler' does not contain 'Millimetres' then **display the hidden menu it contains.**
A menu should appear giving a list of different systems of measurement.
Select the 'Millimetres' option in this menu.
The selection 'Millimetres' should now be in the 'Vertical ruler' box.

6. There are other options in the 'Preferences' dialogue box but all we are concerned with are the 'Measurement system' and the 'Vertical ruler' values. Do not worry if the other settings in figure 5.1 do not match your own.
Place the pointer over the 'OK' in the top right–hand corner of the dialogue box and click the mouse button.
PageMaker has been informed that you have finished with this dialogue box — when it returns to the main PageMaker window the rulers should be in cm and mm.

7. **Move the pointer onto the horizontal ruler at the top of the window** (figure 5.2).

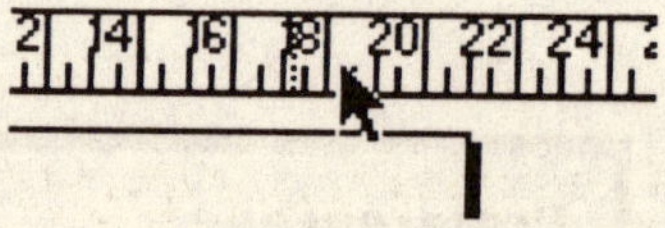

Figure 5.2

8. **With the pointer here, hold down the mouse button.**
You should have 'picked up' an additional guide from the ruler. The pointer changes to a two–headed arrow.

9. **Keeping the mouse button held down, move the pointer down onto the page.**
A guide should be attached to the pointer and move with it. Notice how the vertical position of the guide is kept track of by a small mark on the vertical ruler.

10. **Keeping the mouse button held down move the guide so that the indicator on the vertical ruler is lined up with the 20cm mark.**

11. **With the guide lined up to the 20cm mark release the mouse button.**
You should have 'dropped' the guide here. It should now stay in place when the pointer is moved away (figure 5.3).

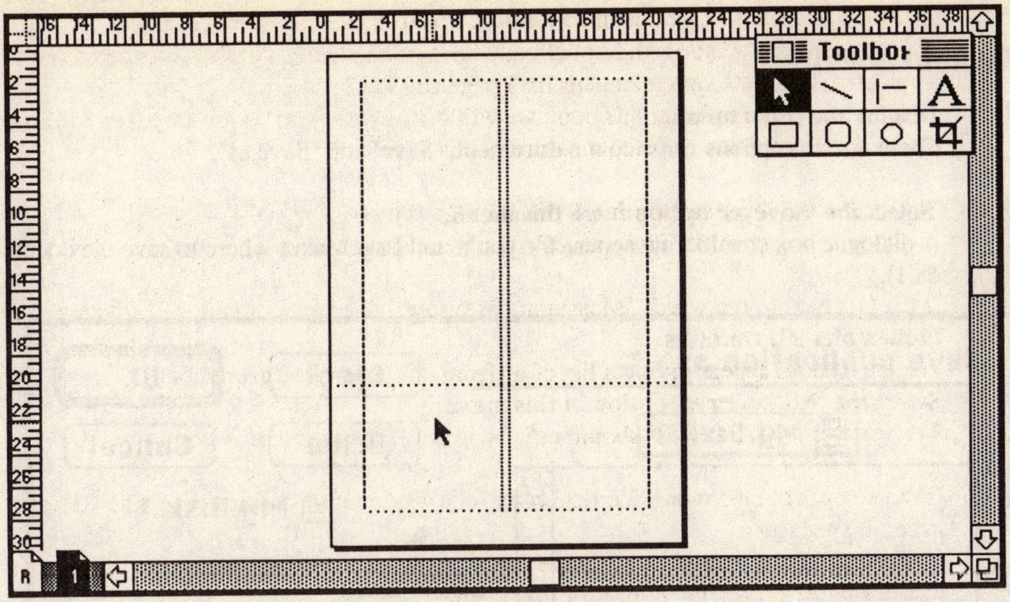

Figure 5.3

12. **Finally, make sure the 'Snap to guides' option in the [Options] menu is active.** With the 'Snap to guides' option active the guides become 'sticky'. This will help later when you try and put text and graphics accurately onto this page.

Independent activity

1. It is easy to move a guide by accident. To make sure the guides cannot be moved ensure the 'Lock guides' option in the [Options] menu is selected.

Activity 6a

Saving a document — Macintosh

Objectives

1. To save a document
2. To use a disc

Introduction

This activity goes through the steps involved in saving or 'storing' a document on your own disc. If you have not already got one then you will need a floppy disc, ready formatted for your particular type of computer. If you are using a PC then go strait to activity 5b.

Guided activity

1. **Display the [File] menu.**
   There are two options for saving a document, 'Save' and 'Save as'.

2. **Select the 'Save as' option from this menu.**
   A dialogue box should now appear for you to tell PageMaker where to save the document (figure 6a.1).

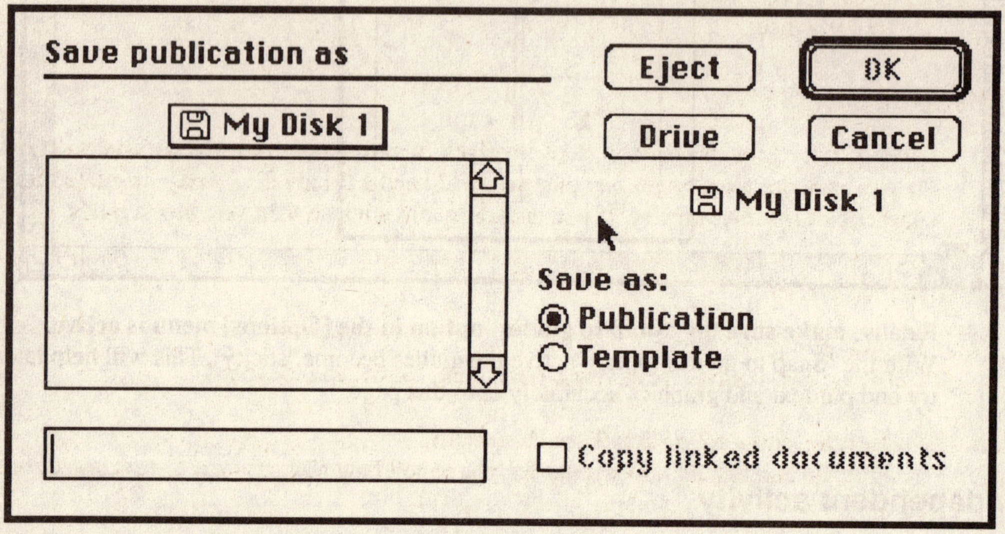

Figure 6a.1

3. If it is not already there then **put your disc into the drive.**

4. The first thing to do is to tell PageMaker the document should be saved on your own disc. By pointing at the word 'Drive' in the top right hand section of the dialogue box and clicking the mouse button you can switch between looking at the 'hard disk' (the one inside your computer) and your own disc.
   Point at the word 'Drive' and click the mouse button until the word 'Eject' is in normal text.
   This indicates that PageMaker is looking at your own disc.

5. The title of the document is held at the bottom of the 'Save publication as' dialogue box.
   Type in 'FirstDoc' (without the quotation marks).

7. **Move the pointer over the word 'OK' in the top right–hand section of the dialogue box and click the mouse button.**
   PageMaker should pause briefly as it saves your document then returns to the page. Your document is now saved.

Activity 6b Saving a document — PC

Objectives

1. To save a document
2. To use a disc

Introduction

This activity goes through the steps involved in saving or 'storing' a document on your own disc. If you have not already got one then you will need a floppy disc, ready formatted for your particular type of computer. If you are using a Macintosh then skip this activity.

Guided activity

1. **Display the [File] menu.**
   There are two options for saving a document, 'Save' and 'Save as'.

2. **Select the 'Save as' option from this menu.**
   A dialogue box should now appear for you to tell PageMaker where to save the document (figure 6b.1).

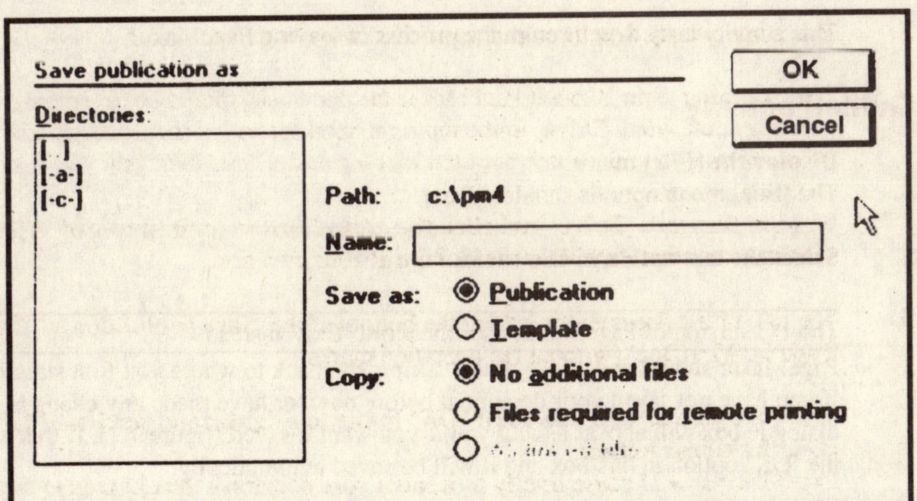

Figure 6b.1

3. If it is not already there then **put your disc into the drive** (if you have two drives then put the disc into drive A:).

4. The first thing to do is to tell PageMaker the document should be saved on drive a:. The box on the left–hand side of the dialogue box holds a list of different 'directories'.
Point over the '[–a–]' in this box and click the mouse button to select drive 'a:'.
The box holding the 'Name' of the document you are saving should now contain 'a:'.

5. **Move the pointer so that it is just after the 'a:' in the 'Name' box. Click the mouse button to place the cursor here.**

6. **Type in 'FirstDoc'** (without the quotation marks).

7. **Move the pointer over the word 'OK' in the top right–hand section of the dialogue box and click the mouse button.**
PageMaker should pause briefly as it saves your document then returns to the page. Your document is now saved.

Activity 7

Leaving PageMaker

Objectives

1. To leave the PageMaker program

Introduction

This activity leads you through the process of leaving PageMaker.

Guided activity

1. **Display the [File] menu.**
The [File] menu options should appear.

2. **Select the last option in this menu, 'Quit'[PC].**

[PC] The PC version of PageMaker uses the word 'Exit' instead.

PageMaker should now close down, taking you back to where you first started it.
If you have not saved your document before now, or have made any changes since the last save, a dialogue box will appear asking you if you want it saved (figure 7.1). If this happens then click on the 'OK' option in this box and it will be saved automatically.

Independent activity

1. Restart the PageMaker program as described in the 'Getting started' section.

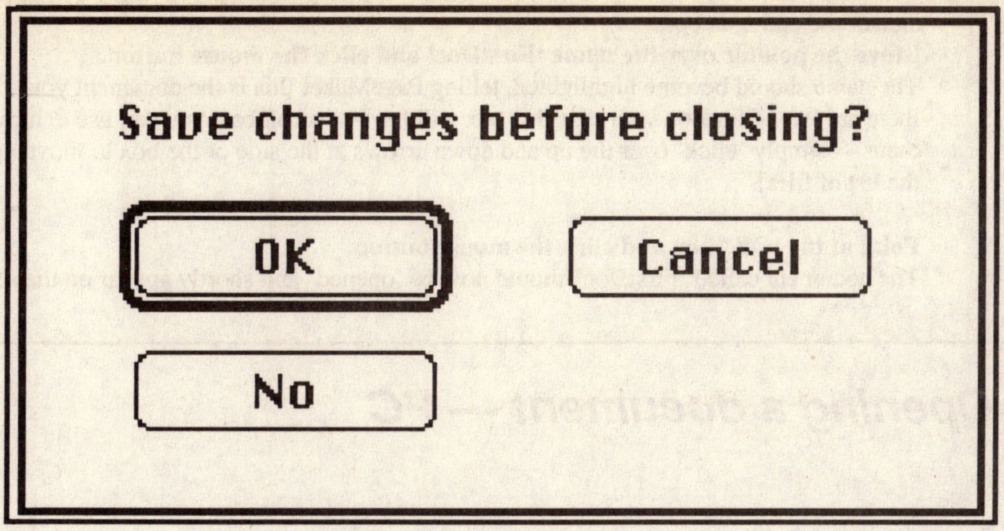

Figure 7.1

Activity 8a Opening a document — Macintosh

Objectives

1. To open an existing PageMaker document

Introduction

When you want to use a document that has already been created you must start the PageMaker program and then 'open' the document you want. This activity leads you through the process of opening the document you have just created. If you are using a PC then move strait to activity 8b.

Guided activity

1. When PageMaker is fully started **display the [File] menu.**
   The [File] menu options should appear.

2. **Select the 'Open' option.**
   A dialogue box should appear for you to tell PageMaker what the document you want to open is called and where it is.

3. Just like saving a document, PageMaker needs to know where it is held.
   Click in the 'Drive' box until PageMaker is looking at your disc (the word 'Eject' should be in normal text).

4. The PageMaker document held on your disc should now be displayed in the box on the left–hand side of the dialogue box.
Move the pointer over the name 'FirstDoc' and click the mouse button.
The name should become highlighted, telling PageMaker this is the document you want to use (if there are lots of files on your disc this box will have a 'scroll bar' you can use to move between them — simply 'click' over the up and down arrows at the side of the box to move up and down the list of files).

5. **Point at the 'OK' box and click the mouse button.**
The document called 'FirstDoc' should now be 'opened' and shortly appear on the screen.

Activity 8b

Opening a document — PC

Objectives

1. To open an existing PageMaker document

Introduction

When you want to use a document that has already been created you must start the PageMaker program and then 'open' the document you want. This activity leads you through the process of opening the document you have just created. If you are using a Macintosh then skip this activity.

Guided activity

1. When PageMaker is fully started **display the [File] menu.**
The [File] menu options should appear.

2. **Select the 'Open' option from this menu.**
A dialogue box should appear for you to tell PageMaker what the document you want to open is called and where it is.

3. Just like saving a document, PageMaker needs to know where it is held.
Point to the '[–a–]' in the 'Files/Directories' box on the left hand side of the dialogue box and click the mouse button.

4. **Click on the 'OK' box.**

5. The PageMaker document held on your disc should now be displayed in the box on the left–hand side of the dialogue box.
Move the pointer over the name 'FirstDoc' and click the mouse button.
The name should be highlighted, telling PageMaker this is the document you want to use (if there are lots of files on your disc this box will have a 'scroll bar' you can use to move between them — simply 'click' over the up and down arrows at the side of the box to move up and down the list of files).

6. **Point at the 'OK' box and click the mouse button.**
The document called 'FirstDoc' should now be 'opened' and shortly appear on the screen.

Note

You should now be able to save documents whenever you wish. It is good practice to save your work regularly — just in case the unexpected happens (powercut, computer faults, children, etc.). For the purpose of the following chapters in this book save your document when you wish to take a break or finish for the day. When you are ready to start again simply start PageMaker and open the document. Then just pick up where you left off.

Once you have saved a document using the 'Save as' option the document can be quickly saved using the 'Save' option. Selecting 'Save' will automatically save your document without bringing up any dialogue boxes — the document will be saved under the name it is currently called.

End of chapter summary

What I want to do	How I do it
• Start a new document	• Select 'New' from [File] menu and fill in dialogue box
• Change attributes of page (margins, size, etc.)	• Select 'Page setup' from [File] menu
• Add columns to my page	• Select 'Column guides' from [Options] menu
• Add additional guides to my page	• 'Drag' guide from rulers located at top of window or to left of window
• Change the system of measurement PageMaker is using	• Select 'Preferences' from [Options] menu and change value in 'Measurement system'
• Save a document	• Select 'Save as' from [File] menu
• Open an existing document	• Select 'Open' from [File] menu and locate required file
• Leave PageMaker	• Select 'Quit' or 'Exit' from [File] menu

Trouble-shooting

Problem	Possible reason	Solution
• Page does not show guides	• Guides are not switched on	• Switch on guides — select 'Guides' option in [Options] menu
• Cannot move guides	• Guides are 'locked'	• Unlock guides — select 'Lock guides' option in [Options] menu
• Margins appear to be in wrong proportions	• Wrong margin settings entered	• Select 'Page setup' from [File] menu and check margin values — change if necessary
• 'Save' dialogue box contains 'Desktop' rather than 'Drive'	• System difference	• Click on 'Desktop' box then on icon of disc and 'OK' — then treat as normal
• Cannot save	• Disk damaged / disk full / disk locked	• Change disk and try again

Chapter 2

Entering text

• entering text on a word processor
• using the 'Story editor'

Introduction to chapter 2

This chapter deals with the process of putting the main text of a document into PageMaker. Once it is there you will probably want to change it in some way — this will be looked at in later chapters. This chapter looks solely at how to get the raw text in. There are two main methods which will be described in order of preference.

The best way to prepare text is to use a word processing package. If you have access to a word processor then follow activity 1. Failing this, it is possible to enter text using PageMaker's 'built in' word processor. If you do not have access to a word processor then follow activity 2.

Activity 1

Entering text on a word processor

Objectives

1. To enter text using a word processor

Introduction

For most pieces of text that are needed in a document it is preferable to type in the text itself using a word processor and then bring it in to PageMaker. At first this may seem like a long way to do things. In the long run, as you start producing longer and more complex documents, the advantages of this method will become obvious. Anything longer than this paragraph should be entered this way. PageMaker can bring in or 'import' most common word processed files. Check your PageMaker manual if you are unsure whether or not the one you are using is suitable.

Guided activity

1. **Load an appropriate word processing package and type in the text shown in figure 2.1.** It is best to keep the format of the text as simple as possible (i.e. excluding any bold or italic text and any indents — this will be done in PageMaker itself). Type the text as shown (including the expression '<Body text>'), only pressing the 'ENTER' or 'RETURN' key at the end of each paragraph.

2. **Save the text on your own disc under the file name 'Text1'.**

Activity 2

Using the 'Story editor'

Objectives

1. To use the story editor to enter text into PageMaker

Introduction

If you are not familiar with a word processor then it is possible to utilise one of the features of PageMaker. The Story editor can be used like a word processor. This activity takes you through the process of using this feature to produce a text file for use in a later activity.

Guided activity

1. **Start PageMaker and open the document you created in the previous chapter** (called 'FirstDoc').

2. **Select the 'Edit story' option from the [Edit] menu.**
The story editor 'window' appears for you to enter text.

3. **Type in the text shown in figure 2.1** (including the expression '<Body text>') as it is shown, only pressing the RETURN (or 'ENTER') key at the end of each paragraph.

4. **Select the 'Export' option from the [File] menu.**
A dialogue box appears for you to tell PageMaker where you want to save this text and what to call it.

5. **Make sure PageMaker is looking at your own disc.**

6. **Click the pointer next to the 'Name' box and replace the contents of this box** (if it has any) **with the name 'Text1'[PC].**

PC users need to include the file name extension '.TXT' after the name.

---

7. PageMaker can save text in a number of different formats.
Click over 'Text Only' or 'ASCII Text Export' in the 'File format' box (you may need to use the 'scroll bar' at the side of this box if 'Text Only' is not displayed).

8. **Click on 'OK'.**
PageMaker should now save this file to your own disc under the name 'Text1'.

9. **Select the 'Close story' option from the [Story] menu.**
A box appears asking if you want to 'Place', 'Discard' or 'Cancel' this story.

10. **Click over 'Discard'** to select this option.
The story editor window disappears, returning you to the main PageMaker window.

Note for PC users

PC users need to ensure all their files have an appropriate extension (like the '.TXT' above). Consult your PageMaker manuals if you are unsure which file extension to use for a particular file.

NB .DOC files do not work. - select WS from input box

Text from WPerfect has some erratic chars at beginning.

<Body text>A talk by Professor C Package on the impact of desk top publishing on the process of creating documents. The talk begins with a look at the history of publishing and the major dramatic changes in these processes. Questions will be welcomed from the audience in the second part of the talk which consists of a discussion on how publishing will change in the future.
Professor Package is a well known figure in desk top publishing having written a number of books on the subject - among them being 'Desk top publishing for children' and 'Life, the universe and desk top publishing'.
Future events are planned to continue from this talk where visitors will get the opportunity for 'hands on' experience of some of the more well known desk top publishing packages. Anyone interested in participating in these events should write to the address shown below. Book early to avoid disappointment.

Figure 2.1

End of chapter summary

What I want to do	How I do it
• Enter text for use in PageMaker via a word processor	• Select a word processor PageMaker can 'read' and use as normal
• Enter text for use in PageMaker via the 'Story editor'	• Select the 'Edit story' option from the [Edit] menu, type in the text, 'Export' to a disc and 'Discard' story

Trouble-shooting

Problem	Possible reason	Solution
• PageMaker won't save on my disc	• Disc is damaged / full / locked	• Get another disc and try again
• 'Text Only' not available in 'File format' box	• 'Text Only' export filter not installed	• Install 'Text Only' filter (see PageMaker manuals) or use different file format

Chapter 3

Working with blocks of text

- placing text into columns
- changing the page view
- removing text blocks
- flowing text across columns
- moving guides
- moving text blocks
- changing the length of text blocks
- changing the text of a story
- abandoning a document

Introduction to chapter 3

PageMaker's ability to manipulate text in so many ways is one of its most powerful features. PageMaker lets us manipulate 'blocks' of text and also change single words or characters. This chapter looks at how we can put blocks of text, previously prepared in chapter 2, onto a page and manipulate them so they fit into the spaces allocated.

Activity 1

Placing text into columns

Objectives

1. To put previously prepared text onto a page
2. To fit text into a column

Introduction

In this activity we will attempt to put the text you prepared in the previous chapter onto the page.

Guided activity

1. **If necessary, start PageMaker and open the document you created in chapter 1** (called 'FirstDoc').
We must now tell PageMaker to place the text you created in chapter 2 ('Text1') onto the blank page.

2. Ensure the rulers, guides, toolbox and scroll bars are 'active' (switched on). **If any of these are not then select the option in the appropriate menu now** (see chapter 1).

3. When you put text onto a page PageMaker can make it 'flow' automatically from one column to the next. This facility is called 'Autoflow'. In this case we do not want the text to flow automatically.
Before putting the text onto the page check that the 'Autoflow' option in the [Options] menu is not active (does not have a tick against it). **If it is active then select this option to make it inactive.**
We are now ready to put the text onto your page.

4. **Select the 'Place' option from the [File] menu.**
The 'Place' option is used to get a text file from disc and place it onto the page. A dialogue box should now appear for you to tell PageMaker where the document is and what it is called — it should look similar to the 'Save as' dialogue box we used in the previous chapter.

5. The document is on your own disc. **Make sure PageMaker is looking at this.**
The different files on your disc should now be displayed in the box on the left–hand side of the dialogue box. The text file you saved should be among them — if there are lots of files on your disc then you may need to use the scroll bar at the right of this box to get to it.

6. **When your text file name, 'Text1', is in view move the pointer over it and click to highlight it.**
The title of your text file should now be highlighted.

7. **Move the pointer over the box next to 'Read tags' and click the mouse button.**
The box next to 'Read tags' should now have a cross in it indicating it is active. The word 'Body text' at the start of the text you typed in the previous chapter is a 'tag' — it tells PageMaker what the text should look like when it is placed. The concept of 'tags' will be explained in detail in section 3.

8. **Click on 'OK' to tell PageMaker this is the text you want to place onto the page.**
(If the text was entered using the 'Story editor' you may now get a box entitled 'Smart ASCII import filter' appearing in the window. This is simply because the text you entered was saved as 'strait text' — free of the formatting added by using a word processor. Simply **click on 'OK'** in this box to continue.)
After a moment PageMaker has brought the text in ('imported' it) ready for you to put it somewhere on the page. The pointer should now have become a little box, the text placing icon, containing a few horizontal lines. This indicates that PageMaker is 'holding' the selected text, ready to put it anywhere in your document.

9. **Move the text placing icon into the left–hand column, against the left–hand margin, and beneath the horizontal guide you placed 20cm from the top of your page.**
The left–hand side of the text placing icon should touch the left–hand margin and the top of the text box icon should touch the horizontal guide (figure 1.1). The 'Snap to guides' option in the [Options] menu being active should make lining these up a little easier.

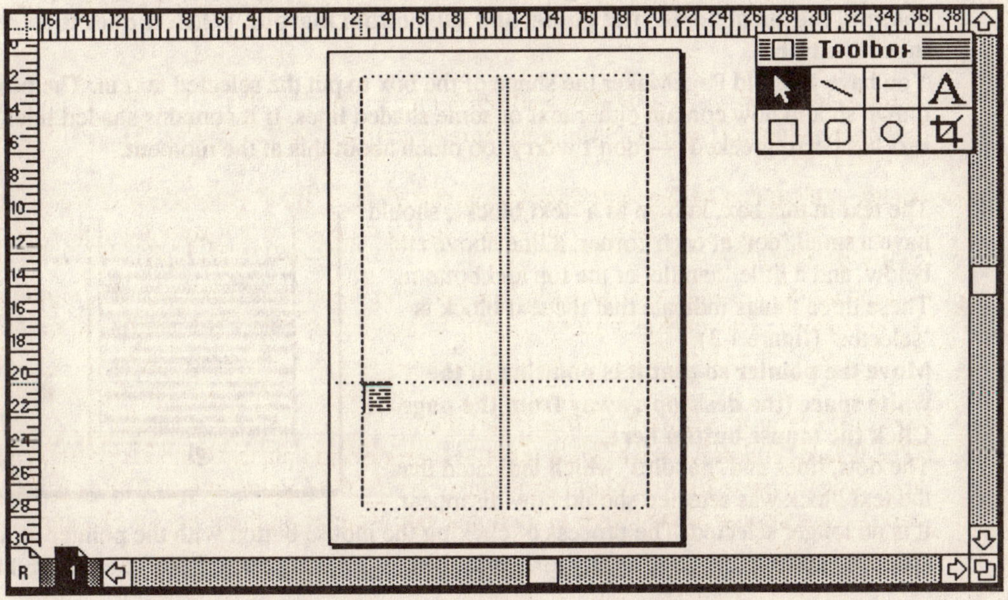

Figure 1.1

10. With the text box icon in this position **hold down the mouse button.**

11. With the mouse button held down **move (or 'drag') the text placing icon to the bottom right–hand corner of the first column.**
As the icon moves it should 'draw' a box as it goes. This is the box that the text from 'Text1' will fill. Notice how the dimensions of this box depend on the way you move the icon.

12. **Line up the box which the icon is drawing so that its bottom right–hand corner fits into the bottom right–hand corner of the first column** (figure 1.2).

Move text : point inside text block, hold mouse (4 headed arrow) drag to reposition. p46 manual.

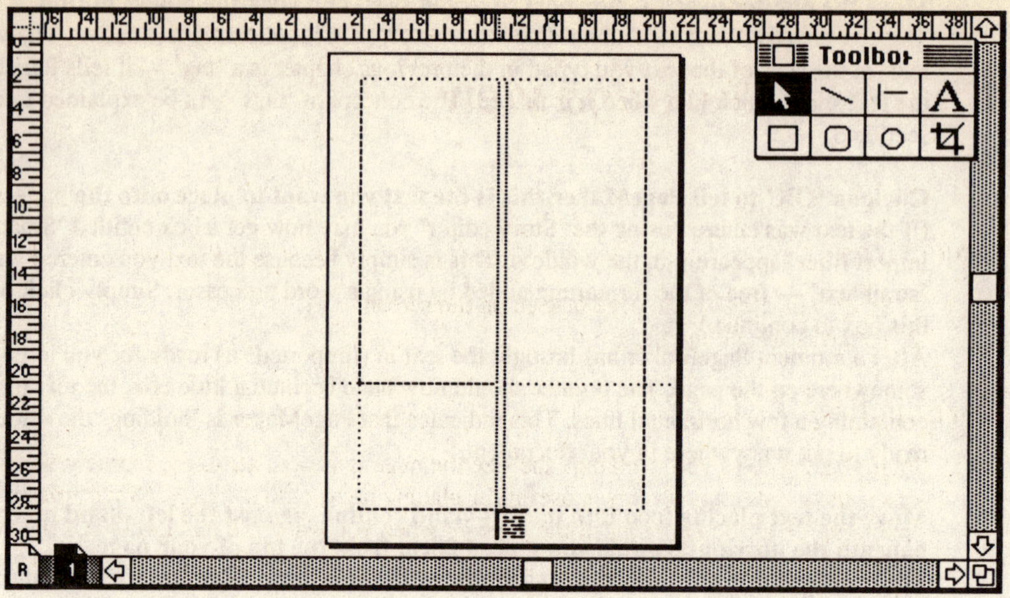

Figure 1.2

13. **The box you have been drawing should fit the box made by the two vertical guides of the first column, the 20cm horizontal guide, and the bottom margin. When it does then release the mouse button.**
You have just told PageMaker the shape of the box to put the selected text in. The box you have drawn should now contain either text or some shaded lines. If it contains shaded lines then your text has been 'greeked' — don't worry too much about this at the moment.

14. The text in this box, known as a 'text block', should have a small 'dot' at each corner, a line above and below, and a little 'handle' at the top and bottom. These three things indicate that the text block is 'selected' (figure 1.3).
Move the pointer so that it is pointing in the white space (the desktop), away from the page. Click the mouse button here.
The dots, lines and 'handles' which indicated that the text block was selected should now disappear — it is no longer selected. The process of clicking the mouse button with the pointer in the white space, away from the page or any text, is known as 'clicking away from' the selected text.

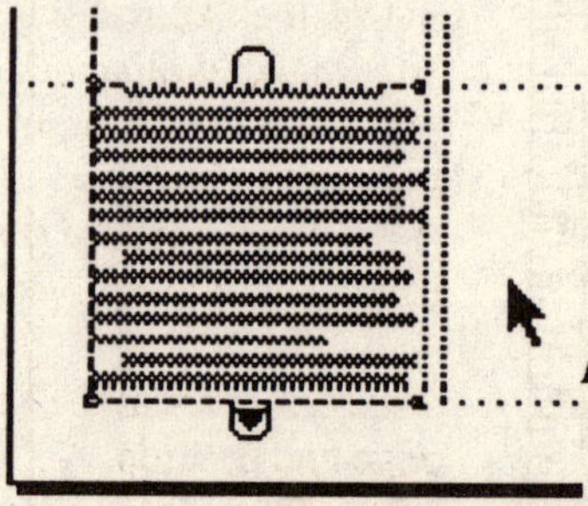

Figure 1.3

Greeked text

'Greeking' text is a method PageMaker uses to speed up what it is doing. When text gets below a certain size (proportional to the size the page is seen at), rather than spend time drawing it on a page, PageMaker puts shaded lines where the text should be. Drawing very small pieces of text can take a long time so by using 'greeked' text PageMaker works considerably faster. Unfortunately this means the text is unreadable — its all 'Greek' to us!

Activity 2

Changing the page view

Objectives

1. To change the size the page is seen on the screen
2. To move around the page

Introduction

PageMaker allows you to change the size the page is viewed at. At the moment you should be able to see the whole page — this is useful for placing items onto the page. Other times it is useful to 'zoom in' on particular areas of the page — when you want to look closely at a piece of text, say. This activity takes you through the process of changing your view of the page and moving around the page to different areas.

Guided activity

1. **Display the [Page] menu.**
   The [Page] menu should appear showing the different sizes the page can be seen at. At the moment there should be a tick against the 'Fit in window' option, indicating the whole page should fit into the PageMaker window.

2. **Select the 'Actual size' option from this menu.**
   PageMaker will now 'zoom in' to show you how the page looks at the actual size it will be when printed. Most monitors cannot fit a full A4 page on the screen so only an area of the page should now be in view.
   If there is nothing in the PageMaker window then you have probably 'zoomed in' to an area on the desktop or a blank piece of the page — don't worry, the page is still there!

3. The scroll bars at the bottom and right of the window can be used to move your view around the page and desktop.
   Move the pointer over the arrow at the right–hand side of the horizontal scroll bar (located at the bottom of the screen) **and click the mouse button.**
   The box inside the scroll bar (known as the 'scroll box') moves a little to the right, indicating your view has moved to the right — if a part of your page was in view then this will move slightly to the left (as your 'eyes' look to the right).

4. **Move the pointer over the arrow at the left–hand side of the horizontal scroll bar and click the mouse button.**
   The box in the middle of the scroll bar moves left slightly, indicating your view has moved to the left — again, if part of your page was in view this will move to the right a little.

5. **Use the arrows on either end of the horizontal scroll bar in this way to place the scroll box in the centre of the scroll bar.**

6. **Move the pointer over the arrow at the top of the vertical scroll bar** (located at the right of the screen) **and click the mouse button.**
The vertical 'scroll box' moves up a little, indicating your view has moved up — if a part of your page was in view then this will move slightly down (as your 'eyes' look up).

7. **Move the pointer over the arrow at the bottom of the vertical scroll bar and click the mouse button.**
The box in the middle of the scroll bar moves down slightly, indicating your view has moved down — again, if part of your page was in view this will move up a little.

8. **Use the arrows on either end of the vertical scroll bar in this way to place the scroll box in the centre of the scroll bar.**
You should be looking at the centre of the desktop, somewhere near the centre of your page. The scroll boxes on the horizontal and vertical scroll bars indicate where on the desktop you are.

Independent activity

1. With the view set to 'Actual size' use the scroll bars to move to the block of text you previously placed. It should now be readable.

2. Move back to 'Fit in window' and select the text block. With the text block selected choose 'Actual size' from the [Page] menu.
PageMaker zooms in to the selected text. If an item on the page is selected PageMaker will automatically zoom in to that item.

Page views

PageMaker allows you to view the page at different sizes.

'Fit in window' — all of page is visible

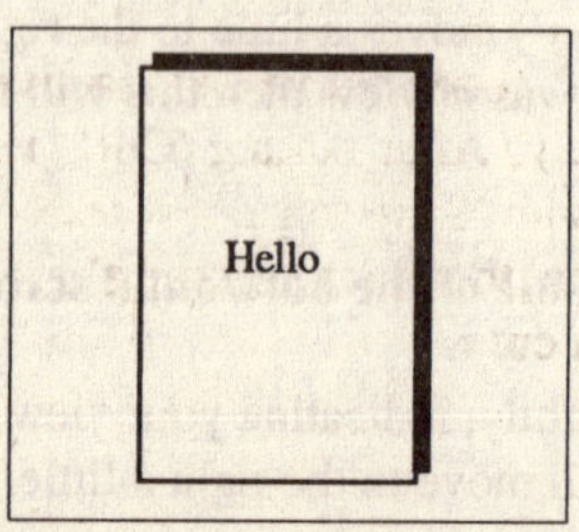

'Actual size' — page is seen at size it will be printed at

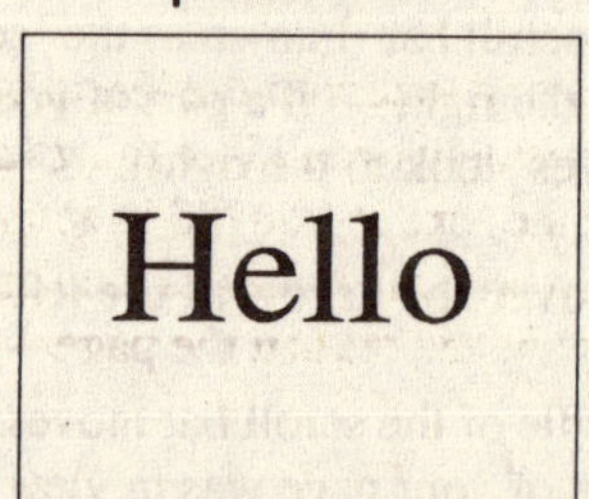

'200% size' — page is magnified to twice its actual size

Activity 3

Removing text blocks

Objectives

1. To remove a block of text from a page

Introduction

Putting text onto a page can be a very fiddly process — especially to the beginner. It is more than likely that you will make a few mistakes. Luckily, we can remove unwanted text blocks quite easily. This activity takes you through the process of removing (or 'cutting') a block of text from a page.

PageMaker refers to the process of removing unwanted bits of text from a page as 'cutting'. This dates back to the times when pre–printed sheets of text were literally 'stuck' onto a page — any unwanted lines or paragraphs being 'cut' out beforehand.

Guided activity

1. **Select the 'Fit in window' option from the [Page] menu.**
   The page should be in full view.

2. **Move the pointer so that it points in the middle of the block of text and click the mouse button.**
   The dots, lines and 'handles' should appear, indicating that the text block is 'selected'.
   To cut a block of text out of a page PageMaker needs to know which block of text you are referring to. It needs to be 'selected'. PageMaker then knows that whatever it is told to do it must do to this particular block of text.

3. With the text block selected **choose the 'Cut' option from the [Edit] menu.**
   The text block should now disappear as it is 'cut' from the page.

Independent activity

1. Experiment with placing text with the 'Snap to guides' option active and inactive — see how having 'sticky' guides helps you place things accurately? After placing 'Cut' the text from your page. Finally, place the text as you did in activity 1 (with 'Snap to guides' active) so that it fits the box made by the two vertical guides of the first column, the 20cm horizontal guide, and the bottom margin. This time leave the text on the page — do not cut it.

Activity 4

Flowing text across columns

Objectives

1. To continue a block of text in another column

Introduction

PageMaker gives you a lot of flexibility over where text blocks go. If all of the text in a text file will not fit into one column or if it is desirable to spread text over a number of columns it can be continued in another column or on another page. The text you placed in the previous chapter does not all fit into the text box you made for it. In this activity we will try and make this text continue to the second column.

Guided activity

1. If the text block in the first column is not already selected then, **with the pointer located in the middle of the text, click the mouse button** to select it.
   The text block should take the form of a 'selected' block of text.
   In the handle at the bottom of the text block there should be a little arrow. This indicates that not all the text fitted into the box you made for it and there is still more to come. The handle at the top of the text block is empty, indicating that this is the start of the text.

2. **Move the pointer inside the handle at the bottom of the text block, over the arrow, and click the mouse button** (make sure you 'click' the mouse button and do not hold it down for any length of time).
   The pointer should change to the text placing icon. By clicking over the arrow in the bottom handle you have taken the rest of the text that wouldn't fit into the text box and PageMaker is now 'holding' it for you to place somewhere on your page.

3. **Move the text placing icon into the right–hand column, against the guide on the left–hand side of this column, and beneath the horizontal guide you placed 20cm from the top of your page.**
   The left–hand side of the text placing icon should touch this guide and the top of the icon should touch the horizontal guide (figure 4.1).

4. With the text box icon in this position **hold down the mouse button.**

5. With the mouse button held down **'drag' the text placing icon to the bottom right–hand corner of the second column.**
   As before, the box icon draws a box as it moves. This is the box the text will fill.

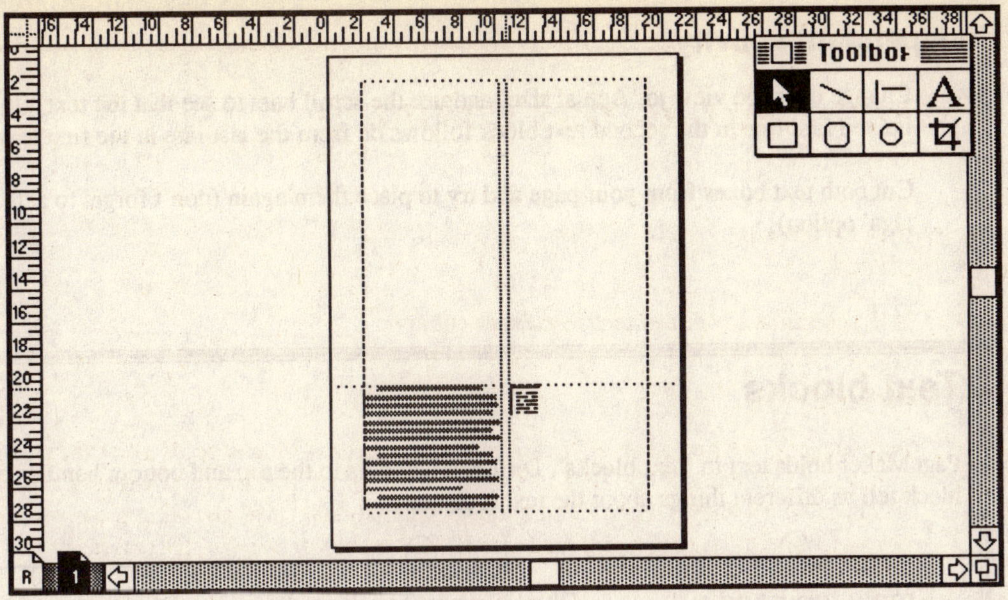

Figure 4.1

6. **Line up the box which the icon is drawing so that its bottom right–hand corner fits into the bottom right–hand corner of the second column.**

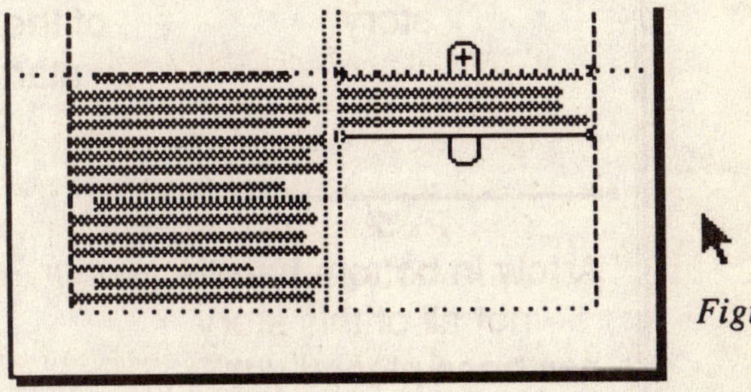

Figure 4.2

7. The box you have been drawing should fit the box made by the two vertical guides of the second column, the 20cm horizontal guide, and the bottom margin. When it does then **release the mouse button.**
PageMaker puts the remaining text from 'Text1' in this box. Again, the box you have drawn should now contain either text or some shaded lines indicating 'greeked' text (figure 4.2). The text block you have just placed should not be as long as the box you drew. This is because there wasn't enough text to fill the box — the text block only goes as far down the column as the last line of text.

8. **Select the text block in the first column by moving the pointer over the middle of it and clicking the mouse button.**
It takes the form of a selected text block.
The handle at the bottom of this text box now contains a '+' indicating that the text in this block is continued in another text block.

9. **Select the text block in the second column.**
The handle at the top of this text block now contains a '+' indicating that the text in this block is a continuation from another text block. The handle at the bottom of the text block is empty, indicating this is the end of the text.
The text has now been placed into two columns. The complete text from the file you placed, now spanning two columns, is known as a 'story'. Your 'story' starts in the first column and continues in the second column.

Independent activity

1. Change the page view to 'Actual size' and use the scroll bars to see that the text 'flows' properly i.e. the first line in the second text block follows on from the last line in the first text block.

2. Cut both text boxes from your page and try to place them again (don't forget to activate the 'Read tags' option).

Text blocks

PageMaker holds text in 'text blocks'. Different symbols in the top and bottom handles of a text block tell us different things about the text it contains.

Empty top handle — this is the start of the story

Plus sign in top handle — this is a continuation of the story — the story started in a previous text block

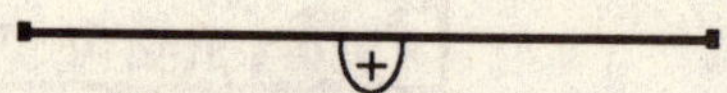

Plus sign in bottom handle — this story is continued in another text block

Arrow in bottom handle — not all of this story has been placed yet — there is still more to come

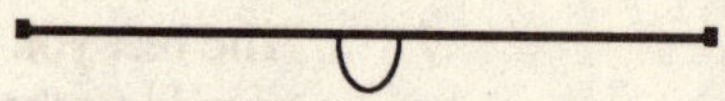

Empty bottom handle — this is the end of the story

Putting text blocks together

If text blocks are broken, combine by:—

① drag last text handle of last text block past its top handle until text disappears

② Repeat ① for all blocks – from end to 1st (this pushes text into the window above)

③ 1st text block has red marker at end to indicate it is incomplete – drag this handle down to reveal all the text

NB If you accidentally roll up all the text it will reappear by clicking on 'Select All' from Edit (p54 manual)

Activity 5

Moving guides

Objectives

1. To move a guide on the page

Introduction

As your page develops you may wish to move your guides to different positions. This activity deals with the process of moving guides.

Guided activity

1. **Display the [Options] menu.**
The [Options] menu should now be displayed and its contents visible.

2. Check if there is a tick against the 'Lock guides' option — if there is then **select this option** to remove the tick and make 'Lock guides' inactive.
When the 'Lock guides' option is active the guides cannot be moved.

3. **Move the pointer so that it is over the guide you placed 20cm from the top of the page and hold down the mouse button** — try and keep clear of the text blocks you placed earlier so as not to move them by mistake (it is best to point at the part of the guide between the edge of the page and the margin).
You have 'picked up' this guide — the pointer should change to a two headed arrow. If it does not then release the mouse button and try again.

4. With the mouse button still held down **'drag' the guide** (which should now move with the pointer) **so that it is lined up with the 11cm mark on the vertical ruler.** Use the small mark on the vertical ruler to keep track of the guides position.

5. When the guide is lined up with the 11cm mark on the vertical ruler **release the mouse button.**
You have now 'dropped' the guide. When you move the pointer the guide should remain at the 11cm mark.

6. **Select the 'Lock guides' option from the [Options] menu.**
With the 'Lock guides' option active the guides cannot be moved by accident. It is good practice to ensure that the guides are normally locked. Only 'unlock' them when you want to move a guide. (From now on it is assumed you unlock and lock the guides as required).

Independent activity

1. Get an additional guide from the horizontal ruler at the top of the window. Place this so that it lines up with the 16cm mark on the vertical ruler.

Activity 6

Moving text blocks

Objectives

1. To move a text block to a different position on a page

Introduction

When a text block has been put onto your page it is not restricted to remaining in the position it was originally placed. PageMaker allows you to move text blocks both around and between pages. This activity goes through the process of moving text blocks around a page.

Guided activity

1. **Move the pointer so that it is located in the middle of the text block in the first column. When it is here, hold down the mouse button.**
   You have 'picked up' this block of text — after a moment the pointer should change to a four–headed arrow. It is now ready to be moved.

2. With the mouse button still held down **'drag' the block of text** (which should now move with the pointer) **so that its top touches the guide you placed at the 11cm mark and its left–hand side touches the left–hand margin** (figure 6.1).

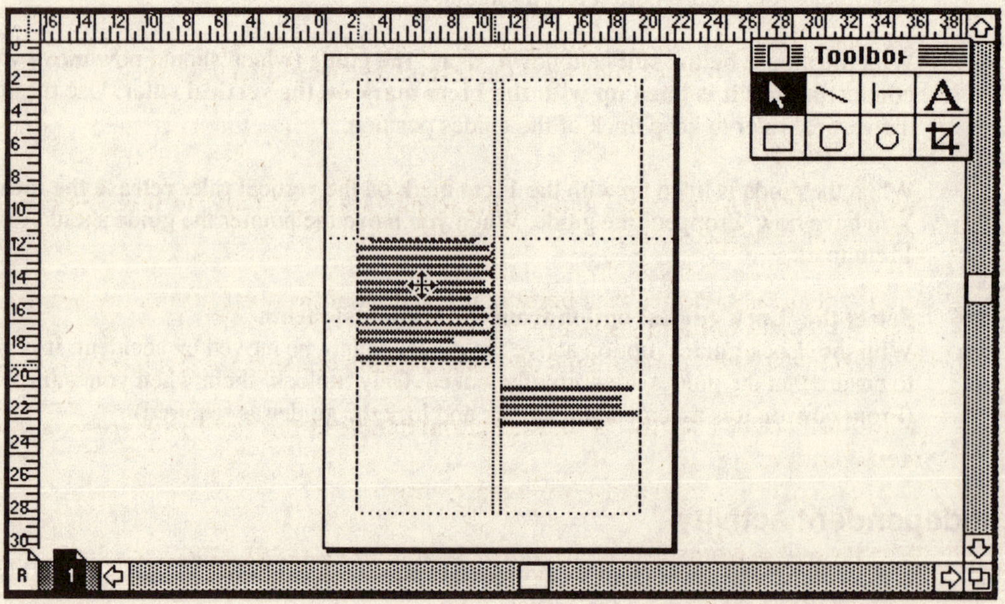

Figure 6.1

3. When the text block is lined up with the 11cm guide and the right and left–hand guides of the first column, **release the mouse button to 'drop' the text block here.**
The text block should now remain in this new position when the pointer is moved away.

Independent activity

1. Move the text block in the second column so that its top touches the 11cm guide and its sides touch the right and left–hand guides which form the second column.

Activity 7

Changing the length of text blocks

Objectives

1. To change the length of a text block currently on a page

Introduction

The 'story' you have placed, which consists of two text blocks, is lined up with the 11cm horizontal guide. The bottom of the text blocks are not lined up. It would be nice if the bottoms of the text blocks lined up also — this would make the story look neat. Although we do not have any control over the quantity of text in the story we placed, we can change the size of the text blocks which hold it. By making the text block in the first column a bit shorter and the one in the second column a little longer we should be able to make the text line up at the bottom. PageMaker doesn't mind how long each text block is. It will continue to display all of the story as long as the combined size of the two text blocks is big enough to hold it. In this activity we will look at how to make these two text blocks line up at the bottom by changing their length.

Guided activity

1. **Set the view to 'Actual size' and use the scroll bars to get both the text blocks as fully into the window as possible.**

2. If it is not already selected then **point in the middle of the text block in the first column and click the mouse button to select it.**
The text in the first column should now take the form of a selected text block.

3. **Move the pointer over the '+' in the bottom handle of this text block and hold down the mouse button.**
The pointer should change to a two–headed arrow.

4. With the mouse button held down **move the pointer up the text block a couple of lines.**
The handle and the line marking the bottom of the text block should move with the pointer (figure 7.1).

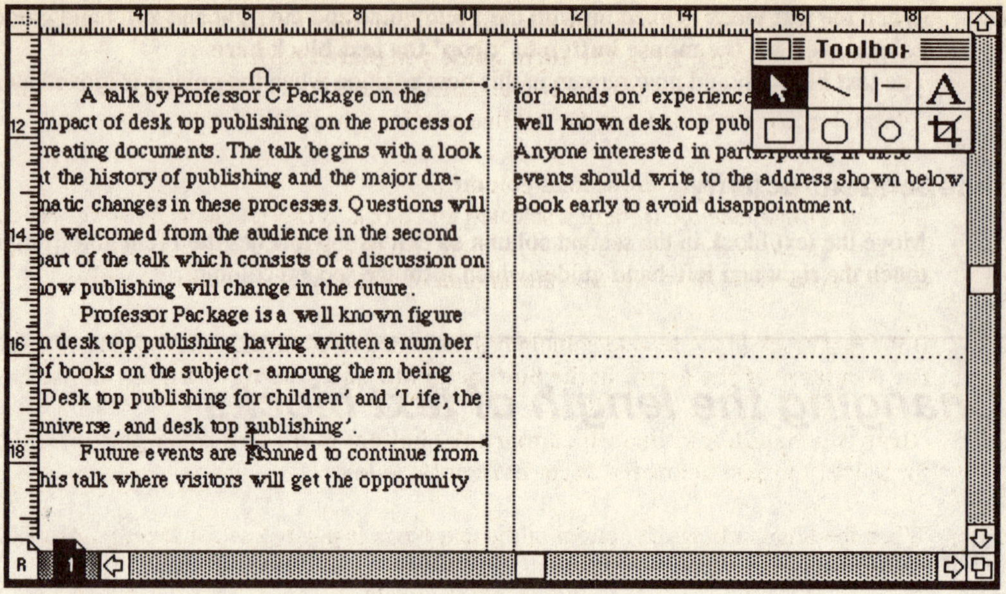

Figure 7.1

5. **Release the mouse button.**
The handle and the line marking the end of the text block should remain here when you move the pointer away. The text below the new position of this line should disappear from the text block. You have used the handle like a 'shutter' to reduce the size of the text block — it is no longer big enough to hold the last couple of lines. The lines of text which have 'disappeared' should now be visible in the top of the text block in the second column — the story still flows the way it should.

6. **Move the pointer over the '+' in the bottom handle of the first text block and hold down the mouse button.**
Again, the pointer changes to a two–headed arrow.

7. With the mouse button held down **move the pointer down the text block a couple of lines.**
The handle and the line marking the bottom of the text block should move with the pointer (figure 7.2).

Figure 7.2

8. **Release the mouse button.**
The handle and the line marking the end of the text block should remain here when you move the pointer away. The text from the text block in the second column should come back to fill the space moving this handle made. You have used the handle like a 'shutter' to increase the size of the text block — it is now big enough to hold more lines of text. The lines of text which have 'appeared' should no longer be visible in the top of the text block in the second column — the story still flows the way it should!

9. **Move the handle of the text block in the first column so that the line marking the bottom of the text block is just below the 16cm guide you placed earlier.**
   The text should flow between the two text blocks such that the first line of text in the second column is a continuation from the last line of text in the first column.

10. **Select the text block in the second column.**
    The text should take the form of a selected text block. If the handle at the bottom of this text block contains an arrow it means there is now more text to come. By altering the size of the text block in the first column we have changed the amount of text held in the second column.

11. If the text block in the second column has more text to come then **pick up the shutter by moving the pointer over the arrow in the bottom handle and holding down the mouse button.**

12. **'Drag' the handle and line which mark the bottom of the text block** (they should move with the pointer) **to just below the 16cm horizontal guide.**

13. When the line marking the bottom of the text block is just below the 16cm guide **release the mouse button.**
    The text which did not fit into this text block should now be visible. The handle at the bottom of the text block should be empty, indicating there is no more text to come.
    The story should still flow in the expected way and the bottom and top of each text block should now be lined up.

Independent activity

1. Try experimenting with the text block 'shutters'. Make the text blocks different lengths again by making one of the text blocks a little longer. Check the story still flows as expected. Make sure the text blocks are lined up again when you have finished.

Activity 8

Changing the text of a story

Objectives

1. To get a tool from the toolbox
2. To select all the text in a story
3. To change the size of text in a story

Introduction

Text has a number of attributes which can be changed to alter its appearance. In this activity we will try and change the size of the text in the story you have placed.

Guided activity

1. Ensure the toolbox is displayed somewhere in the PageMaker window. If it is not then **select the 'Toolbox' option from the [Window] menu.**
   Up until now you have been using the pointer tool. We are going to select a different tool from the toolbox.

2. **Move the pointer over the large letter 'A' in the toolbox** — this is the symbol for the 'text tool'.

3. **With the pointer located here click the mouse button to select it.**
   The symbol for the text tool should become 'highlighted' to show the text tool has been selected and, as you move away from the toolbox, the pointer should be replaced by the text tool.

4. **Move the text tool over the text in the first column. With it located somewhere within the text click the mouse button.**
   A small flashing vertical line, about the same height as the text, should appear in the text where the text tool was 'clicked'. This is the 'cursor' and is used for altering text.

5. We want to change all the text in this story. **Choose the 'Select all' option from the [Edit] menu.**
   The text of the story should become 'highlighted' to show it has been selected (figure 8.1).
   Whatever we now ask PageMaker to do it will do to this highlighted text.

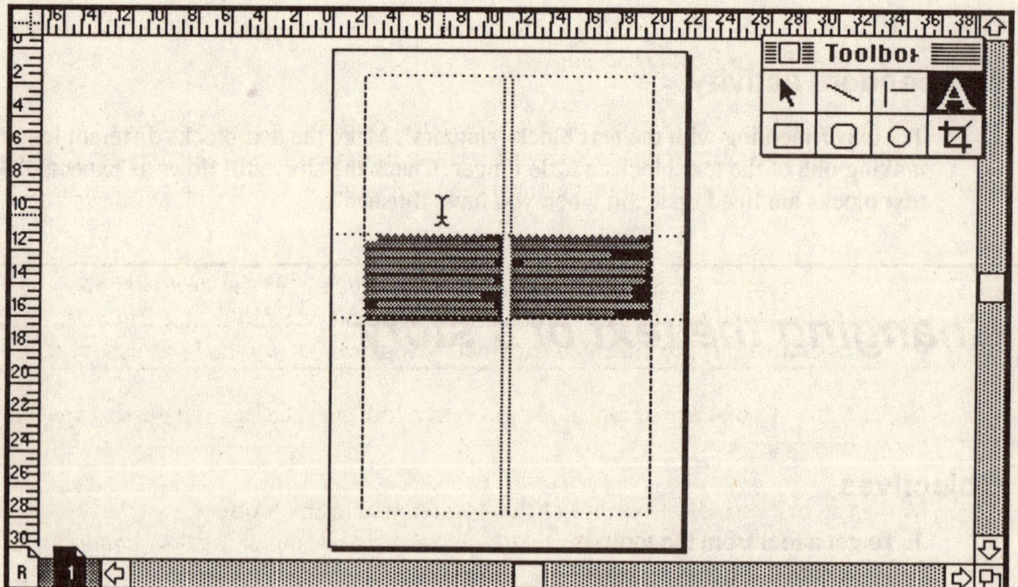

Figure 8.1

6. Some of PageMaker's menu options hold a further menu. This is the case for the 'Size' option in the [Type] menu. To change the size of the highlighted text Macintosh users should:[PC]

   • **Display the [Type] menu by pointing at the menu word and holding down the mouse button.**
   The [Type] menu should be displayed.

   • **With the mouse button held down move down to the 'Size' option in this menu.**
   Another menu should appear displaying a list of numbers — these are the different text sizes available. There should be a tick against the '12' option in this menu indicating that the highlighted text has a size of 12.

   • **Keeping the mouse button held down, move the pointer across to the list of sizes and down to the number '14'.**
   The different sizes should become highlighted as you move across them.

   • When the pointer is located over the number '14' and this number is highlighted, **release the mouse button.**
   After a moment the text in the highlighted story should increase in size (figure 8.2). The text no longer fits into the space allocated for it and 'overflows' out of the last block of text.

   PC users should:

   • **Display the [Type] menu by pointing at the menu word and clicking the mouse button.**
   The [Type] menu should be displayed.

   • **Move over the 'Size' option in this menu and click the mouse button.**
   Another menu should appear displaying a list of numbers — these are the different text sizes available. There should be a tick against the '12' option in this menu indicating that the highlighted text has a size of 12.

   • **Move the pointer across to the list of sizes and click over the number '14'.**
   After a moment the text in the highlighted story should increase in size (figure 8.2). The text no longer fits into the space allocated for it and 'overflows' out of the last block of text.

   Don't worry if you have to repeat this process a few times before you get to grips with it — it will come with practice.

7. **Move the text tool over symbol of the pointer tool in the toolbox.**
   As you move over the toolbox the text tool changes to a pointer to allow you to select a tool.

8. With the pointer located over the symbol of the pointer tool, **click the mouse button to select it.**
   The pointer symbol should become highlighted to show it has been selected. When you move from the toolbox the pointer remains. The text is no longer highlighted.

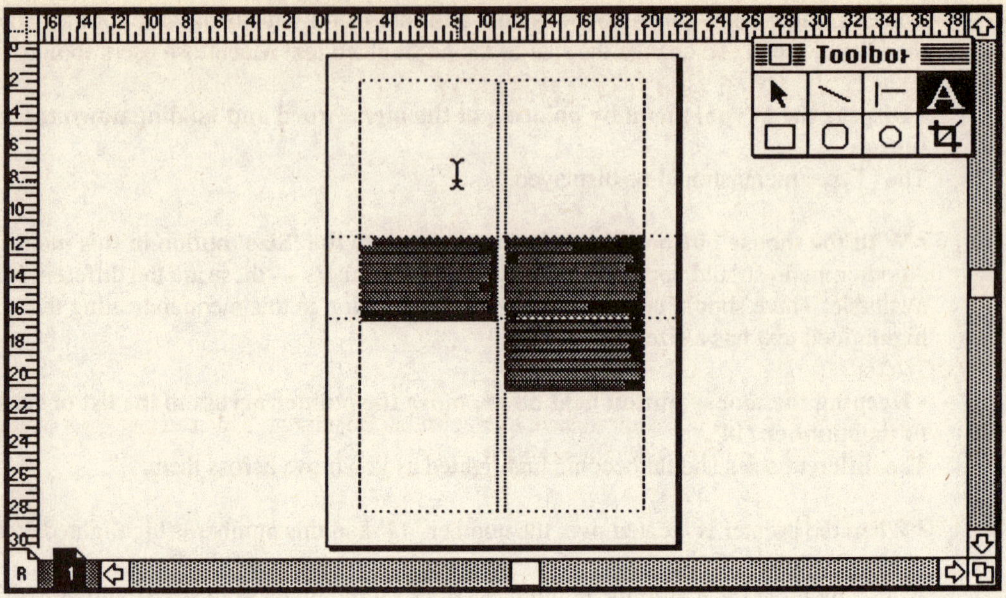

Figure 8.2

Independent activity

1. Repeat the process described above to make the text into size 12 again.

How text is measured

Text in the publishing industry is measured in 'points' — abbreviated to 'pt'. There are 72 points in an inch. As an example of proportions, the main text in this book is in 10pt. PageMaker uses this points system to measure text — the text in the story you placed was originally 12pt, then became 14pt and finally should have been changed to 12pt text.

Text blocks and text

The difference between selecting a text block with the pointer tool and selecting text by highlighting it with the text tool may seem very subtle at first. We use the pointer tool to select a text block when we want to do something with the box which holds the text (move it around the page, change its shape, etc.). The text tool is used to select text when we want to change the actual text inside the text block.

Activity 9

Abandoning a document

Objectives

1. To abandon a document

Introduction

Sometimes you will not want to save a PageMaker document. This activity goes over the process of 'closing' a document without saving it.

Guided activity

1. **Select the 'Close' option from the [File] menu.**
PageMaker knows that you have not saved your document. A small box appears in the window for you to tell PageMaker whether you want to save it or not.

2. **Move the pointer over the 'No' box and click the mouse button.**
You have told PageMaker you do not want to save the document. The PageMaker 'window' should disappear leaving only the menu bar at the top of the screen.

3. **Exit PageMaker by selecting the appropriate option in the [File] menu.**

Independent activity

1. Well done! In this chapter you have covered a lot of basic PageMaker techniques. It would be good practice to repeat this whole process again before starting chapter 4. Restart PageMaker and repeat the activities in this chapter — try and refer to the guided activities as little as possible.

PageMaker shortcuts

Many options in the PageMaker menus have a series of characters by the side. These are the 'keyboard shortcuts' and can be used instead of selecting options from the menus using the pointer. For example, the 'Place' option in the [File] menu has the characters '⌘D' next to it (PC users have the characters '^D'). By holding down the command key (the CTRL key for PC users) and pressing 'D', the 'Place' dialogue box appears — the same as if that option was selected using the menus. As you use PageMaker more and more you will find some of these shortcuts very useful in saving time. The effect of using a keyboard shortcut is no different from selecting the option from a menu.

End of chapter summary

What I want to do	How I do it
• Import previously prepared text	• Select 'Place' from the [File] menu and locate file to place
• Get rest of text from a text block	• Click over arrow in bottom handle of text block
• Put text onto page	• Move text placing icon to where top left–hand corner of text is to start and drag to where bottom right–hand corner of text ends
• Remove item from page	• Select item then choose 'Cut' option from [Edit] menu
• Zoom in on an item on the page	• Select item then choose 'Actual size' from [Page] menu
• See whole page	• Select 'Fit in window' from [Page] menu

Trouble–shooting

Problem	Possible reason	Solution
• Text file prepared on word processor is not displayed in the 'Place' dialogue box	• Word processor is not compatible with PageMaker	• Check in PageMaker manuals if your word processor is compatible — use different word processor or 'Story editor' if not or install filter
• Placed text does not look like that in pictures	• A number of things could be different from example	• Check attributes of text correct (font, size, etc.) — check margin settings are as suggested — check additional guides in correct position — if still inconsistent place again ensuring 'Read tags' is active
• Cannot get the text to place from handle in bottom of first column	• You are not directly over arrow in handle or not 'clicking' fast enough	• Try again ensuring pointer directly on arrow — click in fast movement
• Cannot move guides	• Guides are locked	• Select 'Lock guides' from [Options] menu and try again

Chapter 4

Working with small pieces of text

• entering small pieces of text
• moving text onto a page
• centring text
• changing text

Introduction to chapter 4

In the last chapter we looked at how to add and manipulate text in 'blocks'. As well as having large blocks of text in a document we will also need smaller pieces of text for headings and such like. For pieces of text of this size it is inefficient to type them on a word processor and 'import' them — instead they will be typed directly into PageMaker. This chapter explains the processes of adding small pieces of text to a page, moving them around the page and changing the way they look.

Activity 1 Entering small pieces of text

Objectives

1. To enter a small piece of text directly into PageMaker
2. To change the 'Size' of a small piece of text
3. To change the 'Font' of an area of text
4. To give text a 'Type style'

Introduction

When we want to add a small piece of text to a page, like a heading, we don't usually type it directly into the page. Instead it is typed in the space around the page (the desktop) and moved onto the page. In this activity you will be entering text in this way, changing its size and its 'font', and then moving it onto the appropriate place on the page.

Guided activity

1. If the page is not already in the 'Fit in window' view then **select this option from the [Page] menu.**

2. **Select the text tool from the toolbox.**
The large 'A' in the toolbox should become highlighted showing the text tool is selected — when you move away from the toolbox the pointer has changed to the text tool.

3. **Move the text tool so that it is on the desktop near the left–hand side of the window and click the mouse button.**
You have just put the 'cursor' on the desktop — it is indicated by a small, flashing vertical line. This can now be used to enter text directly onto the desktop — the cursor showing where the text is to start. Before we begin entering text set the size of the text you want.

4. **Select '36' from the 'Size' option in the [Type] menu.**
The list of sizes available may vary from one copy of PageMaker to the next. If the list of sizes the 'Size' option contains does not include a '36' then you could either choose the 'Other' option and specify '36' or choose the size nearest to 36.
The flashing cursor should now change to the appropriate size for 36 point text.

5. **Display the [Type] menu again and then the list held in the 'Font' option.**
A list of different 'fonts' is displayed. The names of these will vary by manufacturer. Two common ones are 'Times' (which may be called 'Times Roman' or 'Dutch') and 'Helvetica' (which may also be called 'Swiss') — the names of these may be abbreviated ('Helvetica' may be called 'Helv', say). Different fonts give text a certain 'look' and 'feel'. For example, the main text of this book is in the 'Times' font. But this sentence is in the 'Helvetica' font. The 'Times' font looks more 'flowing' while 'Helvetica' gives words a 'modern' feel.

6. **Select the 'Helvetica' option from the list of fonts available.**

7. **Type in the following words:**
`You are invited to a talk on`
Notice how the text appears where you 'placed' the cursor. The text you are now looking at has a size of 36 point and is in the Helvetica font. It is known as '36pt Helvetica'. Don't worry if the text flows onto another line.

8. To make these words 'stand out' a little lets try changing their 'Type style' to 'Bold'. First the text needs to be highlighted to tell PageMaker which piece of text we are talking about.
Move the text tool so that it is within the text you just typed and click the mouse button.
The flashing cursor should now be visible inside this text. If it is not then try 'placing' the cursor again using the text tool.

9. **Select the 'Select all' option from the [Edit] menu.**
The text becomes highlighted.

10. **Select 'Bold' from the 'Type style' option in the [Type] menu.**
The text becomes a little thicker as it is made 'bold'.

11. **Select the pointer tool from the toolbox.**
The highlighted text returns to non–highlighted text. The picture of the pointer in the toolbox becomes highlighted to show it has been selected. When you move from the toolbox the pointer tool remains.

Fonts

There are many different fonts. Each one gives text its own 'look' and 'feel'. Some common fonts are:

Helvetica
Times
Courier
Brush Script

Type styles

PageMaker can give text different 'type styles'. These change the way text looks and give different emphasis and effect. Some common type styles are:

Normal
Bold
Italic
Underline
Outline

More than one type style can be 'active' at one time, for example:

This is Bold Outlined text
This is Italic Underlined text

Activity 2

Moving text onto a page

Objectives

1. To move a piece of text entered on the desktop onto a page

Introduction

We are now ready to move the text entered in the previous activity to an appropriate place on the page. This activity deals with the process of taking text from the desktop and putting it onto a page.

Guided activity

1. **With the pointer tool, point into the middle of the text you just typed and click the mouse button.**
The text should take the form of a selected text block. Whatever method we use to enter text into PageMaker ('Placing' it from a word processed file or typing it in directly) it is always held in a text block.

2. **'Pick up' the text block holding this text** — with the pointer located in the middle of the text hold down the mouse button.

3. **Move the text block** (which should move with the pointer as long as the mouse button is held down) **onto the page so that the top line of the text block is lined up with the top margin and the left–hand side of the text block is lined up with the left–hand margin** (figure 2.1).

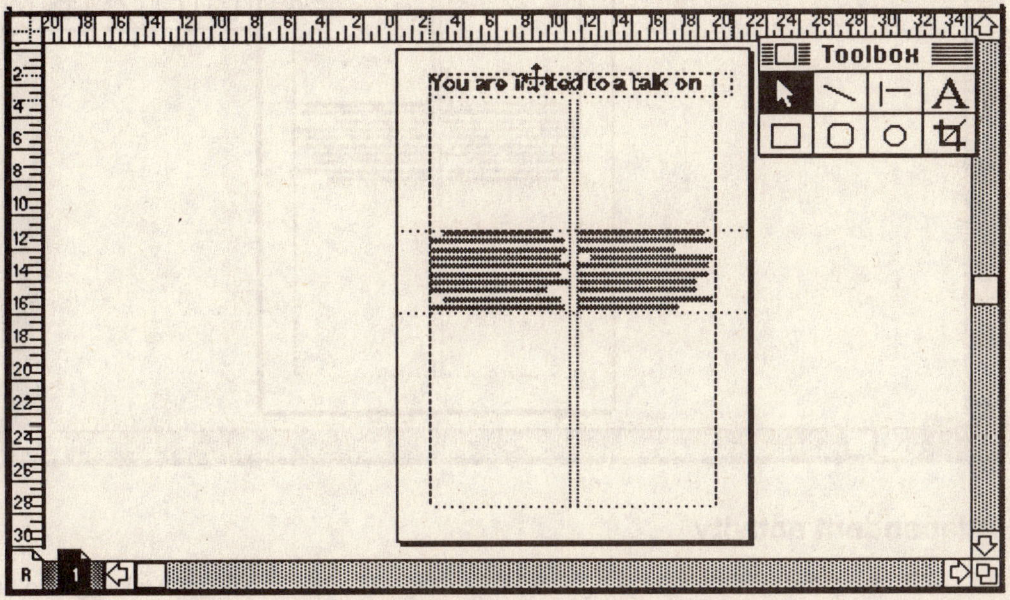

Figure 2.1

It is important that the text block fits into the space between the left and right–hand margins exactly — if it does not then the text will not span the space between these two margins and end abruptly. The two dots on the left–hand side of the text block should be lined up with the left–hand margin and the dots on the right should line up with the right–hand margin (as in figure 2.2). You have just lined up the left–hand side of the text block with the left–hand margin but the right–hand side may not reach or may go past the right–hand margin. If this is the case then you need to change the shape of the text block so that the right–hand side is lined up correctly. If the right–hand side of the text block does not rest on the right–hand margin then ...

• **Move the pointer so that it points at the dot in the top right–hand corner of the selected text block and hold down the mouse button.**
You have just 'picked up' this corner of the text block.

• **With the mouse button held down move the pointer so that it touches the right–hand margin.**
An outline of the new shape of the box should be drawn as you move — make sure the top of this box remains lined up with the top margin.

• **When the pointer rests in the corner so that it touches the right and top margins release the mouse button.**
The text block should now change to fit the new shape you have just specified and should span the space between the left and right–hand margins. It should also be touching the top margin.
If it does not then try picking up the dot and moving it to the right–hand margin again.

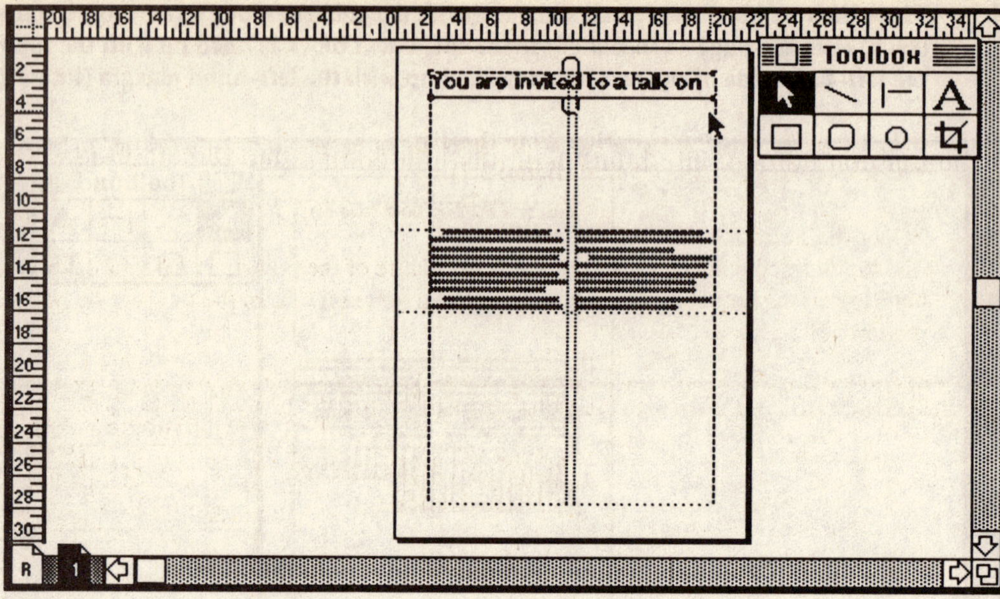

Figure 2.2

Independent activity

1. Change the size of the text you just added to 48pt. The text should now take up two lines — don't worry about this.

Activity 3

Centring text

Objectives

1. To centre text within its text block

Introduction

The sample document you are creating would probably look better if the text in the box you just added was 'centred'. This activity explains the process of centring text.

Guided activity

1. **With the text tool, place the cursor in the middle of the text block at the top of the page.** The flashing cursor should appear in the text.

2. **Select the 'Select all' option from the [Edit] menu.** The text should become highlighted.

3. **PageMaker refers to how text is lined up inside a text block as its 'alignment'. Dsplay the list in the 'Alignment' option in the [Type] menu.**
   A list of different alignments is displayed.

4. **Select the 'Align centre' option from this list.**
   The text should become centred (figure 3.1).

5. **Select the pointer tool from the toolbox.**
   The highlighted text returns to normal. The picture of the pointer in the toolbox becomes highlighted to show it has been selected. When you move from the toolbox the pointer tool remains.

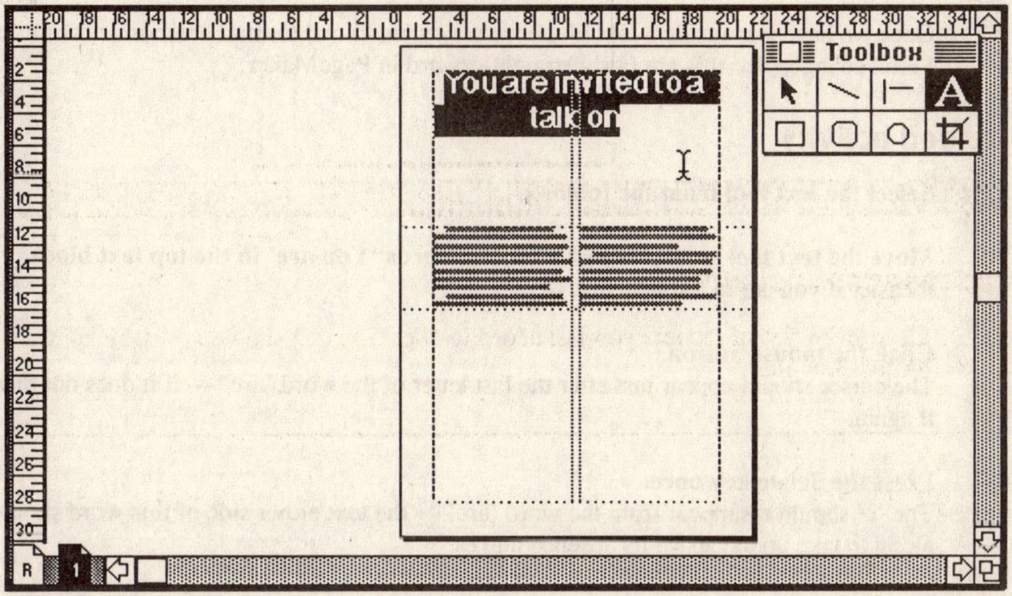

Figure 3.1

Text alignment

Text alignment refers to how a piece of text is lined up within its text block. The four main alignments are 'align centre', 'align right', 'align left' and 'justify'. Each type of alignment gives text a very definite 'look'.

Align centre

Text alignment refers to how a piece of text is lined up within its text block. The four main alignments are 'align centre', 'align right', 'align left' and 'justify'. Each type of alignment gives text a very definite 'look'.

Align right

Text alignment refers to how a piece of text is lined up within its text block. The four main alignments are 'align centre', 'align right', 'align left' and 'justify'. Each type of alignment gives text a very definite 'look'.

Align left

Text alignment refers to how a piece of text is lined up within its text block. The four main alignments are 'align centre', 'align right', 'align left' and 'justify'. Each type of alignment gives text a very definite 'look'.

Justify

Text alignment refers to how a piece of text is lined up within its text block. The four main alignments are 'align centre', 'align right', 'align left' and 'justify'. Each type of alignment gives text a very definite 'look'.

Activity 4

Changing text

Objectives

1. To change the contents of text in a text block

Introduction

Once we have text inside a text block we may want to make small amendments to its content. Small changes like this are fairly straightforward in PageMaker.

Guided activity

1. **Select the text tool from the toolbox.**

2. **Move the text tool so that is just after the words 'You are' in the top text block** (you may find it easier if you are in 'Actual size').

3. **Click the mouse button.**
The cursor should appear just after the last letter of the word 'are' — if it does not then try placing it again.

4. **Press the delete key once.**
The 'e' should disappear from the word 'are' — the text either side of this word should 'shuffle' along to take up the space its absence makes.

5. **Press the delete key three more times.**
The 'ae' and the space after the word 'You' should be deleted. The text should now read:
`You invited to a talk on`
And the cursor should be just after the 'u' in 'you'.

6. **Type in**
`'re`
These letters should appear making the word "You're". The text should now read:
`You're invited to a talk on`

7. **Select the pointer tool from the toolbox.**

Independent activity

1. Change the text in the block at the top of the page back so that it reads:
`You are invited to a talk on`

2. **Add the text**

   `The impact of desk top publishing on 'the person in the street'`
   under the text block at the top of the page. To do this:
   - **Get an additional guide from the horizontal ruler and place it on your page so that it lines up with the 6cm mark on the vertical ruler.**
   - **At the side of the page type in the following text in 36pt Helvetica (text with a size of '36' and a font of 'Helvetica'):**

   `The impact of desk top publishing on 'the person in the street'`
   - **Move it onto your page so that the text block is lined up with the left and right–hand margins and its top touches the guide you just placed.**
   - **Centre this text.**

3. **Repeat the process to place the following text in 30pt Helvetica starting 17cm down your page and centred:**

```
Start time : 7.30pm
Finish time : 9.30pm
on 1st April
at
The Community Centre
45 Publishing Road
Topsmoor
Sheffield
```

End of chapter summary

What I want to do	How I do it
• Change the 'Size' of a story	• 'Select all' of the story and select a new size from the list in the 'Size' option of the [Type] menu
• Change the 'Font' of a story	• 'Select all' of the story and select a new font from the list in the 'Font' option of the [Type] menu
• Change the 'Type style' of a story	• 'Select all' of the story and select a new type style from the list in the 'Type style' option of the [Type] menu
• Change the 'Alignment' of a story	• 'Select all' of the story and select a new alignment from the list in the 'Alignment' option of the [Type] menu
• Change the shape of a text block	• Point at one of the dots in each corner of the text block and drag it to a new position

Trouble–shooting

Problem	Possible reason	Solution
• Cursor doesn't appear where it is placed by the text tool	• Text alignment not to left	• Ensure 'Alignment' set to 'Left' after placing cursor
• Text entered is already in italics or other type style	• Text has a 'default' type style assigned	• Ensure 'Type style' is set to 'Normal' after placing cursor
• Text in end of block of text missing although it was typed in	• Text has overflowed block	• Select text block concerned and ensure the bottom handle is empty — if not then increase length of text block
• Text not centred	• Text block incorrectly lined up	• Check right and left–hand sides of text block reach right and left–hand margin guides

Chapter 5

Lines and boxes

- adding a line
- moving and stretching a line
- adding a box
- changing the shape of a box
- printing a document

Introduction to chapter 5

In this chapter we will make some finishing touches to the first sample document in this book. We will add a line to divide the page up a little and a border around the whole page. Finally this chapter shows how to print the final document.

Activity 1

Adding a line

Objectives

1. To add a line to a page

Introduction

Lines can be added to a document to break up the text and add a bit of variety and interest. This activity deals with the process of adding a line.

Guided activity

1. **Put an additional horizontal guide 10.5cm from the top of the page.**

2. **Select the 'Perpendicular–line' tool from the toolbox** (figure 1.1).
As you move away from the toolbox the pointer becomes a '+'.

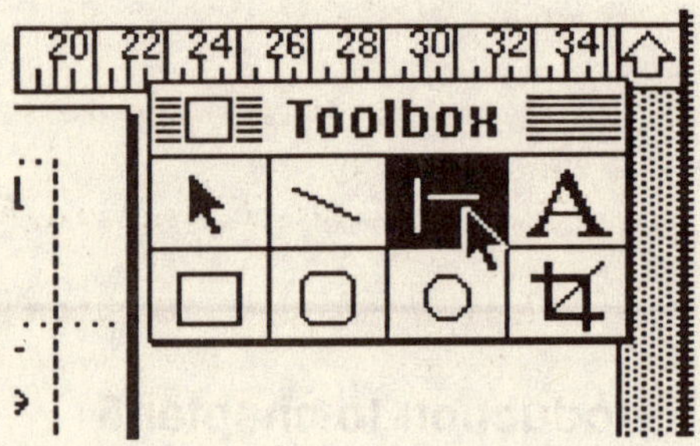

Figure 1.1

3. **Move the cross so that it rests on the guide you just placed, where it touches the left–hand margin, and hold down the mouse button.**

4. **With the mouse button held down move the pointer to the right–hand side of the guide where it touches the right margin.**
As you move a line should be drawn (though it may be obscured by the guide you are using).

5. **With the cross resting on the point where the 10.5cm horizontal guide and the right margin meet, release the mouse button.**
A line appears along the guide. At either end of this line there should be a 'dot' (just like the ones on a selected text block) — indicating it is currently 'selected'.

6. **Select the pointer from the toolbox.**
The dots at either end of the line disappear — it is no longer selected. Changing your tool causes anything currently selected to become de–selected.

7. **Make the guides inactive** so you can see your line clearly.

8. **Activate the guides once more.**

Activity 2

Moving and stretching a line

Objectives

1. To move a previously placed line around a page
2. To change the length of a line

Introduction

Once a line has been drawn on a page it does not have to stay in the position it was originally placed. PageMaker allows us to move lines and change their length.

Guided activity

1. **Ensure the 'Lock guides' option in the [Options] menu is active** — we do not want to move the guide by mistake.

2. **Move the pointer so that it is located somewhere along the line you just drew and click the mouse button.**
   The line has just been selected. A dot appears at either end.

3. **Move the pointer so that it points on the line you just placed** (but keep away from the dots at each end).

4. **Hold down the mouse button.**
   The pointer changes to a four–headed arrow.

5. **With the mouse button held down, drag the line** (which moves with the pointer) **so that it rests on the top margin.**
   As you move the pointer the line follows. It has been 'picked up'.

6. **With the line resting on the top margin, release the mouse button.**
   You have 'dropped' the line here. When the pointer is moved away the line should stay in place.

7. **Move the pointer so that it points at the dot at the right–hand end of the line you just moved.**

8. **Hold down the mouse button.**
   You have just 'picked up' this end of the line — the pointer changes to a cross.

9. **Move the cross to middle of the top margin.**
   The line should decrease in length, following the pointer.

10. **With the cross located in the middle of the top margin, release the mouse button.**
    The right hand side of the line should now end where you 'dropped' the dot.

Independent activity

1. Stretch the line so that it reaches the right–hand margin again.

2. Move the line back to rest on the 10.5cm horizontal guide, between the left and right margins.

Activity 3

Adding a box

Objectives

1. To add a box to a page

Introduction

Using PageMaker you can add boxes to a page. They can be filled with a variety of shades or patterns, or they can be empty. An empty box can act as a frame or 'border' around a document. In this activity we will try and add a border to the sample document you have been creating.

Guided activity

1. **Select the 'Square corner box' tool from the toolbox** (figure 3.1). We are going to use this to draw a box around the page.

2. **Move down to the 'Line' option in the [Element] menu.**
   A list of different types of line is displayed. We want a line 1 pt (1 point) in thickness.

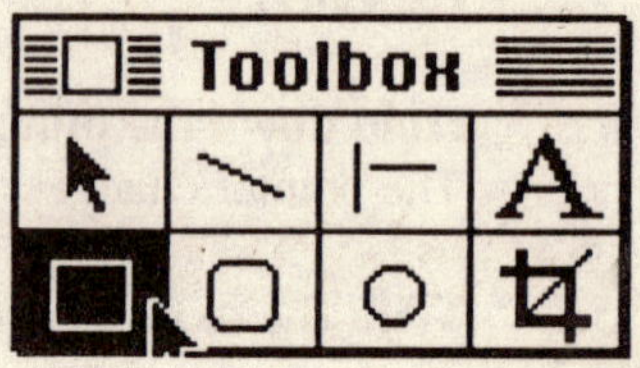

Figure 3.1

3. **Select the '1 pt' option from this list.**

4. **Move to the 'Fill' option in the [Element] menu.**
   A list of different shades and patterns a box can be filled with appears. We want the box to be empty — to act like a border around the page.

5. **Select the 'None' option from this list.**

6. **Move the cross so that it is in the top left–hand corner of the page, just outside the margins** (figure 3.2).

7. With the cross located here, **hold down the mouse button.**

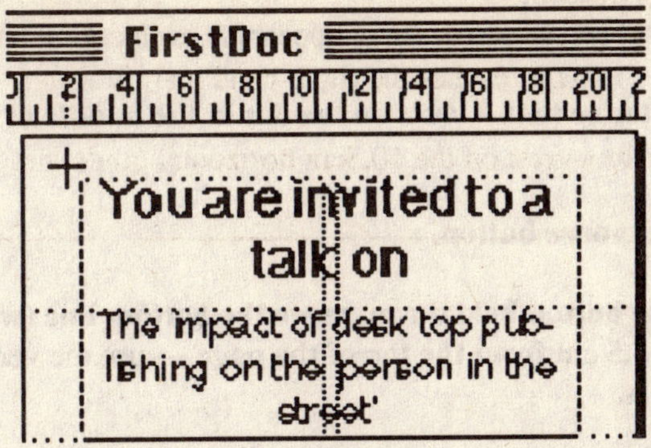

Figure 3.2

8. **Move the cross to the bottom right–hand corner of the page, just outside the margins.**
As you move PageMaker draws a box.

9. **With the cross located here, release the mouse button.**
A box should be drawn around your page — the line which marks it is 1pt wide. The box is empty (so you can see your text!) In each corner and in the middle of each line there is a dot — indicating the box is selected.

10. **Select the pointer tool from the toolbox.**
The dots indicating the box is selected disappear.

11. **Make the guides inactive** so you can how the page looks.

12. **Activate the guides once more.**

Activity 4

Changing the shape of a box

Objectives

1. To change the shape of a previously drawn box

Introduction

Just as with lines, we do not have to leave boxes as they were when we first drew them. In this activity you will change the shape of the box you just drew.

Guided activity

1. **Ensure the 'Lock guides' option in the [Options] menu is active.**

2. **Move the pointer so that it is located somewhere along the line of the box you just drew and click the mouse button.**
   The box has just been selected. A dot appears at each corner and in the middle of each line.

3. **Move the pointer so that it rests on the dot in the middle of the bottom line of the box you have just drawn.**

4. **Hold down the mouse button.**

5. **With the mouse button held down, move the bottom line** (which should move with the pointer) **so that it rests 5.5 cm from the top of the page** — use the vertical ruler to keep track of where the bottom line is.

6. **With the pointer located here, release the mouse button.**
   The box should have been redrawn so that the bottom line rests in the new position.

7. **Click away from the page** (move the pointer to the space on the desktop and click the mouse button).
   The dots indicating a selected box should now disappear.

8. **Make the guides inactive** so you can how the page looks.

9. **Activate the guides once more.**

Independent activity

1. Replace the box in its original position.

Activity 5 Printing a document

Objectives

1. To print a document

Introduction

This activity goes through the process of printing the sample document you have been creating. We will use PageMaker's default settings to make a simple print.

Guided activity

1. **Select the 'Print' option from the [File] menu.**
   A dialogue box should appear.

2. **Click in the 'OK' or 'Print' box.**
   After a moment PageMaker should print your page.

Smart quotes

Most word processors only allow you to use a 'keyboard quote'. For keyboard quotes the opening quotation mark is the same as the closing quotation mark (since the same key is used for both). PageMaker allows the use of ‘smart’ quotes.

Ordinary keyboard quotes	Smart quotes
'This is a quote'	‘This is a quote’
"This is a quote"	“This is a quote”

To obtain smart quotes it is necessary to press a series of keys — these are shown below:

Type of quote	Keys to press (Macintosh)	Keys to press (PC)
‘	OPTION and]	CTRL and [
’	OPTION, SHIFT and]	CTRL and]
“	OPTION and [	CTRL, SHIFT and [
”	OPTION, SHIFT and [	CTRL, SHIFT and]

Independent activity

1. Change the quotation marks surrounding the words 'the person in the street' to ‘smart’ quotes and print the document again.

End of chapter summary

What I want to do	How I do it
• Add a line to a page	• Select the line drawing tool and drag from where you want the line to start to where it should end
• Move a line around the page	• Hold down pointer tool over middle of line and drag to new position
• Change the length of a line	• Hold down pointer tool over dot at end of selected line and drag to new length
• Add a box	• Select the box drawing tool and drag from top left–hand corner of where box should be to bottom right–hand corner of where box should be
• Change the shape of a box	• Hold pointer tool over dot at corner or in middle of lines of box and drag to new position
• Print a document	• Select 'Print' from [File] menu and click on 'OK' or 'Print' in dialogue box

Trouble–shooting

Problem	Possible reason	Solution
• When adding line or box the text seems to move as if it can't go near the line or box	• Text wrap is switched on	• See section 3 — chapter on 'Text wrap' then choose appropriate wrap option to switch text wrap off
• Can't select line or box	• Too far away / text block in the way / unlocked guide in way	• Change view so that line or box is closer and try again — if not successful then 'click away from' the page before going closer — if still not successful ensure 'Lock guides' is active and try again
• Can't print	• Any number of reasons	• Outside scope of this book — printer and connections need to be checked and possibly default print settings also

Additional Exercises

- advertisement for talk
- advertisement for services
- handout

Introduction

The following pages hold additional exercises to give you practice at what you have learned in this section. Each exercise or 'project' is divided into three parts:

- **'Project'** shows what the document you are to create looks like.
- **'Guides'** suggests some positions for guides and margins (in diagrammatic form) which may be helpful.
- **'Elements'** shows the different elements on the page.

For clarity the sample document you have been creating in this section is included as the first exercise.

Project

Advertisement for Desk Top Publishing Talk

You are invited to a talk on

The impact of desk top publishing on the 'person in the street'

A talk by Professor C Package on the impact of desk top publishing on the process of creating documents. The talk begins with a look at the history of publishing and the major dramatic changes in these processes. Questions will be welcomed from the audience in the second part of the talk which consists of a discussion on how publishing will change in the future.

Professor Package is a well known figure in desk top publishing having written a number of books on the subject - amoung them being 'Desk top publishing for children' and 'Life, the universe, and desk top publishing'.

Future events are planned to continue from this talk where visitors will get the opportunity for 'hands on' experience of some of the more well known desk top publishing packages. Anyone interested in participating in these events should write to the address shown below. Book early to avoid disappointment.

Start time : 7.30pm
Finish time : 9.30pm
on 1st April
at
The Community Centre
45 Publishing Road
Topsmoor
Sheffield

Guides

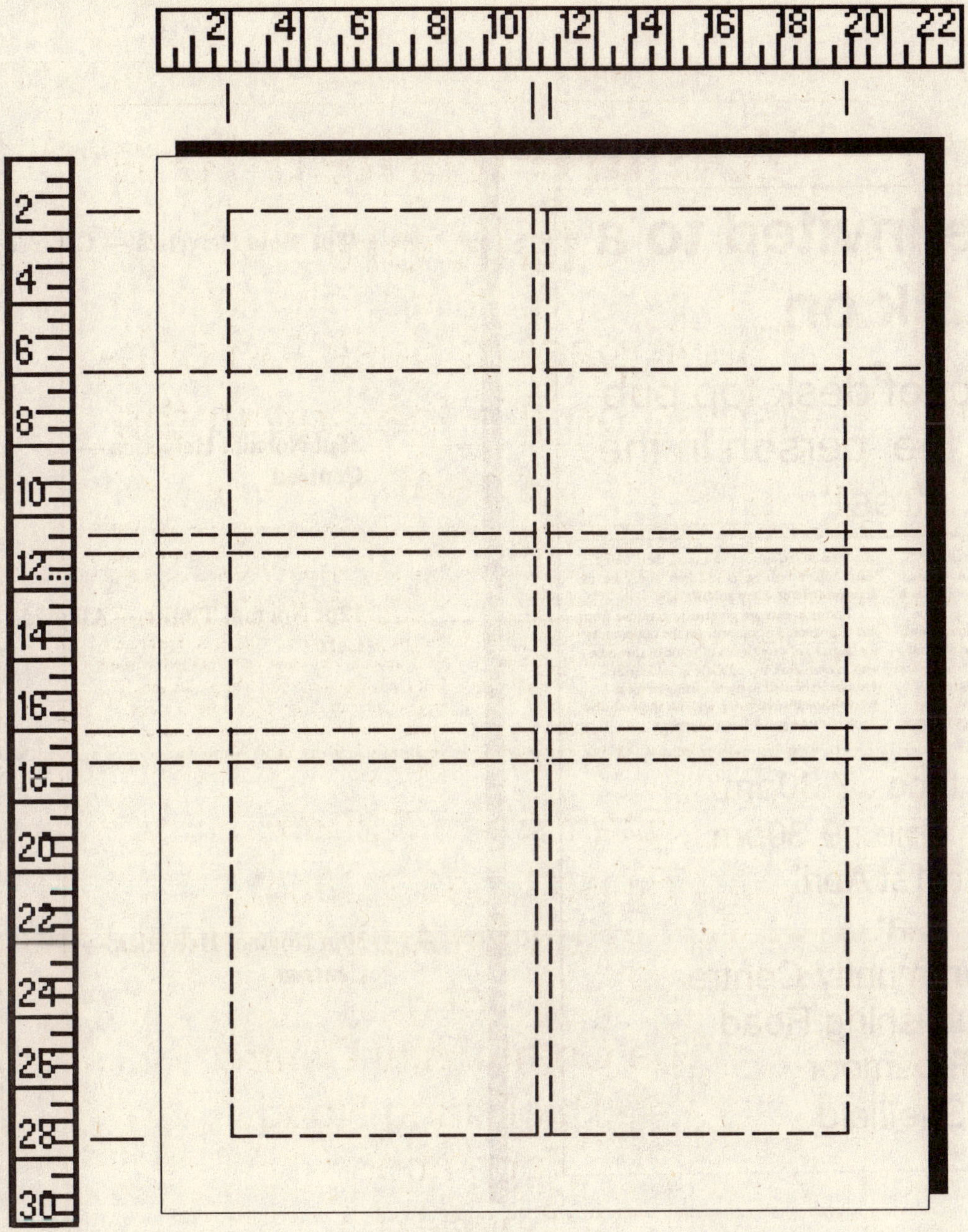

Elements

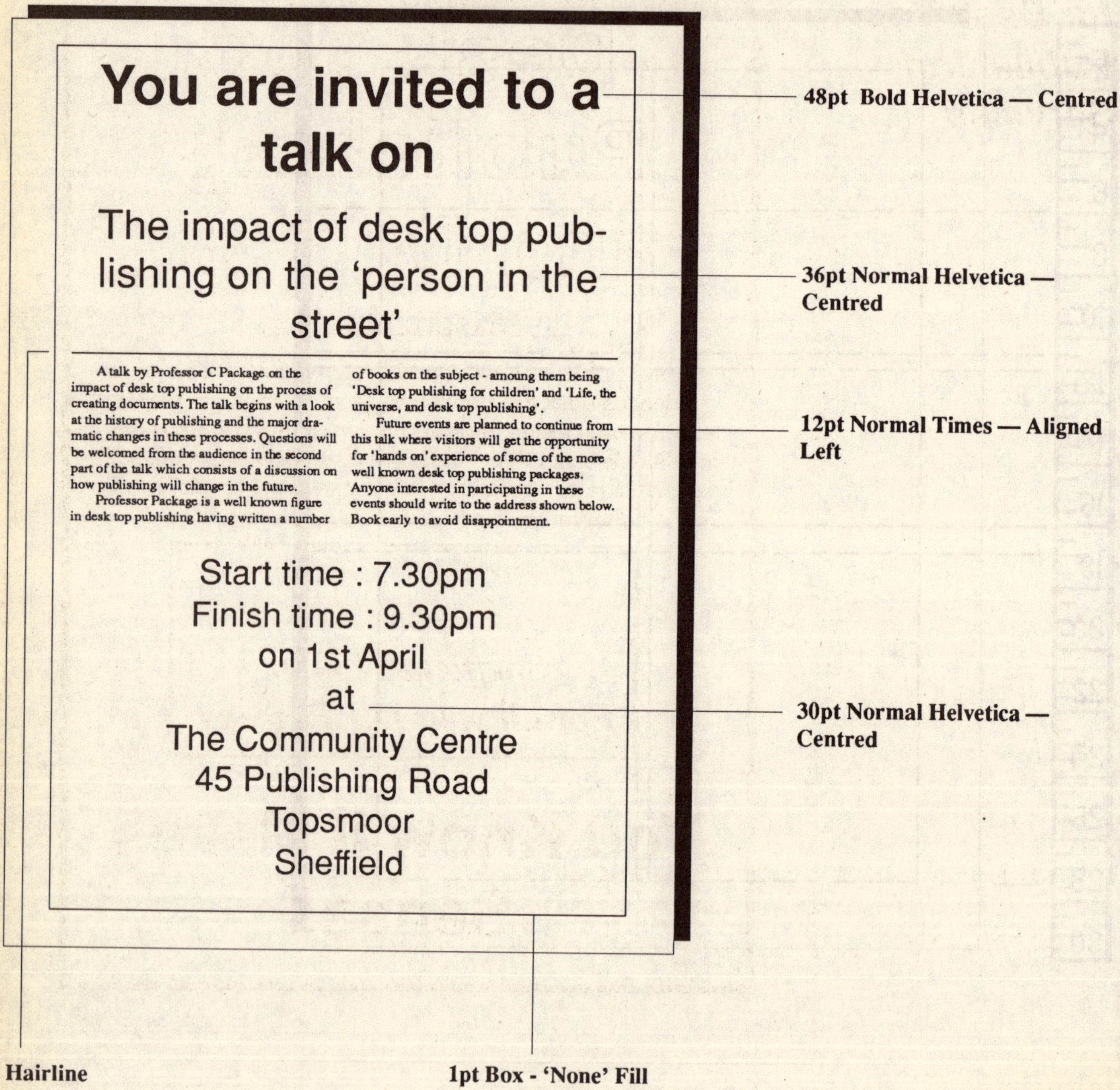

You are invited to a talk on

The impact of desk top publishing on the 'person in the street'

A talk by Professor C Package on the impact of desk top publishing on the process of creating documents. The talk begins with a look at the history of publishing and the major dramatic changes in these processes. Questions will be welcomed from the audience in the second part of the talk which consists of a discussion on how publishing will change in the future.

Professor Package is a well known figure in desk top publishing having written a number of books on the subject - amoung them being 'Desk top publishing for children' and 'Life, the universe, and desk top publishing'.

Future events are planned to continue from this talk where visitors will get the opportunity for 'hands on' experience of some of the more well known desk top publishing packages. Anyone interested in participating in these events should write to the address shown below. Book early to avoid disappointment.

Start time : 7.30pm
Finish time : 9.30pm
on 1st April
at
The Community Centre
45 Publishing Road
Topsmoor
Sheffield

Project

Advertisement for Desk Top Publishing Services

Desk Top Publishing and Design

at reasonable rates

Desk top publishing work and design of documents by experienced desk top publishers on modern, high quality equipment. Design and production of most publications from single sheet flyers to large newsletters undertaken at reasonable rates. A sliding scale is available. For a free consultation with no further obligation contact:

Pitsmoor Publishers
on
Sheffield 123456
For all your D.T.P. needs

You Know It Makes Sense!

Guides

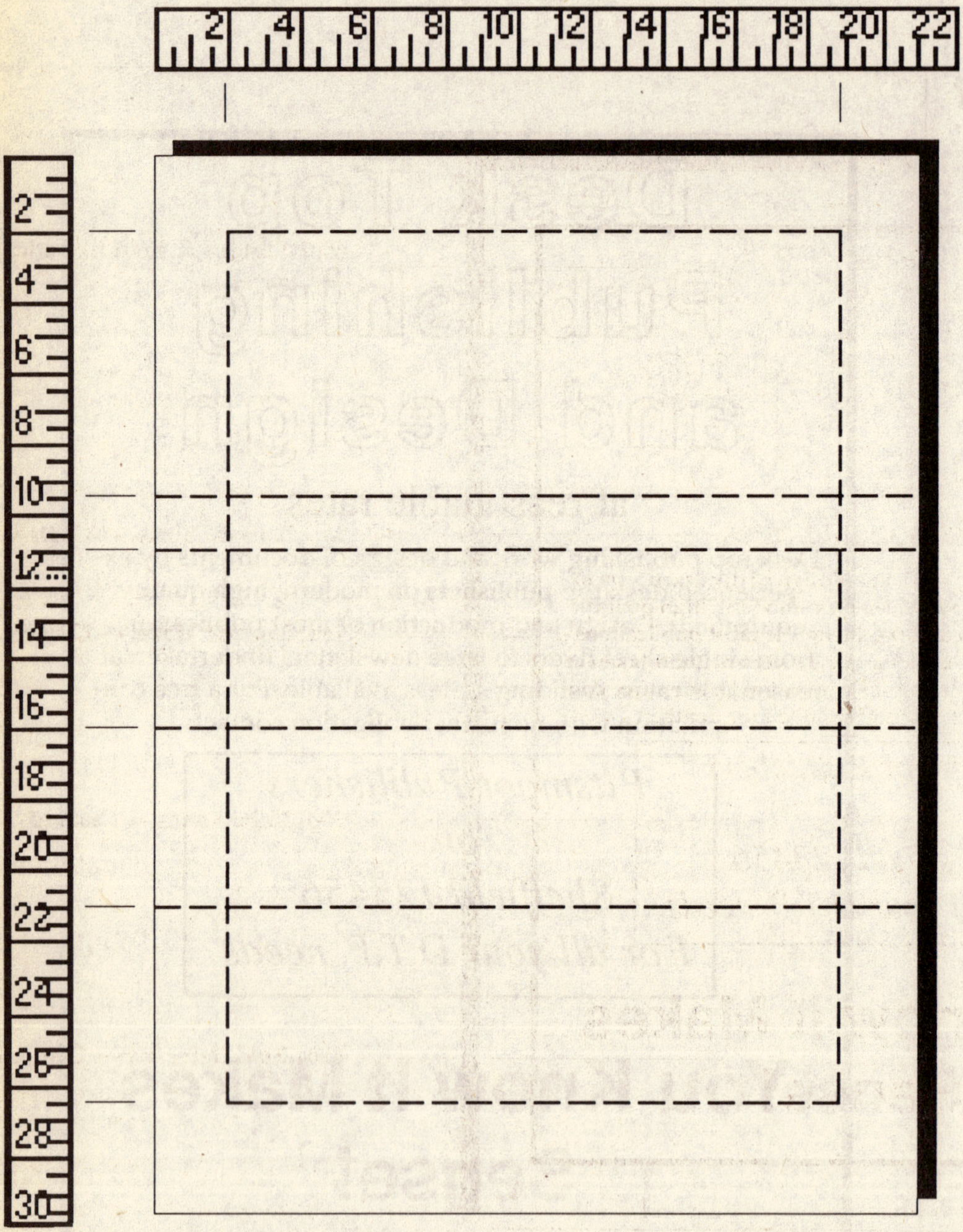

Elements

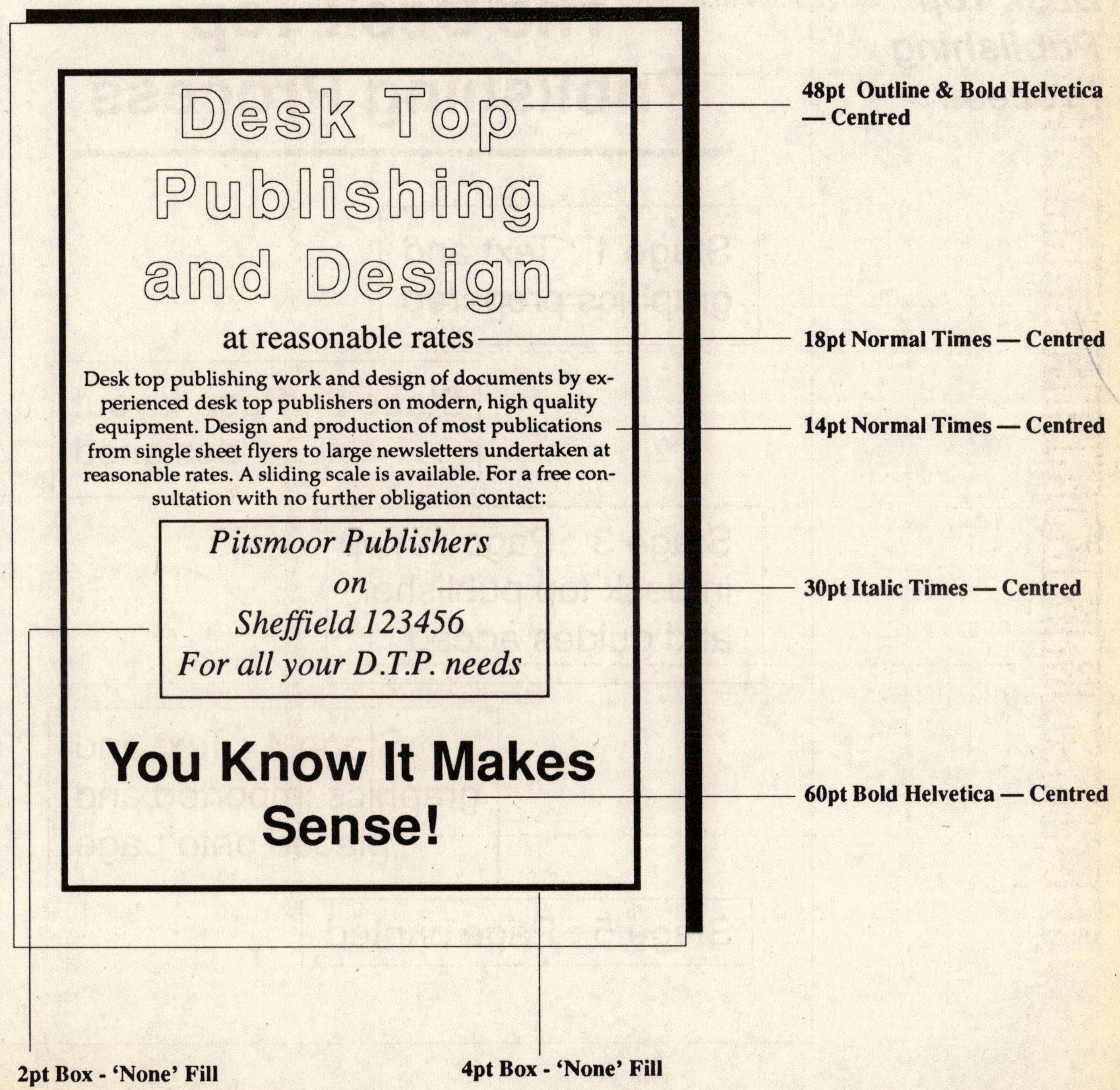
Desk Top Publishing and Design
at reasonable rates
Desk top publishing work and design of documents by experienced desk top publishers on modern, high quality equipment. Design and production of most publications from single sheet flyers to large newsletters undertaken at reasonable rates. A sliding scale is available. For a free consultation with no further obligation contact:
Pitsmoor Publishers
on
Sheffield 123456
For all your D.T.P. needs
You Know It Makes Sense!
48pt Outline & Bold Helvetica — Centred
18pt Normal Times — Centred
14pt Normal Times — Centred
30pt Italic Times — Centred
60pt Bold Helvetica — Centred
2pt Box - 'None' Fill
4pt Box - 'None' Fill

Project

Handout on Desk Top Publishing Process

The Desk Top Publishing Process

Stage 1 : Text and graphics prepared

Stage 2 : Page layout designed

Stage 3 : Page set up in desk top publisher and guides added

Stage 4 : Text and graphics imported and placed onto page

Stage 5 : Page printed

Guides

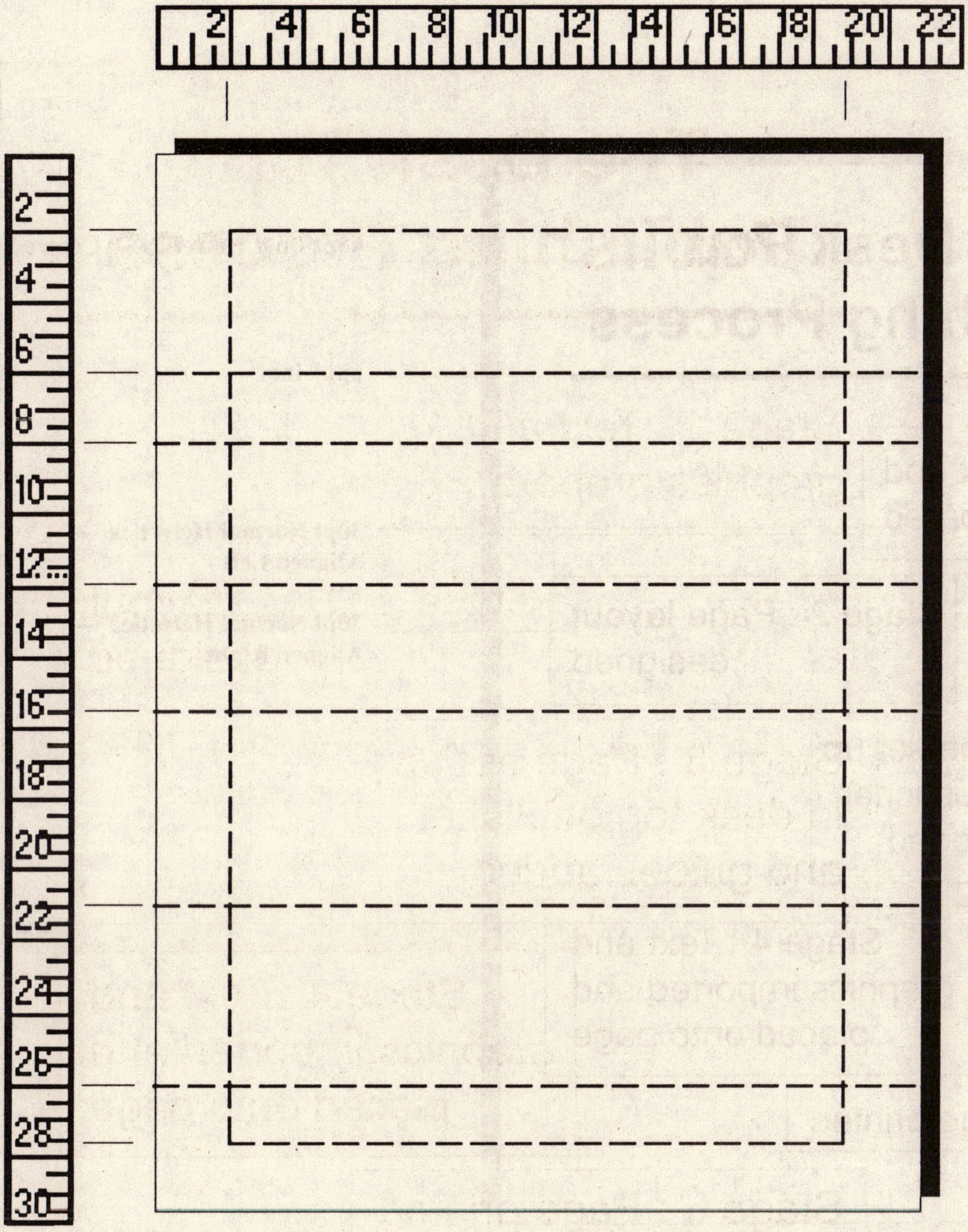

Elements

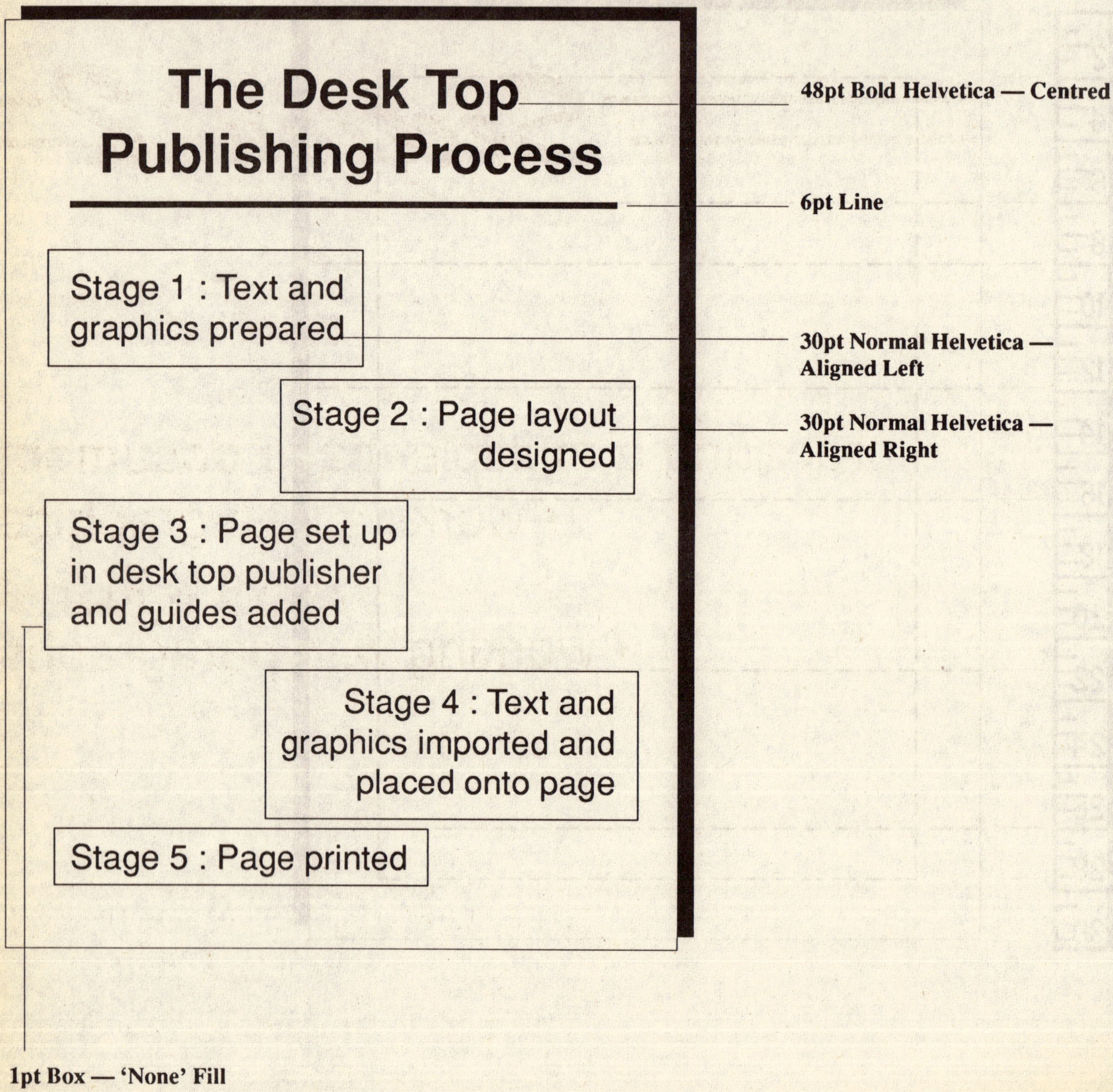
The Desk Top Publishing Process
Stage 1 : Text and graphics prepared
Stage 2 : Page layout designed
Stage 3 : Page set up in desk top publisher and guides added
Stage 4 : Text and graphics imported and placed onto page
Stage 5 : Page printed
48pt Bold Helvetica — Centred
6pt Line
30pt Normal Helvetica — Aligned Left
30pt Normal Helvetica — Aligned Right
1pt Box — 'None' Fill

Section 2

• preparing a multiple–page document
• working with graphics
• ways with text
• working with paragraphs

Introduction to section 2

Having covered the basics of setting up a PageMaker page and adding text section 2 explains how to use multiple–pages, add graphics to your documents and more on PageMaker's text manipulation caperbilities. To do this we will be creating the first two pages of a four–page newsletter.

The creation of these pages is broken down into a number of stages — covered in the following chapters:

Chapter 1 — Preparing a multiple-page document

Creating multiple–page documents need not be a daunting task. This chapter shows how to set up a document with more than one page. We will see how to make repeating features (like page numbers) appear on each page automatically.

Chapter 2 — Working with graphics

Explains how to add graphics to a page and how to change them so they occupy a given space.

Chapter 3 — Ways with text

Has a closer look at working with text in PageMaker. As well as some basic desk top publishing text manipulation functions we will look at producing special effects with text.

Chapter 4 — Working with paragraphs

Thinking of text as a collection of paragraphs can be a useful concept for the desk top publisher. This chapter looks into why this is the case.

Documents created in this section

In this section you will be creating the first two pages of the four-page newsletter shown below.

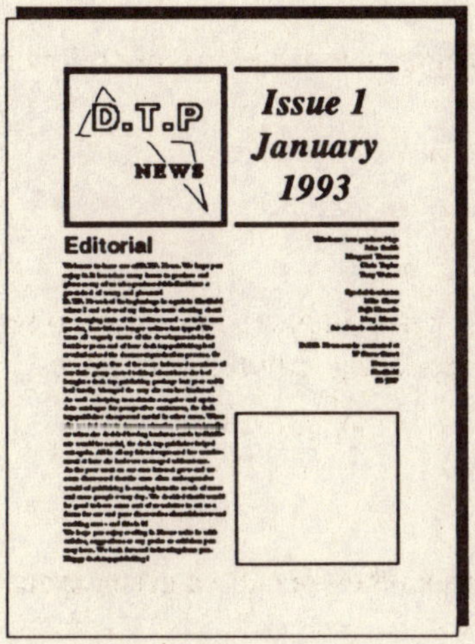

Page 1

Pages 2 and 3

Page 4

Chapter 1

Preparing a multiple–page document

• setting up pages
• adding repeating guides
• additional guides
• adding 'headers' and 'footers'
• page numbers
• 'hiding' master page items

Introduction to chapter 1

In this chapter we will look at how to set up a multiple–page document — that is, a document with more than one page. When working with multiple–page documents it is important to try and keep a degree of consistency between pages. By keeping the same number of columns on each page, the same margins and the same structure to the pages the final document will look more flowing and well–prepared. We will probably want many features of the document to appear on each page so will be using the 'master pages' to assist our preparation.

Activity 1

Setting up pages

Objectives

1. To set up a multiple–page document

Introduction

In this chapter you will use the 'Page setup' dialogue box to tell PageMaker some details about your multiple–page document.

Guided activity

1. Start PageMaker and, when it is fully started, **use the 'Preferences' dialogue box** (in the [Edit] menu) **to ensure the 'Measurement system' is set to 'Millimetres' and the 'Vertical ruler' is set to measure in 'Picas'.**

2. **Select the 'New' option from the [File] menu.**
   The 'Page setup' box should appear for you to tell PageMaker how the pages should look.

3. For the sample document you want a page of 'A4', with an orientation of 'Tall', starting on page '1' and with '4' pages. **Set these options in the dialogue box.**

4. PageMaker can think of a page as having two or 'double' sides (as they actually do). Since we are dealing with more than one page here let's think of the document as having double–sided pages. **Select this option.**
   The 'Facing pages' option should now be in normal text — showing it may be selected.

5. When we work with double–sided pages we can ask PageMaker to show us pages which will be next to or 'facing' each other at the same time.
   Select the 'Facing pages' option so that PageMaker will show each page with the page facing it.

6. When we are using double–sided pages PageMaker refers to side margins as 'Inside' and 'Outside' (figure 1.1).
   Set the 'Inside', 'Outside', 'Top' and 'Bottom' margins to '26.7', '26.7', '25.4', and '34.5' respectively.

7. **Click on 'OK'** to tell PageMaker you are happy with these settings.
   A blank page should now appear.

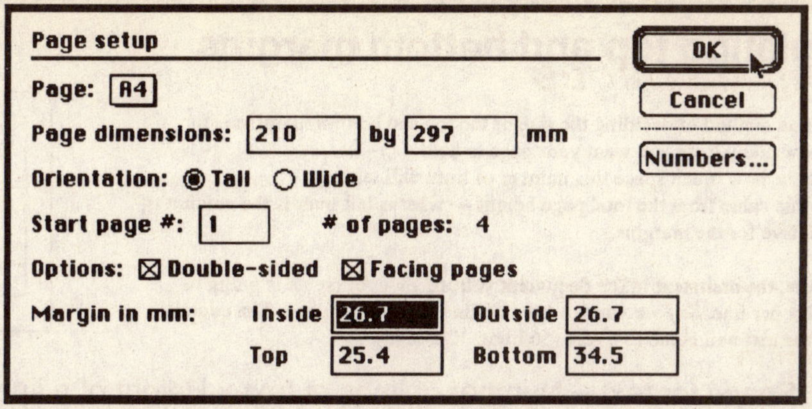

Figure 1.1

Picas

1 pica (1p) = 12 points (12pt)

A pica (abbreviated to 'p') is the equivalent measurement to 12 points. It is often more useful to measure in points and picas rather than millimetres since text itself is measured this way.

Inside and outside margins

When using double–sided pages PageMaker refers to the margins either side of a page as 'Inside' and 'Outside' margins.

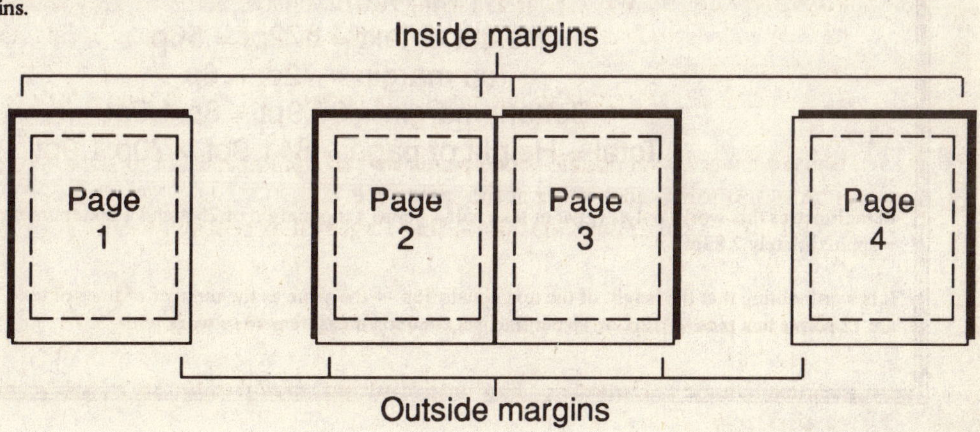

The inside margins are those on the inside of a finished publication and the outside margins are seen on the outside of a finished publication.

Calculating top and bottom margins

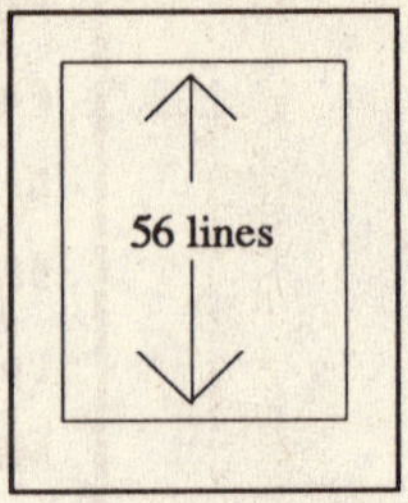

One common method of deciding the size of the top and bottom margins is to:
- decide how many lines you want your page to hold
- calculate the how much space this number of lines will take up
- subtract this value from the total page height — what is left over is the amount of space you have for the margins.

For example, the main text in the document you are about to create is going to take up 12pt per line. Say we want to have 56 lines of text per page. The overall height of the text will come to 672pt (56 lines, 12pt high).

Space for text = Number of lines of text x Height of a line of text

The total height of the page is 841.9pt (or 297mm). So, if the text takes up 672pt that leaves us 169.9pt (841.9pt - 672pt) for the top and bottom margins.

Space for margins = Height of page - Space for text

In this case we will make the top margin 72pt and the bottom margin 169.9pt.

To summarise:

Height of text = 56 lines of 12pt = 672pt
Top margin = 72pt
Bottom margin = 97.9pt
Total = Height of page = 841.9pt

It is common to represent large values in points and picas (rather than just points). This would give us:

Height of text = 672pt = 56p
Top margin = 72pt = 6p
Bottom margin = 97.9pt = 8p 1.9pt
Total = Height of page = 841.9pt = 70p 1.9pt

In millimetres this works out as (give or take half a point) a top margin of 25.4 and a bottom margin of 34.5 (since 1mm = approximately 2.83pt).

It is worth noting that the height of the text equals 56p — the same as the number of lines of text. This is because there are 12 points in a pica — 12pt or 1p per line is a common measurement to work with.

Calculating inside and outside margins

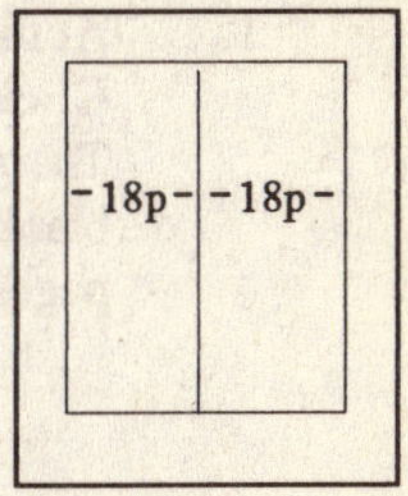

To calculate the inside and outside margins we can use a similar method to the one we used for calculating the top and bottom margins.

If we have two columns 18p wide on our pages — separated by a 1p space then the width of our text will be:

$$18 + 18 + 1 = 37p$$

The overall width of the page is 49p 7.3pt (or 210mm). So, the space left for our inside and outside margins is:

$$49p\ 7.3pt - 37p = 12p\ 7.3pt$$

If we split this up evenly between the margins then they are 6p 3.65pt each.

To summarise:

Width of each column = 18p
Width of space between columns = 1p
Inside margin = 6p 3.65pt
Outside margin = 6p 3.65pt
Total = 49p 7.3pt

In millimetres this works out as (give or take half a point) an inside margin of 26.7mm and an outside margin of 26.7mm (since 1mm = approximately 2.83pt).

Activity 2

Adding repeating guides

Objectives

1. To use the page icons
2. To add repeating guides using the 'master pages'

Introduction

In this activity we will be using the 'master pages'. These are special pages which are very useful when producing multiple–page documents. Anything we put onto a master page will be repeated on all of the pages in a document. Thus, if we wanted all the pages in a document to have 2 columns, by putting two columns onto the master pages this would be achieved. We will also be splitting each page into sections to form a 'grid'. Such 'page grids', as they are known, help give an extra structure for adding text and graphics.

Guided activity

1. At the bottom left–hand corner of the PageMaker window are the 'Page icons' (figure 2.1).
Click over the pages containing 'L' and 'R'.
These are the master page icons — 'L' stands for the 'Left' page and 'R' for the 'Right' page. Two blank pages should appear side by side. There are two pages because we selected the 'Facing pages' option in the 'Page setup' box.

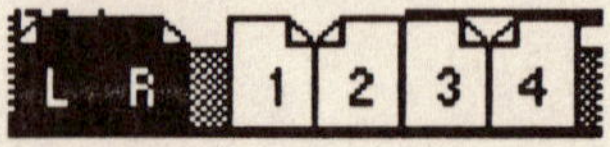

Figure 2.1

2. What you are now looking at are the master pages. We will put some column guides onto them.
Select the 'Column guides' option from the [Options] menu.
The 'Column guides' dialogue box should appear (figure 2.2).

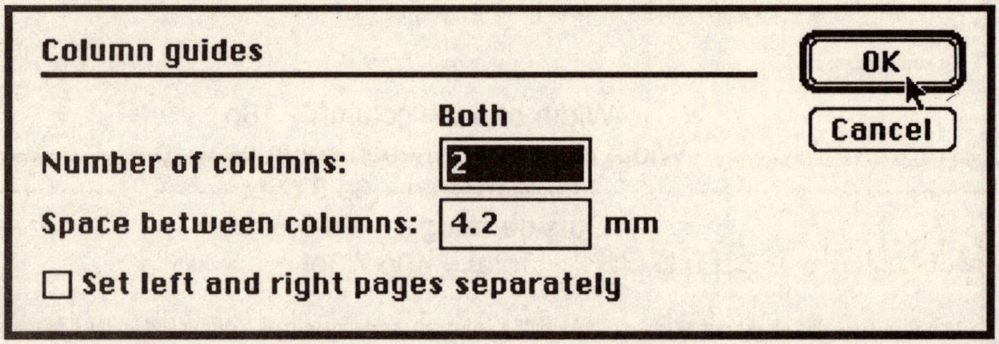

Figure 2.2

3. At the bottom of the dialogue box before you is the option to 'Set left and right pages separately' — if this option were selected then we could give a different number of columns to the left and right pages. In our sample document all the pages are based on a two–column structure so **ensure this option is not selected.**

4. **Select '2' columns '4.2' mm apart and click on 'OK'.**
The pages now have two columns each (provided your 'Guides' option is active!).

5. **Click on the page 1 icon.**
Page 1 should now be displayed. Since the first page of a document has no other pages facing it PageMaker should only display a single page. This page should have the two columns you set on the master pages.

6. **Click on the page 2 icon.**
Pages 2 and 3 should appear containing the columns you set on the master pages.

Master pages

Master pages are special pages used with multiple-page documents. There is a right-hand master page and a left-hand master page. Anything put onto the right master page will appear on every right-hand page of the document (pages 1, 3, 5, etc.) and everything put onto the left master page will appear on all of the left-hand pages (pages 2, 4, 6, etc.).

Master pages

Document pages

Activity 3

Additional guides

Objectives

1. To change the zero mark on the vertical ruler
2. To add additional horizontal guides to a document

Introduction

In this activity we will add some additional horizontal guides to our pages to give them a little extra structure when adding text and graphics. The first guide is going to be 18p (18 picas) from the top margin. To make measuring easier it would be good if zero on the vertical ruler was at the top margin rather than the top of the page. PageMaker gives us control over where the zero begins so let's try changing it.

Guided activity

1. **Move to the master pages** (click on the 'L' or 'R' page icon).

2. **Ensure the 'Zero lock' option in the [Options] menu is not active.**
With the 'Zero lock' option active the zero positioning on the rulers cannot be changed — they are 'locked'.

3. **Move the pointer over the box in the top left–hand corner of the PageMaker window, where the two rulers meet (figure 3.1), and hold down the mouse button.**
You have just 'picked up' the zero mark setter.

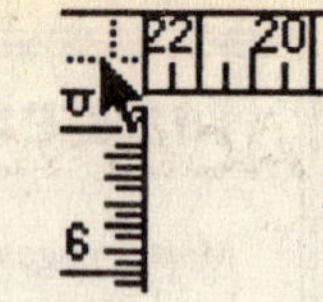

Figure 3.1

4. **With the mouse button held down 'drag' this down the vertical ruler.**
As you move a horizontal line follows the pointer — indicating where the zero on this ruler will start.

5. **Move the pointer so that the zero marker is lined up with the top margin guide. With the marker lined up here, release the mouse button.**
The zero point should now be in line with the top margins (figure 3.2). If it is not then repeat the process of picking up and moving the zero guide setter again. We are not currently concerned with the position of the zero point on the horizontal ruler so ignore this.

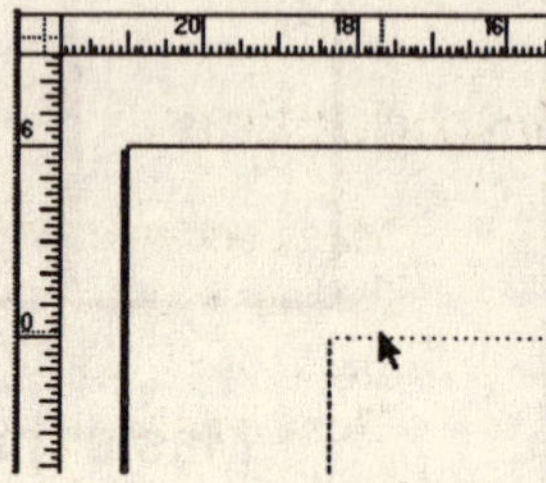

Figure 3.2

6. **Select the 'Zero lock' option from the [Options] menu to make it active.**
The zero indicator cannot now be moved — it is 'locked'.

7. **Add additional horizontal guides at the 18p, 19p, 37p and 38p marks on the vertical ruler.**
We have now split the page up into boxes — creating a 'page grid' (figure 3.3).

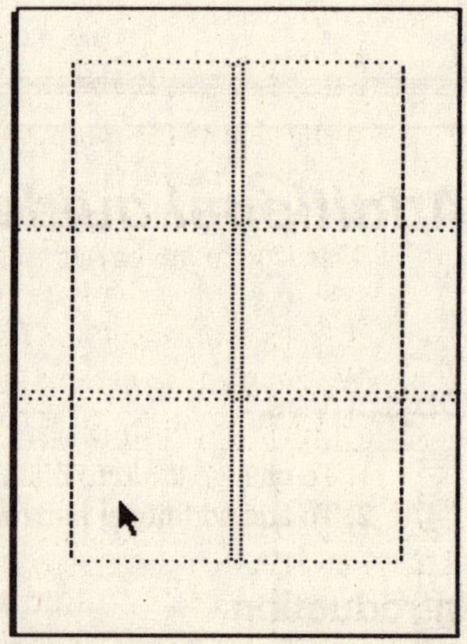

Figure 3.3

Page grids

By splitting the pages in a document into a 'grid' we give them an extra structure to assist us when laying out our document.

The grid we are using is achieved by splitting the page up into 6 'boxes' - each 18p high and 18p wide, separated by 1p.

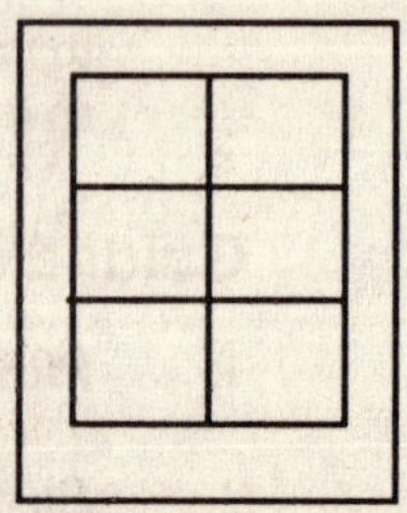

Activity 4

Adding 'headers' and 'footers'

Objectives

1. To add a header to a document

Introduction

Many documents include 'headers' and 'footers'. These are pieces of text at the top of a page (headers) and at the bottom of a page (footers) which give the reader some information. Headers and footers usually appear on most pages of a document so we will add them to our master pages. This book has headers on most of its pages saying which section you are on and which chapter.

Guided activity

1. **Ensure your 'Snap to guides' option is active.**

2. **A the side of the page type in**
`D.T.P. News`
in 10pt Helvetica text in italics.
This is going to be our 'header'. It will appear on both the right and the left pages.

2. **Add an additional horizontal guide 4 picas above the top margin** (figure 4.1).
We are going to use this guide to line up the headers.

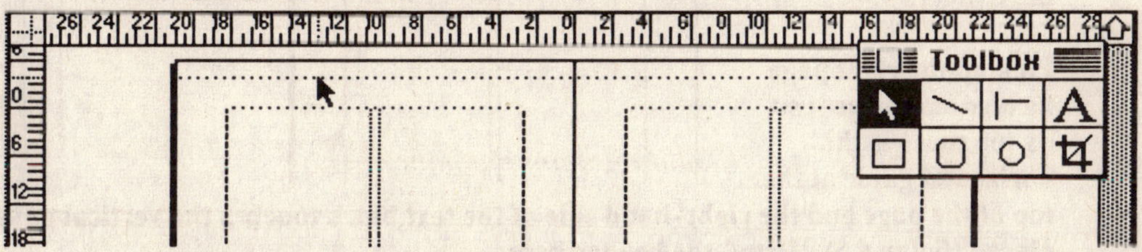

Figure 4.1

3. We want the same header on both pages so let's make another copy of the text block holding the header you just typed.
Using the pointer, select the text block holding the header.

4. With this text block selected, **choose the 'Copy' option from the [Edit] menu.**
PageMaker has now made a copy of this block of text.

5. **Select the 'Paste' option from the [Edit] menu.**
PageMaker puts the copied block of text onto the desktop (or the page). You now have two copies of the header.

6. The header on the left page is to be lined up to the left so **ensure one of the text blocks is 'Aligned left'** (use the text tool to 'Select all' then check 'Alignment' in the [Type] menu).

7. **Add an additional vertical guide so that it lines up with the left–hand side of the first column on the left page** (figure 4.2).

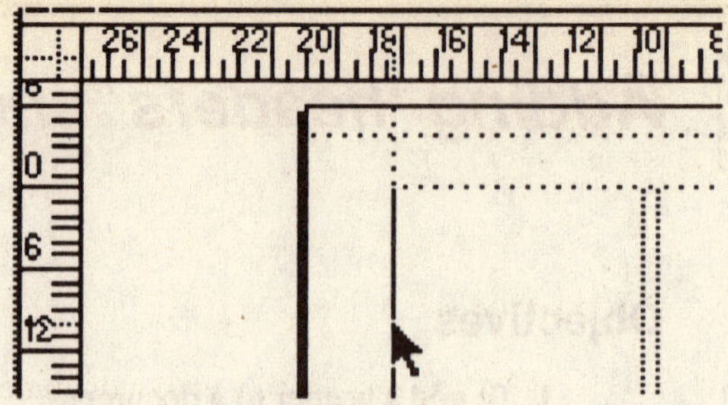

Figure 4.2

8. **Pick up the left page header and place it so its top touches the horizontal guide at the top of the page and the left–hand side of the text block touches the vertical guide you just placed** (figure 4.3). **'Drop' the header here** (you may find it easier in 'Actual size').

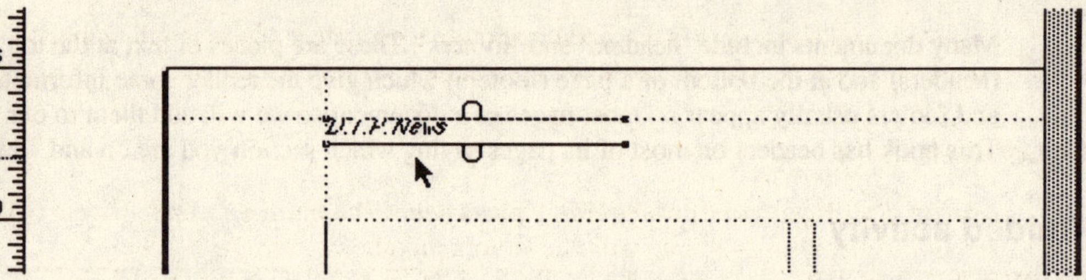

Figure 4.3

9. The header on the right page is to be lined up to the right so **ensure the remaining text block is 'Aligned right'.**

10. **Add an additional vertical guide so that it lines up with the right–hand side of the second column on the right page** (figure 4.4).

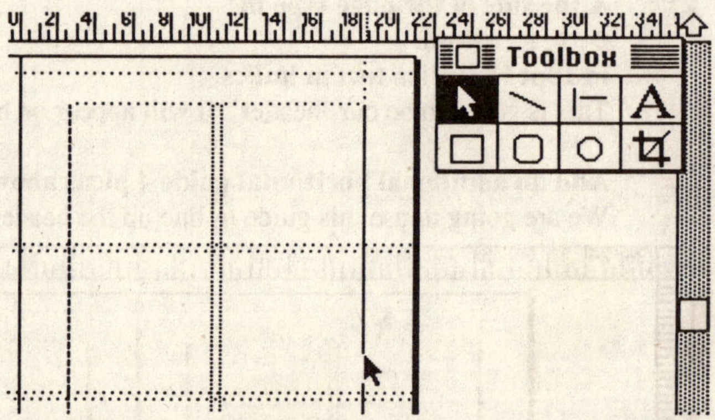

Figure 4.4

11. **Pick up the right page header and place it so its top touches the horizontal guide at the top of the page and the right–hand side of the text block touches the vertical guide you just placed** (figure 4.5). **'Drop' the header here.**

12. It is 'good practice' to remove guides that you will not need anymore — this stops your document becoming 'cluttered'. The horizontal guide which helped you place the headers onto the master pages will not be needed again so...
Remove the guide you placed 4 picas above the top margin by moving it back onto the horizontal ruler (don't forget to stay clear of text blocks when moving the guide).

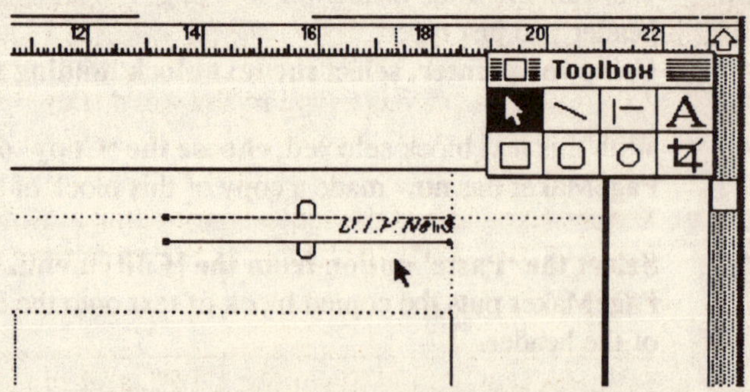

Figure 4.5

Activity 5

Page numbers

Objectives

1. To add page numbers to a document

Introduction

PageMaker allows us to add a special marker to a document where it will automatically put page numbers. This activity explains how to put these onto your document.

Guided activity

1. **Add an additional horizontal guide 5 picas below the bottom margin** (figure 5.1). Moving the zero marker so that it lines up with the bottom margin will help with this.

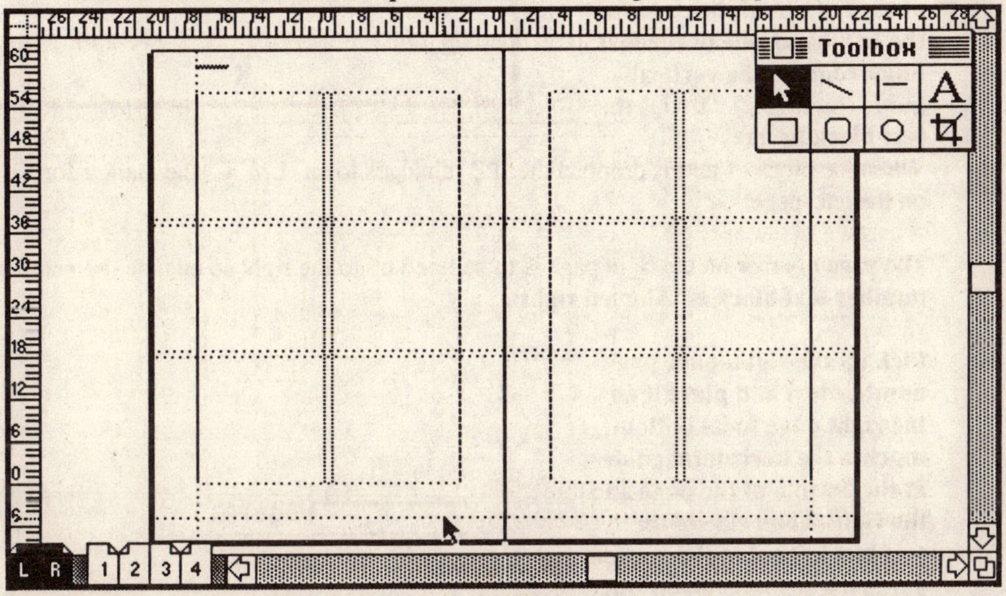

Figure 5.1

2. **At the side of the page type in the word 'Page' in 10pt Helvetica text in italics followed by a space.**

3. We are going to add the special page number marker next. To do this **hold down the OPTION**[PC] **key and the COMMAND key at the same time and, with these keys held down, press the 'P' key.**

PC users should **hold down the CTRL and the SHIFT keys and press '3'** instead.

The letters 'PB' appear next to the word 'Page'. This is the spacial marker. When it is on a page this marker will be replaced by the relevant page number of that page.

4. We want page numbers on both pages so let's make another copy of the text block holding the text you just typed.
Using the pointer, select the text block holding the 'Page PB' text.

5. With this text block selected, **choose the 'Copy' option from the [Edit] menu.**
PageMaker has now made a copy of this block of text.

6. **Select the 'Paste' option from the [Edit] menu.**
PageMaker puts the copied block of text onto the desktop (or the page). You now have two copies of the text block.

7. The page number on the left page is to be lined up to the left so **ensure one of the text blocks is 'Aligned left'.**

8. **Pick up the left–page page number text and place it on the left page so its bottom touches the horizontal guide at the bottom of the page and the left–hand side of the text block touches the vertical guide** (figure 5.2). **'Drop' the text block here.**
When the block of text is dropped the 'PB' changes to an 'LM' — the marker for a page number on the left–page.

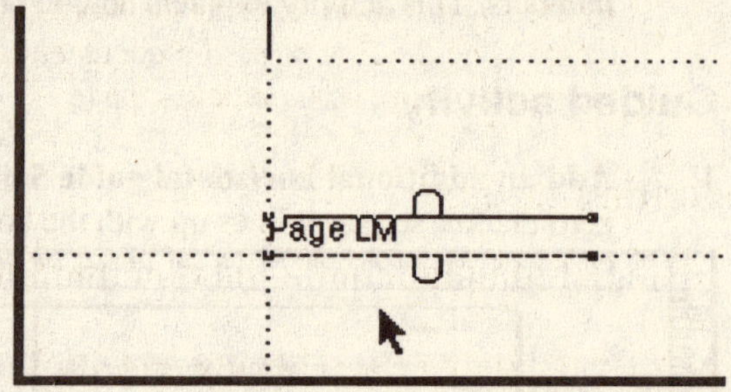

Figure 5.2

9. The page number on the right page is to be lined up to the right so **ensure the remaining page number text block is 'Aligned right'.**

10. **Pick up the right–page page number text and place it on the right page so its bottom touches the horizontal guide at the bottom of the page and the right–hand side of the text block touches the vertical guide** (figure 5.3). **'Drop' the text block here.**
When the block of text is dropped the 'PB' changes to an 'RM' — the marker for a page number on the right page.

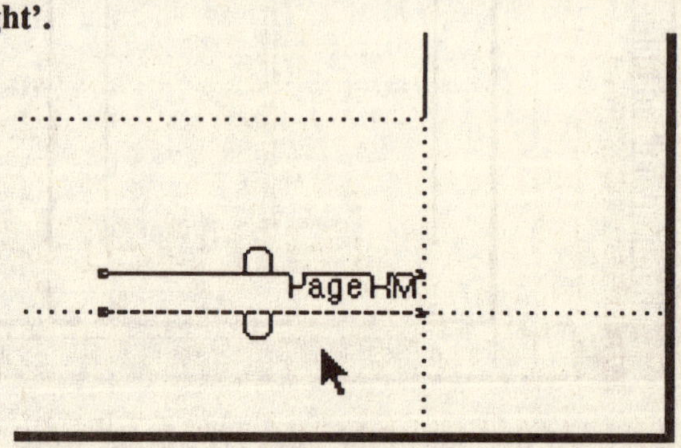

Figure 5.3

11. To keep the document uncluttered **remove the guide you placed 5 picas beneath the bottom margin and the two vertical guides you placed earlier** by moving them back onto the rulers.

12. **Move to page 1.**
The text at the bottom reads 'Page 1'. At the top of the page is the header 'D.T.P. News'. These elements are repeated on each page of the document — you may wish to check this.

Activity 6

'Hiding' master page items

Objectives

1. To hide items repeated from the master page on a particular page

Introduction

Headers and footers (such as the words 'D.T.P. News' and the page numbers) are not normally included on the first page of a document. In this activity we see how to 'hide' repeating items from the master pages on a particular page.

Guided activity

1. **Move to page 1 and zoom in on the 'D.T.P. News' text.**

2. **Select the box drawing tool and draw a small box around these words** (figure 5.1).

Figure 5.1

3. **With the box selected choose a 'Line' of 'None' and 'Fill' it with 'Paper'.**
You have just drawn a box the same shade as the paper and with no line surrounding it. Although the words 'D.T.P. News' are still there, they should no longer be visible (since the box is on top of them). When the page is printed it will look like there is just empty space where this header is. This is a common technique for 'getting rid' of unwanted items from the master pages on a specific page in a document.

Independent activity

1. Use the technique explained in the previous activity to hide the footer 'Page 1' at the bottom of the page.

End of chapter summary

What I want to do	How I do it
• Add column guides to every page in a document	• Move to master pages and add columns
• Change where zero is on rulers	• Ensure 'Zero lock' in [Options] menu is inactive and drag zero mark from box in top left–hand corner of window where rulers meet
• Add headers or footers to every page in a document	• Put headers and footers onto master pages
• Remove a guide	• Ensure 'Lock guides' in [Options] menu is inactive and drag guide back over ruler
• Make a copy of an item	• Select item and choose 'Copy' from [Edit] menu then 'Paste' from [Edit] menu
• Add page numbers to a document	• Hold down OPTION and COMMAND and press 'P' (PC users hold down CTRL and ALT and press '3') to get page number marker — put these on left and right master pages
• Hide a master page item on an ordinary page	• Draw a box over item with 'Fill' of 'Paper' and a 'Line' of 'None'

Trouble–shooting

Problem	Possible reason	Solution
• Can't move guides back to rulers	• Guides are 'locked'	• Select 'Lock guides' from [Options] menu and try again
• Can't move zero mark on rulers	• Zero lock is active	• Select 'Zero lock' from [Options] menu and try again

Chapter 2

Working with graphics

- adding and 'cropping' a graphic
- moving and 'scaling' a graphic

Introduction to chapter 2

In this chapter we will be adding a graphic to the document you have been creating. 'Graphics' is a general term for anything that is not text — photographs, drawings, cartoons, charts, logos, etc. are all graphics in the publishing use of the word.

Where to get graphics from

There are numerous methods of obtaining or creating graphics for your documents — the number of drawing packages alone is astounding. It is outside the scope of this book to guide you through creating graphics using any of these packages (though a browse through the computing section of any major bookstore will exemplify the large and diverse number of guides available for this purpose). For completeness, the most common methods of creating or obtaining graphics are listed below:

Using a drawing package

Graphics can be drawn using one of the numerous drawing packages available (such as Paintbrush or MacPaint). PageMaker can then 'import' these graphics — provided the package they were done on is compatible (check your PageMaker manuals if you plan to use a drawing package to ensure it is one PageMaker can 'read').

Using a scanner

A scanner is a device which takes images on paper and copies them into a file suitable for use by various computer packages. Although scanners are relatively expensive they are usually available in large organisations and colleges. A copy of all the graphics used for the exercises in this book are held in the appendix — these can be 'scanned in' if you have access to a scanner.

Using pre-prepared graphics

Many computer users will have access to 'libraries' of pre-prepared graphic files. One of the more common of these are 'Clip art' files. Pages of drawings and images which have been scanned in.

The graphics used in the following activities can be scanned in if you have access to a scanner (a copy of each graphic used is included in the appendix for this). Alternatively, if you are familiar with a drawing package which produces files PageMaker can use (check your user manual to see which it can) you could draw the graphics beforehand, or at least a basic image of them.
If neither of these methods is suitable then you could, for the purpose of these exercises, substitute alternative pre-prepared graphics from clip art type files.

A disc with all the graphics and text files used in this book is available from the publisher — see 'Preface' for details of this.

Activity 1

Adding and 'cropping' a graphic

Objectives

1. To add a previously prepared graphic to a page
2. To 'crop' a graphic

Introduction

In this activity we are going to try and add the graphic shown in appendix 1a to your document. It is assumed you have a graphic held in a file called 'Pic1', on your own disc, obtained through one of the methods just mentioned (either a scanned image of appendix 1a, a similar graphic drawn on one of the drawing packages available, or a substitute graphic from a pre-prepared graphic file you have access to).

Placing the graphic is a fairly straightforward process — very similar to placing text. PageMaker also lets us cut unwanted pieces off a graphic (called 'cropping') . Both of these functions will be covered in the activity — for this process it is assumed that you are using a graphic similar to the one shown in appendix 1a (though the processes of placing and cropping can be applied to any graphic).

Guided activity

1. **If necessary, restart PageMaker and open the document you have been creating.**

2. **Make sure you have the pointer tool selected and you are on page 1 of your document.**

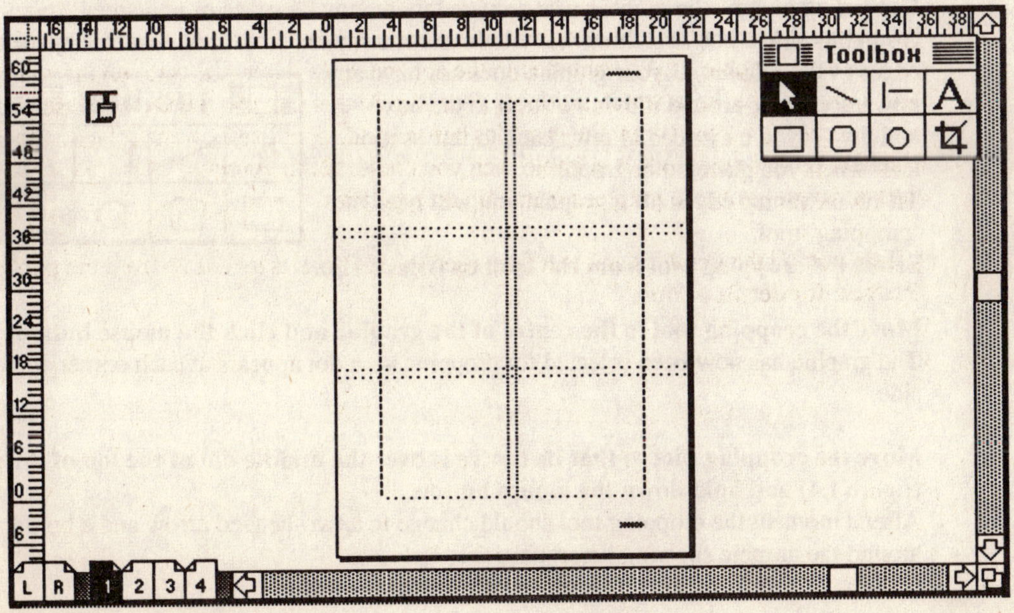

Figure 1.1

3. **Select the 'Place' option from the [File] menu and choose the file 'Pic1' on your own disc.** After a moment the pointer will turn to a small box, similar to the text placing icon. The exact look of this box (which is the graphic placing icon) depends on how the graphic was prepared.

4. **Move the graphic placing icon to the side of the page, on the desktop near the top left-hand corner of the window** (figure 1.1).

5. **With the icon here, click the mouse button** to 'drop' the graphic onto the desktop. The graphic should appear on the desktop (figure 1.2) with a 'dot' at each corner and along each side (indicating it is selected).

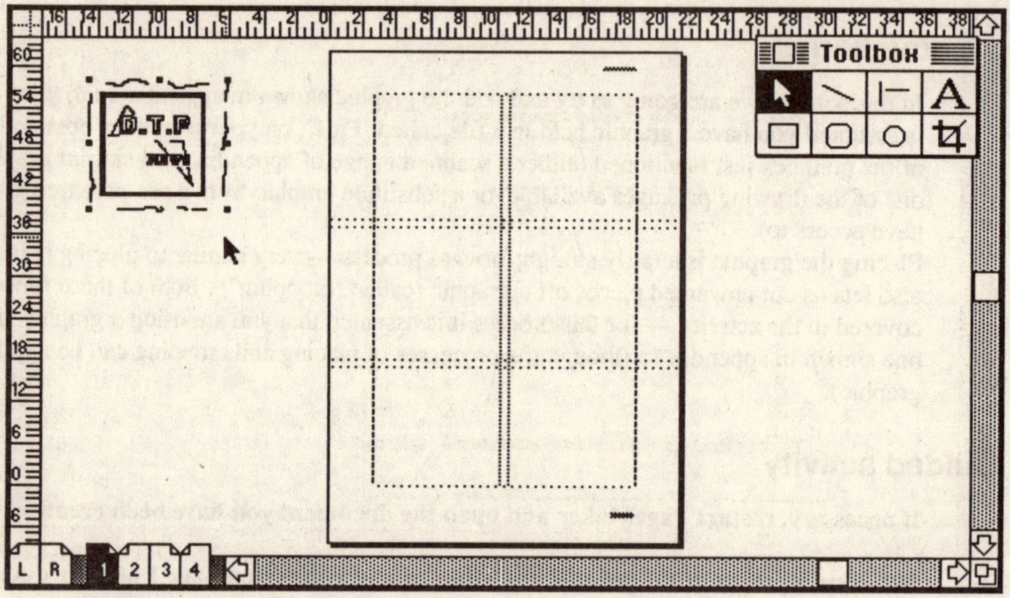

Figure 1.2

6. Depending on how the graphic was prepared there may be space or unwanted 'rough edges' around its sides. The first thing we will do is cut away or 'crop' the unwanted space around the edges of the graphic. If your graphic does not have any unwanted space around it then go strait to the next activity — you may need to refer back to this section later when you place other graphics.
To cut unwanted edges off a graphic you will need the 'cropping' tool.
Select the cropping tool from the toolbox (figure 1.3).

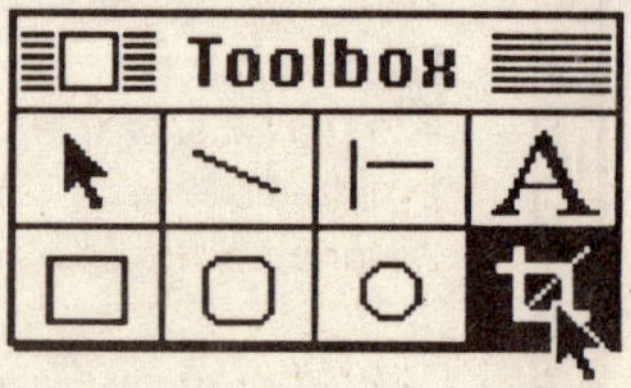

Figure 1.3

7. **Move the cropping tool to the centre of the graphic and click the mouse button.** The graphic has now been selected for cropping — a dot appears at each corner and along each side.

8. **Move the cropping tool so that its centre is over the middle dot at the top of the graphic** (figure 1.4) **and hold down the mouse button.** After a moment the cropping tool should change to a two-headed arrow and a border appears around the graphic showing its proportions.

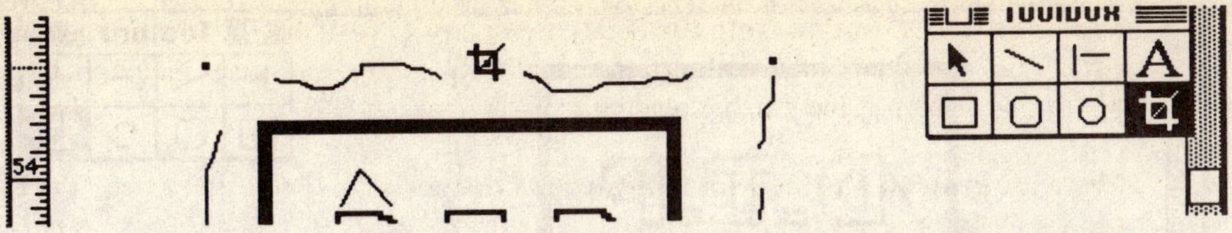

Figure 1.4

9. **Keeping the mouse button held down, move to just above the top of the box in your graphic (figure 1.5).**
   As you move the line indicating the border of the graphic should move down also.

Figure 1.5

10. **Release the mouse button.**
    The top of the graphic has now been 'cropped' away and should no longer be visible. Although you can no longer see it is still there.

11. **Move the cropping tool over the middle dot at the top of the graphic and hold down the mouse button.**
    After a moment the cropping tool change to a two-headed arrow.

12. **With the mouse button held down move the two-headed arrow up.**
    As you move the parts of the image which you cropped away reappear again.

13. **Crop the top of the graphic again so it looks like figure 1.5.**

14. **Move the cropping tool so that its centre is over the middle dot at the left-hand side of the graphic and hold down the mouse button.**
    After a moment the cropping tool should change to a two-headed arrow.

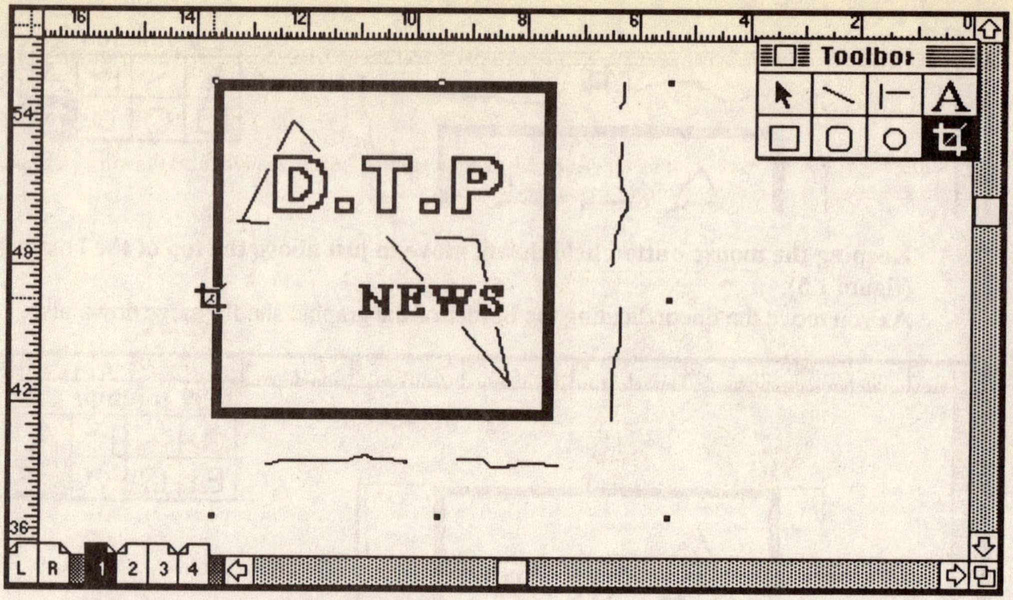

Figure 1.6

15. **Keeping the mouse button held down, move so that the space to the left of the box in your graphic is cropped away** (figure 1.6).
As you move the line indicating the border of the graphic should move left also.

16. **Release the mouse button.**
The left-hand side of the graphic has now been 'cropped' away and should no longer be visible.

Independent activity

1. Crop the graphic you have been using so that the space below and to the right of the image is not showing (figure 1.7).

Figure 1.7

Cropping

Cropping is the process of cutting unwanted edges off a graphic - either to focus attention on a particular aspect of the graphic or to remove unsightly parts around the edges.

Original graphic

Cropped graphic

Activity 2

Moving and 'scaling' a graphic

Objectives

1. To move a graphic about a page
2. To scale a graphic

Introduction

As well as allowing us to cut unwanted pieces off a graphic ('cropping') PageMaker lets us change its size ('scaling') so it can be made to fit the space allocated for it. This process will be covered in the following activity — it is assumed that you are using the graphic you prepared earlier (though the processes of cropping and scaling can be applied to any graphic). This process is quite 'fiddly' so don't be too put off if you have to take a few goes to get it right.

Guided activity

1. **If the pointer tool is not already selected then choose it from the toolbox.**

2. **With the pointer in the middle of the graphic click the mouse button.**
   The graphic takes the form of a selected graphic.

3. **With the pointer tool located in the middle of the graphic, hold down the mouse button.** The pointer changes to a four-headed arrow — the moving icon. You have just 'picked up' this graphic.

4. **With the mouse button held down, move the graphic (which should move with the pointer) so that its top left-hand corner lines up with the top margin and its left-hand side lines up with the left-hand side of the first column** (figure 2.1).

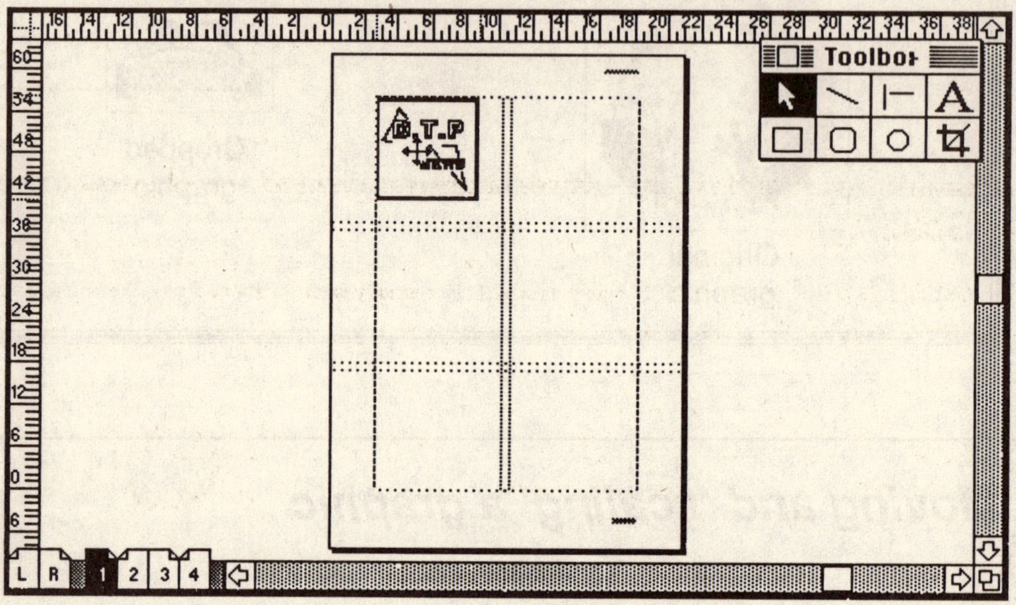

Figure 2.1

5. **With the graphic lined up thus, release the mouse button.** The graphic should be 'dropped' here and stay when the pointer is moved away.

6. **Move the pointer over the dot in the bottom right-hand corner of the graphic and hold down the mouse button.** You have just 'picked up' this corner. The pointer should change to a two-headed arrow.

7. **Keeping the mouse button held down, move the bottom right-hand corner of the graphic (which should move with the pointer) so that it rests on the right-hand side of the first column and the 18p horizontal guide** (figure 2.2). As you move the pointer the graphic 'grows' or 'shrinks' to fill the space made by the box surrounding the graphic.

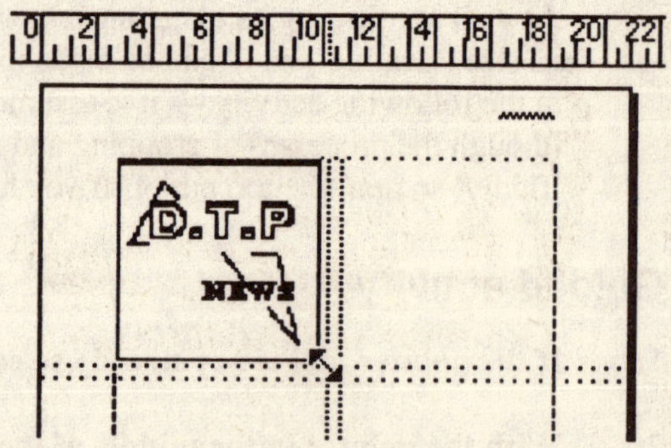

Figure 2.2

8. **With the graphic lined up thus, release the mouse button.** The bottom right-hand corner of the graphic should be 'dropped' here and stay when you move the pointer away (figure 2.3).

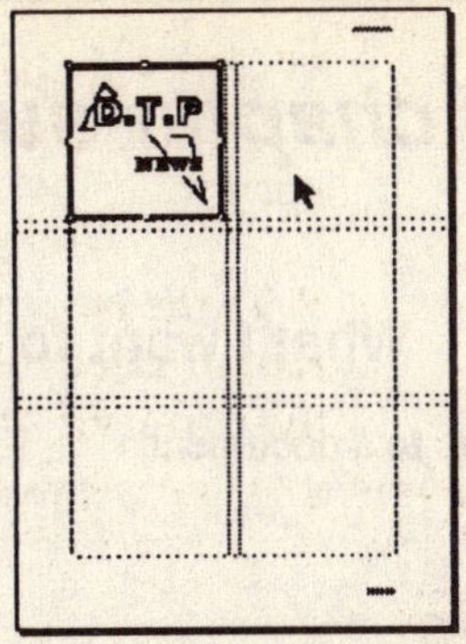

Figure 2.3

Scaling

Scaling a graphic is the process of changing its size. This is usually used if a graphic is too big or too small to fit into a space allocated to it on a page

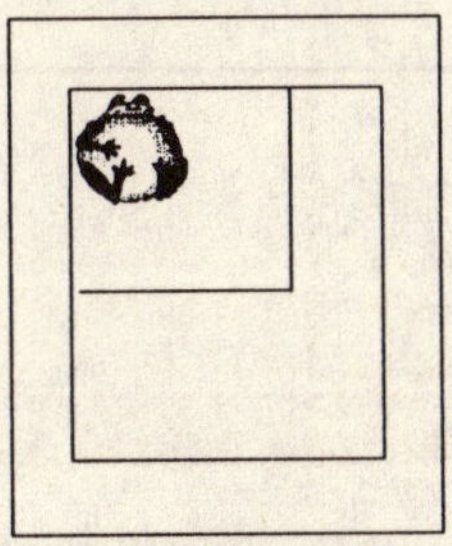

Original graphic

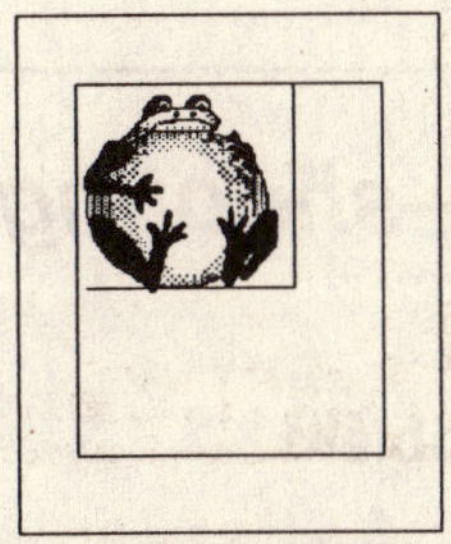

Graphic scaled to fit space allocated

PageMaker allows us to do proportional scaling. That is, reducing or enlarging a graphic so that it does not lose its proportions and look 'warped' or 'squashed'.

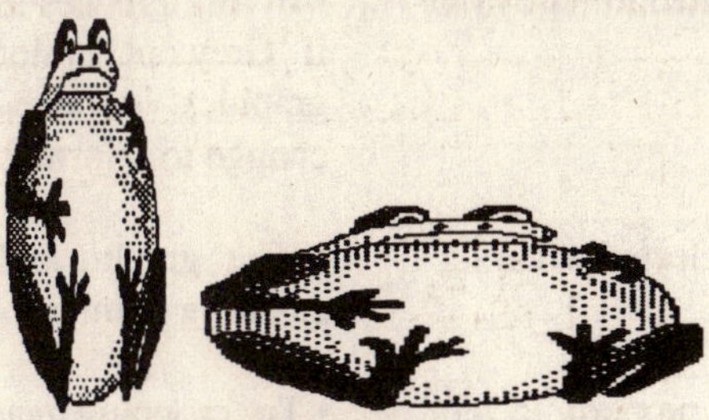

Graphics warped through scaling

Graphic whose proportions were maintained

To achieve this simply keep the SHIFT key held down while scaling.

End of chapter summary

What I want to do	How I do it
• Add a graphic to a document	• Select 'Place' from the [File] menu and locate the file containing graphic
• Crop a graphic	• Choose cropping tool and click on graphic — crop sides by holding cropping tool over selection dots and dragging
• Move a graphic	• Point over graphic and hold down mouse button — drag to new position
• Scale a graphic	• Select graphic with pointer and move over selection dot — drag dot to new position

Trouble–shooting

Problem	Possible reason	Solution
• Graphic file name not present in 'Place' dialogue box	• Type of file not compatible with PageMaker	• If graphic prepared using drawing package check compatibility with PageMaker in manuals — may be necessary to use different method of preparation
• Placed graphic just shaded box	• PageMaker defaulted to 'Grey out' graphics	• In 'Preferences' dialogue box check if 'Grey out' option under 'Detailed graphics' is active — if yes then change to 'Normal'
• Placed graphic cannot be moved sideways	• Pointer tool not selected when placing	• 'Cut' graphic and place again ensuring pointer tool selected
• When trying to crop tool changes to 'hand' and graphic moves around inside border	• Cropping tool not properly located	• Try cropping again ensuring 'eye' of cropping tool over selection dot

Chapter 3

Ways with text

- changing text in text blocks
- changing 'leading'
- 'tracking' and 'width'
- special effects with 'width'

Introduction to chapter 3

In this chapter we will consider some more techniques to use when working with text. We will look at how to change the attributes of a specific piece of text and also introduce some new terms.

Activity 1

Changing text in text blocks

Objectives

1. To select a piece of text within a text block
2. To change the attributes of a piece of text within a text block

Introduction

In this activity the text you add to page 1 of your document contains a heading which forms part of the main body of text. We will make this heading stand out by changing its attributes (font, size, etc.). Unlike before, the heading will not be a separate text block but will be part of the same block as the main story.

Guided activity

1. We are going to add the first story to your document (the text for which is held in appendix 1b). **Enter the text for the 'Editorial'** (in appendix 1b) **via a word processor or using the story editor.**

2. **Save the text on your own disc in a file called 'Editor'.**

3. **'Place' this text into the first column of page 1, beneath the horizontal guide 19p below the top margin, stretching as close to the bottom margin as it will go** (figure 1.1). **Make it 10pt Times text.**
The heading 'Editorial' has the same text attributes as the rest of the story. Since it is a heading we should make it stand out a little.

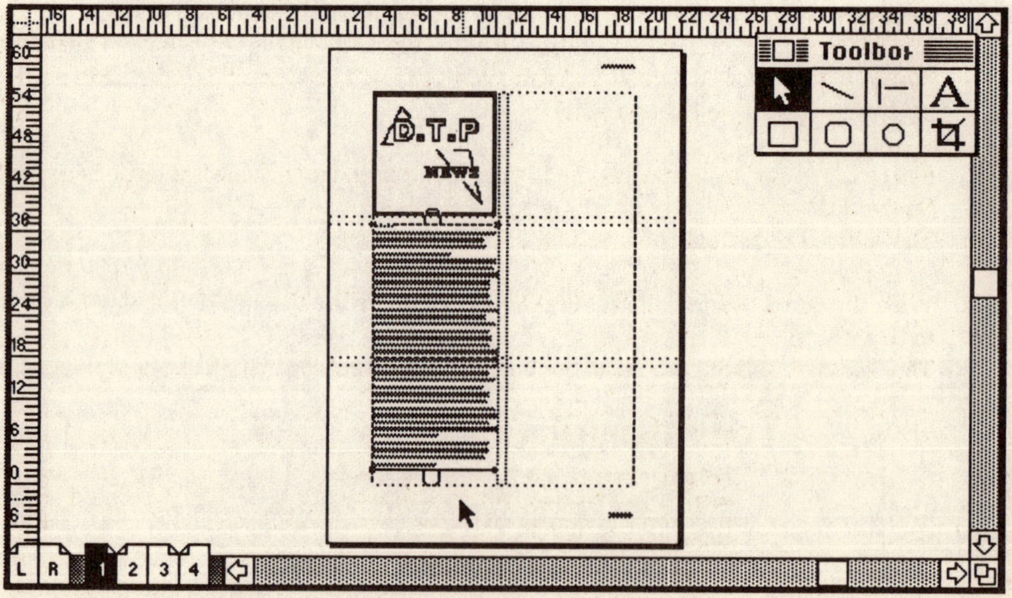

Figure 1.1

4. **Change the page view so you can see the beginning of the text in the first column** (try 'Actual size' from the [Page] menu and use the scroll bars to position the page).

5. **Select the 'Text tool' from the toolbox.**

6. In this case we just want to change some of the text in the text block, not all of it — this can seem a little tricky at first.
Move the text tool so that it is just before the first word 'Editorial' (figure 1.2a) **and hold down the mouse button.**

Figure 1.2a

7. **With the mouse button held down, 'drag' the text tool to just after the word 'Editorial'** (figure 1.2b).
As you move the text tool the text it moves across becomes highlighted.

Figure 1.2b

8. **When the word 'Editorial' is fully highlighted, release the mouse button.**
You have now selected this word from the text block. Anything we now tell PageMaker to do it will do to this selected text only. Again, don't worry if selecting this word takes a few goes (the closer the view is the easier it gets).

9. **Select the 'Font' option from the [Type] menu and, from the list of options available, choose 'Helvetica'.**
The selected text should now be in the 'Helvetica' font.

10. **With the word 'Editorial' still highlighted, change the size of the text to 24pt and the 'Style' to 'Bold'.**
The 'heading' should now stand out but still be a part of the text block (figure 1.3).

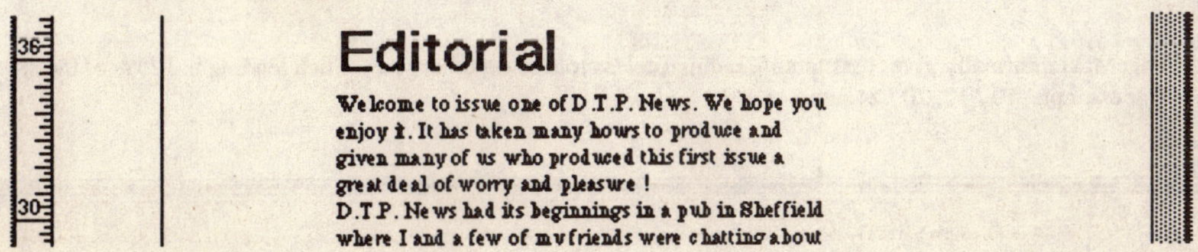

Figure 1.3

Activity 2

Changing 'leading'

Objectives

1. To change the 'leading' of a piece of text

Introduction

The space between lines is known as 'leading' (pronounced 'ledding'). In this activity we will change the leading of a selected piece of text.

Leading

Leading (pronounced 'ledding') determines how far apart the lines in a piece of text are. Just like text, leading is measured in points. The leading of a piece of text is the height of the text plus the space between the lines of text.

10pt text with 12pt leading is known as '10 over 12' or '10 / 12' text. Below are some examples of different leading settings.

8 / 10 text

Leading (pronounced 'ledding') determines how far apart the lines in a piece of text are. Just like text, leading is measured in points. The leading of a piece of text is the height of the text plus the space between the lines of text.

8 / 13 text

Leading (pronounced 'ledding') determines how far apart the lines in a piece of text are. Just like text, leading is measured in points. The leading of a piece of text is the height of the text plus the space between the lines of text.

8 / 18 text

Leading (pronounced 'ledding') determines how far apart the lines in a piece of text are. Just like text, leading is measured in points. The leading of a piece of text is the height of the text plus the space between the lines of text.

PageMaker normally gives text 'auto' leading (unless told to do otherwise). Such leading is 120% of the size of the text (for example, 10 / 12, 20 / 24, etc.).

Guided activity

1. **Select the first word of the text in column one, 'Editorial', by highlighting it.**

2. **With this text highlighted, move to the 'Leading' option in the [Type] menu. From the list of options available choose the '36' option.**
   The space above and below the heading 'Editorial' should increase slightly. This text is now 18pt Helvetica with 36pt leading — known as 18/36 Helvetica.

Activity 3

'Tracking' and 'Width'

Objectives

1. To change the width and tracking of a piece of text

Introduction

The distance between the individual letters and words in a piece of text is controlled by the 'tracking'. This activity explains the process of changing this tracking and also changing the width of text.

Guided activity

1. **Move to page 2 of the document and add the heading**
   `The Shape of Things To Come`
   at the side of the page in 36pt Helvetica text.

2. **Move the heading onto the page and place it in the top left–hand corner of the first column, making the text box span the margin guides either side of the page** (figure 3.1).

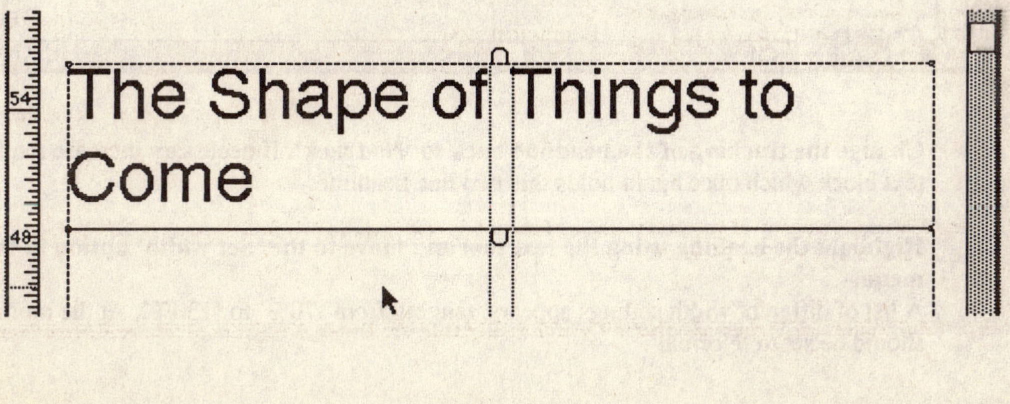

Figure 3.1

3. It would be good if the heading filled one line, rather than having the last word on a line of its own. One way of doing this is to change the 'tracking' of the text. The tracking indicates how close together the letters which make up the text are.
Highlight the heading using the text tool (move to the start of the text, hold down the mouse button and drag to the end of the text) **and move to the 'Track' option in the [Type] menu.**
A list of different tracking settings appears, ranging from 'Very loose' to 'Very tight'. At the moment the tracking should be set to 'No track'.

4. **Select the 'Normal' option from the list of trackings available.**
The letters in the highlighted text should move slightly closer as they are given a tracking of 'Normal'. The difference in closeness is very subtle and may not seem obvious. If the last word is still on a line by itself then...

5. Make the tracking tighter. With the text still highlighted **select a 'Track' of 'Tight' from the [Type] menu.**
This time the further reduction of space between the letters in the highlighted text should make a space at the end of the first line large enough to hold the last word. This is automatically brought up to the first line making the headline span a single line (figure 3.2). If this did not happen then increase the tracking to 'Very tight'.

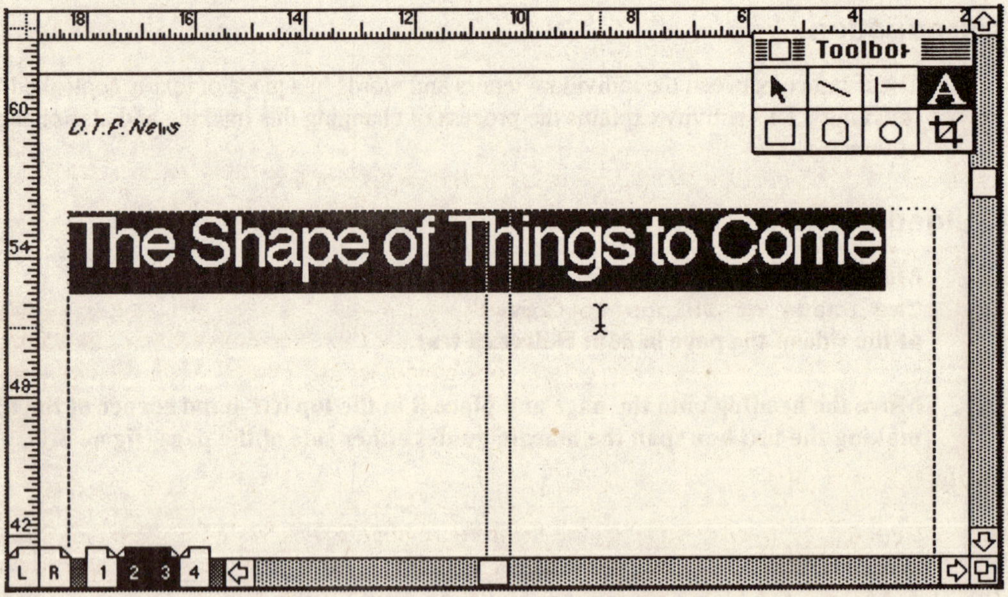

Figure 3.2

6. **Change the tracking of the headline back to 'No track'.** If necessary increase the length of the text block which once again holds this two line headline.

7. **Highlight the heading using the text tool and move to the 'Set width' option in the [Type] menu.**
A list of different width settings appears, ranging from '70%' to '130%'. At the moment the width should be set to 'Normal'.

8. **Select the '90%' option from the list of widths available.**
The letters in the highlighted text should move slightly closer as their width is reduced. The difference in size is very subtle and may not seem obvious. If the last word is still on a line by itself...

9. Make the width smaller still. With the text still highlighted **select a 'Width' of '80%' from the [Type] menu.**
This time the further reduction of space between the letters in the highlighted text should make a space at the end of the first line large enough to hold the last word. This is automatically brought up to the first line making the headline span a single line.

Independent activity

1. Change the 'Width' of the text back to 'Normal' and alter its 'Track' so that it fits onto a single line.

Activity 4

Special effects with 'Width'

Objectives

1. To create a special effect by changing the width of a piece of text.

Introduction

Changing the tracking of a piece of text is a much subtler method of saving space than changing its width. Changing width should not normally be used for such things (except in extreme emergencies!) In this activity we will look at another use for the 'Width' option — to create an eye–catching effect.

Guided activity

1. **Replace the word 'Shape' in the heading on page 2 with 'SHAPE'** (you may like to refer back to the 4th activity in chapter 4 of the last section to refresh your memory on how to do this).

2 **Highlight this word using the text tool.**

3. With the word highlighted, **select a size of '60'.**
The word should increase in size.

4. With the word still highlighted **select the 'Other' option from the list of 'Width' settings available.**
A small dialogue box appears for you to type in the new width.

Figure 4.1

5. **Replace the value currently in this box (which should be 'Normal') with '25' and click on 'OK'.**
When the page returns the word 'SHAPE' should be 25% its Normal width creating an interesting effect (figure 4.1). Zoom in and have a look at this.

Tracking

The tracking of a piece of text is a measurement of how close together its letters and words are. The different trackings are shown below:

Tracking is a measurement of ...	No track
Tracking is a measurement of ...	Very loose
Tracking is a measurement of ...	Loose
Tracking is a measurement of ...	Normal
Tracking is a measurement of ...	Tight
Tracking is a measurement of ...	Very tight

Width

The width of a piece of text is a measurement of how wide its letters are. Some different width settings are shown below:

Width is a measurement of ...	70%
Width is a measurement of ...	80%
Width is a measurement of ...	90%
Width is a measurement of ...	Normal (100%)
Width is a measurement of ...	110%
Width is a measurement of ...	120%
Width is a measurement of ...	130%

Independent activity

1. Before starting the next chapter let's finish page 1 of 'D.T.P. News'.
   • At the side of the page type in:
   `Issue 1`
   `January`
   `1993`
   in 48pt Times text. Make it 'Bold' and 'Italic' and then change the 'Alignment' to 'Align centre'.

   • Place this text in the grid 'box' in the top right-hand corner of the page.

   • Keeping in line with the grid box, draw a 4pt line above and below this text

   • At the side of the page type in:

```
This issue was produced by:
John Smith
Margaret Thomas
Chris Taylor
Tony Waters

Special thanks to:
Mike Shaw
Sajit Hussain
Mary Moore
for all their assistance.

D.T.P. News can be contacted at
17 Straw Street
Pitsmoor
Sheffield
S3 9DP
```

   in 10pt Times and align it to the right.

   • Put this text onto the page in the second column so that the top of the text block touches the guide 19p from the top margin and the right–hand side of the text block touches the right–hand margin (or the 'inside margin').

   • Finally, draw box with a 2pt 'Line' and a 'Fill' of 'None' so that each side touches the sides of the grid box in the bottom right–hand side of the page (we will use this box in section 3).

End of chapter summary

What I want to do	How I do it
• highlight a piece of text inside a text block	• Move text tool to start of text to be highlighted and hold down mouse button — drag to end of text and release
• Change the leading of a piece of text	• With text highlighted select 'Leading' from [Type] menu
• Change the tracking of a piece of text	• With text highlighted select 'Track' from [Type] menu
• Change the width of a piece of text	• With text highlighted select 'Width' from [Type] menu

Trouble–shooting

Problem	Possible reason	Solution
• Cannot highlight text — text tool draws a box which disappears when mouse button released	• Text tool not correctly positioned	• Move page closer and try again
• Width does not appear to change on screen	• Target printer incompatible with width changes (PC users only)	• Change target printer (if this is feasible)

Chapter 4

Working with paragraphs

- type specifications
- paragraph specifications
- indents and tabs
- hyphenation

Introduction to chapter 4

Up until now we have been changing text in one of two ways — either changing the whole story (using the 'Select all' option) or changing just a small area of text (by highlighting just that area). It is often useful to think of the text in a story as a collection of paragraphs and change each paragraph as required (a paragraph in PageMaker terms is a collection of characters ending with the RETURN or ENTER key being pressed — thus the 'Editorial' heading on page 1 of the document you are producing is a paragraph).

This chapter looks at methods of changing whole paragraphs of text. The full potential of this will become more apparent in the next section when you start to use 'style sheets' to format text.

Activity 1

Type specifications

Objectives

1. To change the type specifications of a paragraph

Introduction

'Type specifications' is a general term for which font, what size, type style, etc. text is formatted to. This activity explains how to change all of these specifications using a single dialogue box.

Guided activity

1. **Enter the text shown in appendix 1c via a word processor or the story editor and save it in a file called 'Shape' on your own disc.**

2. **Place the text in the file 'Shape' into the first column on page 2.**
The text should span the space between the guide 19p below the top margin and the bottom margin (figure 1.1).

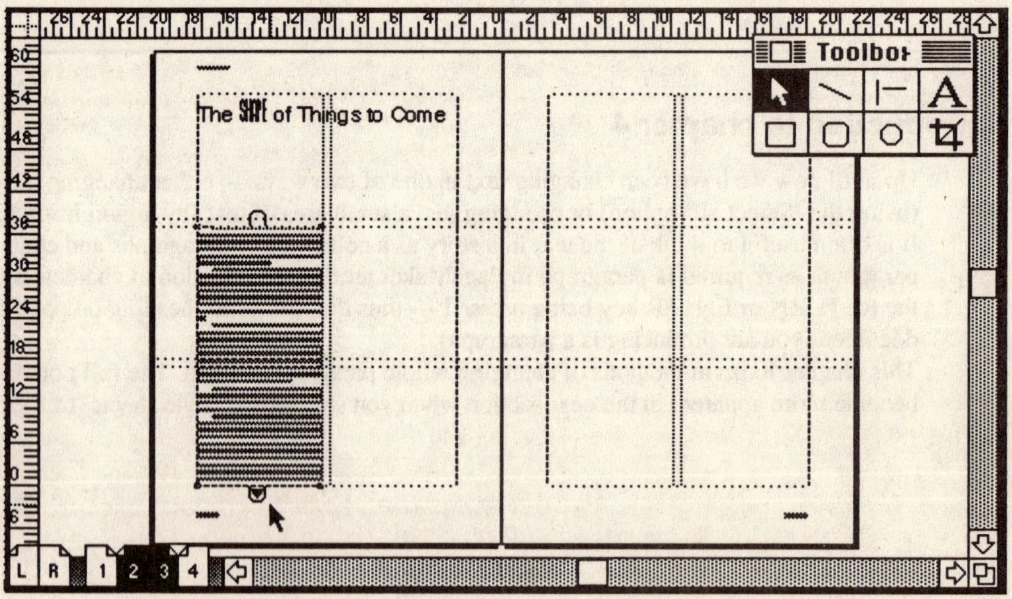

Figure 1.1

3. **With some of the text placed in the first column 'Select all' of the text in the story and change it to 10pt Normal Times (i.e. 10pt Times text with a 'Type style' of 'Normal'). Also change the 'Alignment' to 'Justify'.**

4. There is more text to come.
Place the remaining text into column 2.
The text should start beneath the horizontal guide 19p below the top margin and continue as far down the column as it will go (figure 1.2).

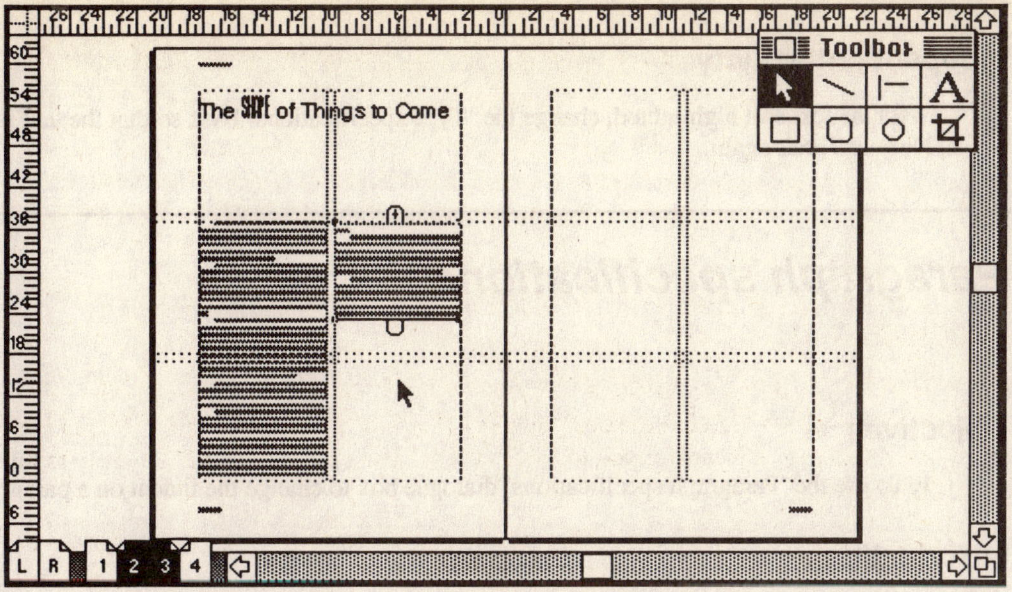

Figure 1.2

5. **'Select all' of this story** (place the cursor anywhere in the text and choose the 'Select all' option from the [Edit] menu).

6. **Select the 'Type specs' option from the [Type] menu.**
A dialogue box appears (figure 1.3).
The dialogue box before you is used to specify most of the text attributes you have covered so far

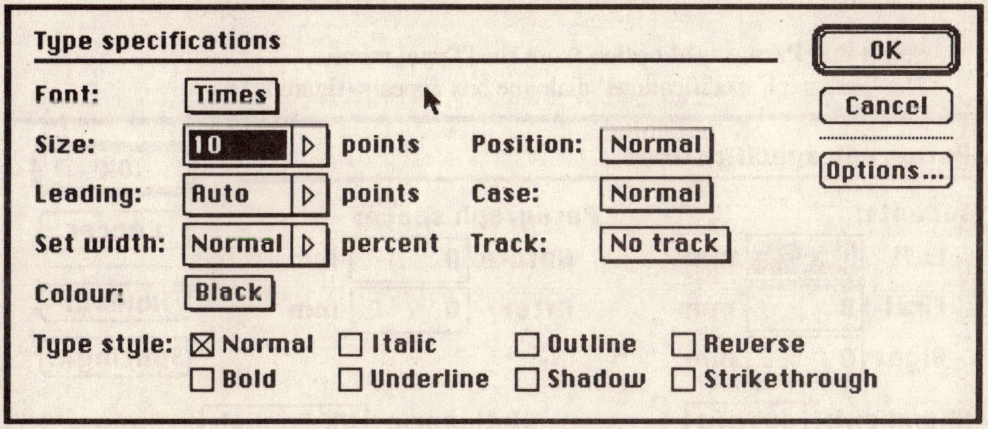

Figure 1.3

7. The 'Font' in the 'Type specifications' holds a hidden menu. Using this menu **change the font of the selected text to 'Helvetica'.**

8. **Change the 'Size' of the selected text to '12'pt.**

9. **Click over the box next to 'Italic' to make the selected text italic.**

10. **Click over 'OK'**
When the page returns the selected text has changed to the new specifications — check and see.

Independent activity

1. With the text still highlighted, change the 'Type specifications' back so that the text is 10pt Normal Times again.

Activity 2

Paragraph specifications

Objectives

1. To use the 'Paragraph specifications' dialogue box to change the indent on a paragraph.

Introduction

One common feature of a paragraph is that the first line is often in a little from the edge of the column. This is known as an 'indent'. In this activity we will look at how to give a paragraph an indent or change an existing indent using the 'Paragraph specifications' dialogue box.

Guided activity

1. **Highlight the whole story you used in the previous activity.**

2. **Select the 'Paragraph' option from the [Type] menu.**
   The 'Paragraph specifications' dialogue box appears (figure 2.1).

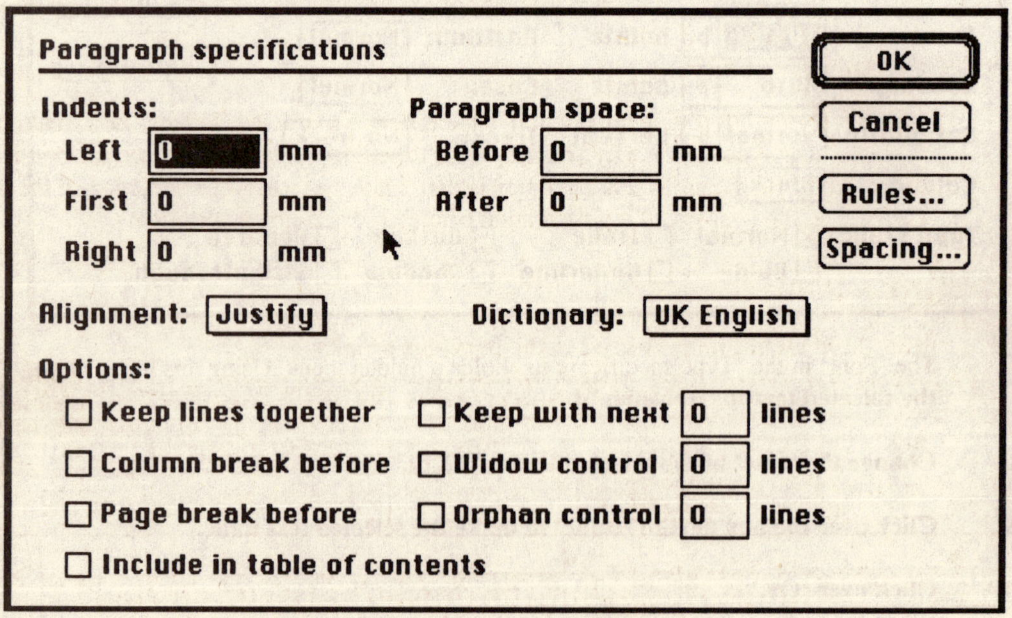

Figure 2.1

3. We are going to add an 'indent' to the highlighted paragraphs.
Replace the value in the 'First' box with '10'.

4. **Click over 'OK'.**
When the page returns the paragraphs of the highlighted text should have an indent of 10mm in the first line.

5. **Select the 'Paragraph' option from the [Type] menu and give the paragraphs an indent of zero again.**

6. **Click over 'OK'.**
When the page returns the highlighted paragraphs once again have no initial indent .

Independent activity

1. Use the 'Paragraph specifications' dialogue box to change the 'Alignment' of the highlighted text to 'Right'. After observing this change in the highlighted text return the 'Alignment' to 'Justify'.

Activity 3

Indents and Tabs

Objectives

1. To use the 'Indents / tabs' dialogue box to set a paragraph indent

Introduction

Another method of setting an indent in a paragraph is to use the 'Indent / tabs' dialogue box in the [Type] menu. One reason why you may wish to set indents using this dialogue box rather than the 'Paragraph specifications' dialogue box is that it gives a visual representation of the indent — as opposed to the non–visual representation offered by 'Paragraph specifications'.

Guided activity

1. **Highlight all of the story used in the previous activity.**

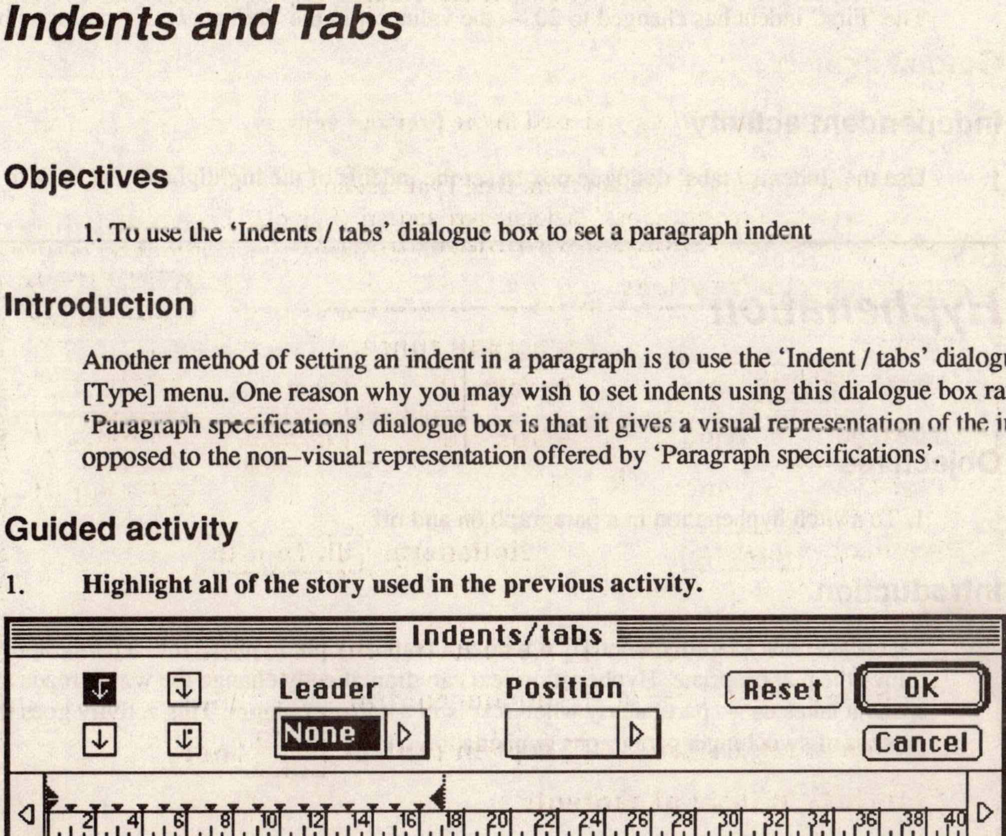

Figure 3.1

2. **Select the 'Indents / tabs' option from the [Type] menu.**
The 'Indents / tabs' dialogue box appears (figure 3.1).

3. The paragraph indent marker is represented by the small triangle shown in figure 3.2.
Move the pointer over this marker and 'drag' it so that it rests above the 20mm mark on the ruler displayed in this dialogue box.
As you move the value of the indent is displayed in the 'Position[PC]' box to help you place it accurately.

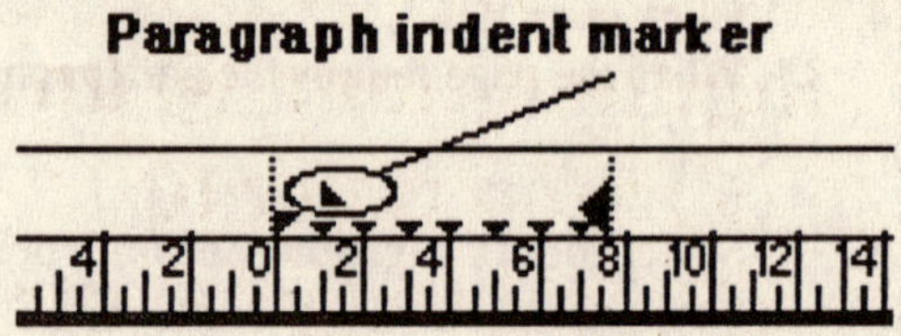

Figure 3.2

PC users have the position of the indent recorded in a box entitled 'Tab action' instead

---

4. **Click over 'OK'.**
When the page returns the highlighted paragraphs have been set to the new value of 20mm.

5. With the text still highlighted **select the 'Paragraph' option** once again.
The 'First' indent has changed to 20 — the value set in the 'Indents / tabs' dialogue box.

Independent activity

1. Use the 'Indents / tabs' dialogue box to set the indents of the highlighted text back to 10mm.

Activity 4

Hyphenation

Objectives

1. To switch hyphenation in a paragraph on and off

Introduction

PageMaker has a facility whereby it will automatically put hyphens into a paragraph where it thinks them appropriate. Hyphenating text can dramatically change the way it reads and how much space it takes up — particularly when text is in a narrow column. This activity goes through the process of switching a paragraphs hyphenation on and off.

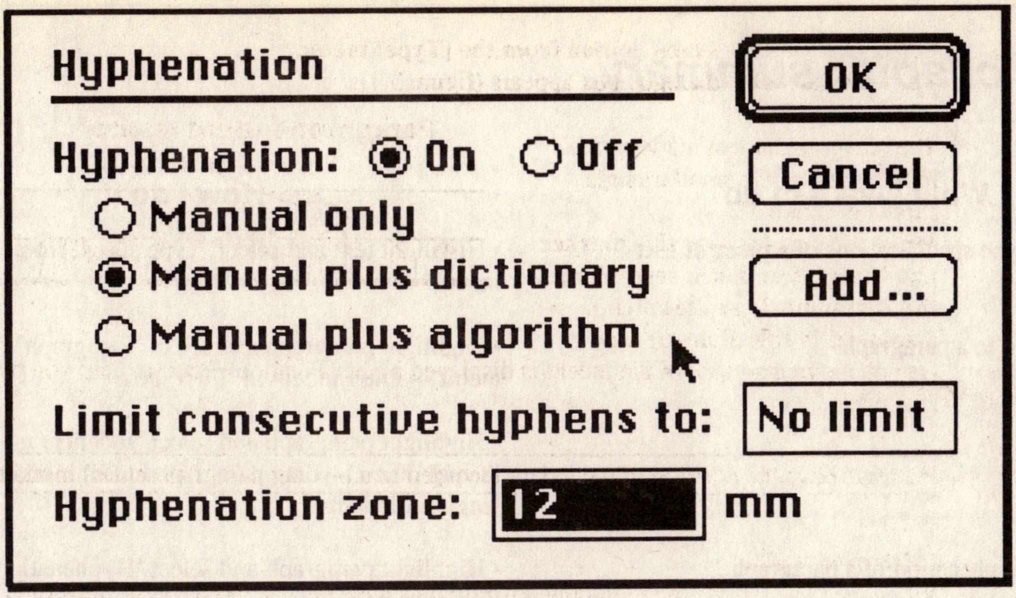

Figure 4.1

Guided activity

1. **Highlight the story you used in the previous activity.**

2. With the text highlighted, **select the 'Hyphenation' option from the [Type] menu.**
The 'Hyphenation' dialogue box appears (figure 4.1).

3. Hyphenation is probably set to 'On' with 'Manual plus dictionary' selected. This means that PageMaker will use its own dictionary to decide which words may be hyphenated.
Switch hyphenation to 'Off'.
(If the hyphenation was initially set to 'Off' then change it to 'On').

4. **Click over 'OK'.**
When the page returns the selected text should no longer be hyphenated. Go to 'Actual size' and have a look.
(If you switched hyphenation 'On' the paragraphs should now be hyphenated).

Independent activity

1. Switch the hyphenation in the highlighted text on again.

2. Finish page 2...

   • Add the graphic in appendix 1d to the space between the heading at the top of the page and the beginning of the main text — crop and scale as necessary.

   • Add the graphic in appendix 1e to the space remaining in the bottom of the second column between the end of the text and the bottom margin — crop and scale as necessary.

End of chapter summary

What I want to do	How I do it
• Change the type specifications of a piece of text	• Highlight text and select 'Type specs' from [Type] menu
• Add an indent to a paragraph	• Highlight paragraph and select 'Paragraph' from [Type] menu — enter indent in 'First' box *or* • Highlight paragraph and select 'Indents / tabs' from [Type] menu — drag paragraph indent marker to specify length of indent
• Change the hyphenation of a paragraph	• Highlight paragraph and select 'Hyphenation' from [Type] menu

Trouble–shooting

Problem	Possible reason	Solution
• Cannot move paragraph indent marker in 'Indents / tabs' dialogue box	• Pointer not located correctly	• Persistence!

Additional Exercises

- leaflet for pottery exhibition

Project

Leaflet for Pottery Exhibition

Front

Pitsmoor Pottery

An exhibition of work
on 1st April
at

The Community Centre
Pitsmoor

Back

All products made locally and available for sale at reasonable prices.

Satisfaction guaranteed on all goods sold — total refund if returned within seven days.

Free help and advice on antique pottery.

Valuations available on request.

All breakages must be paid for!

Front

Pitsmoor
Pottery

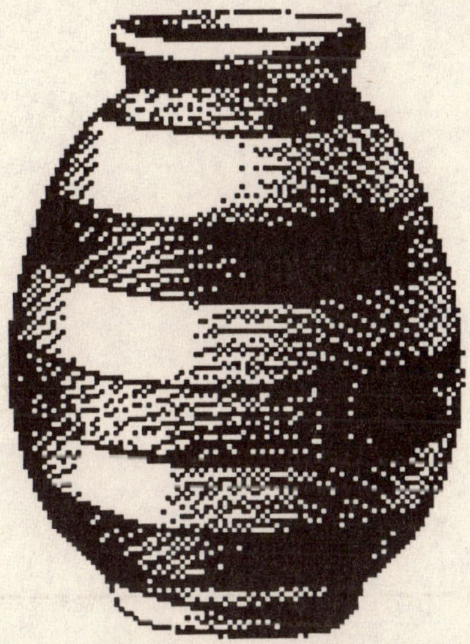

An exhibition of work
on 1st April
at

The Community Centre
Pitsmoor

Guides

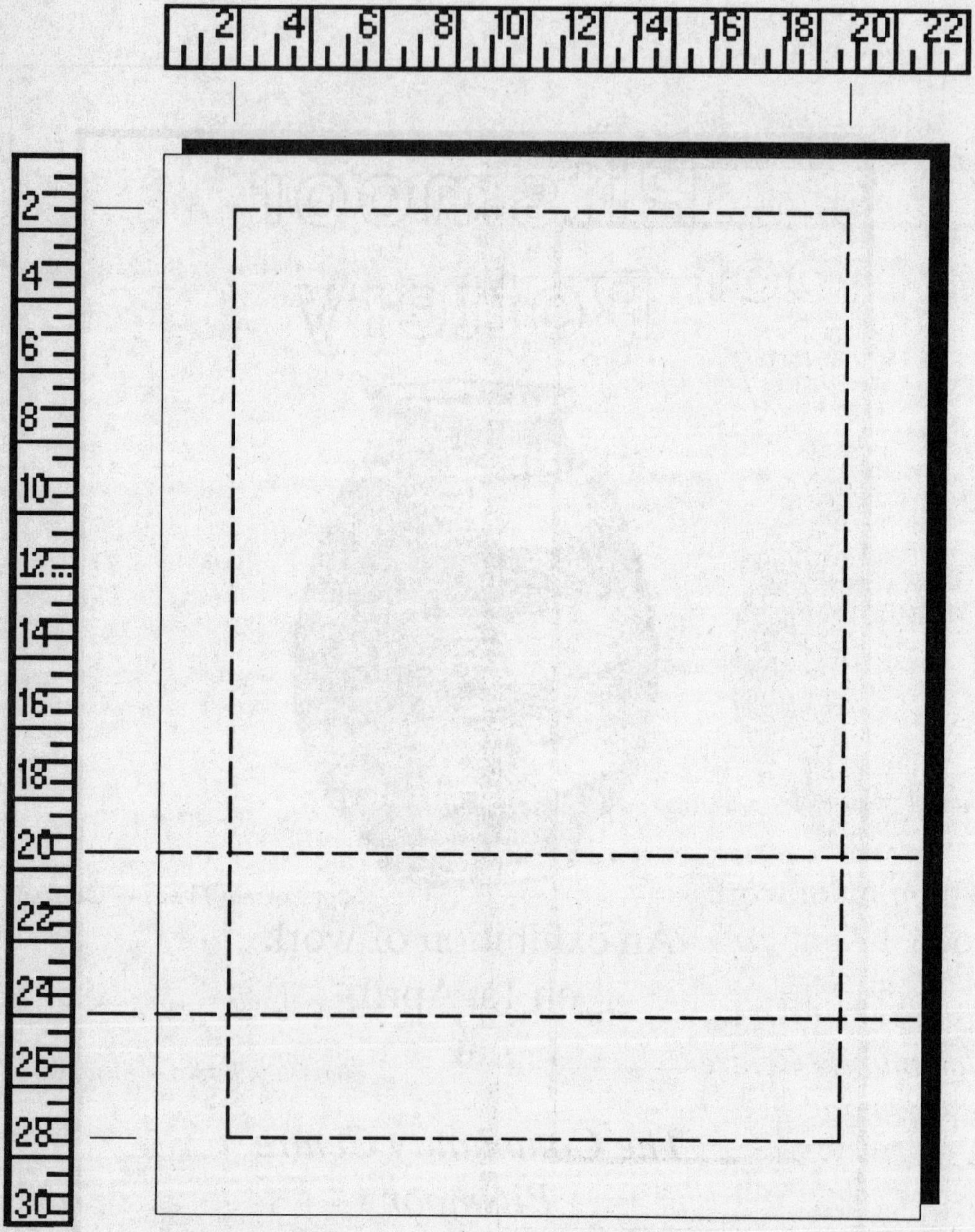

Elements

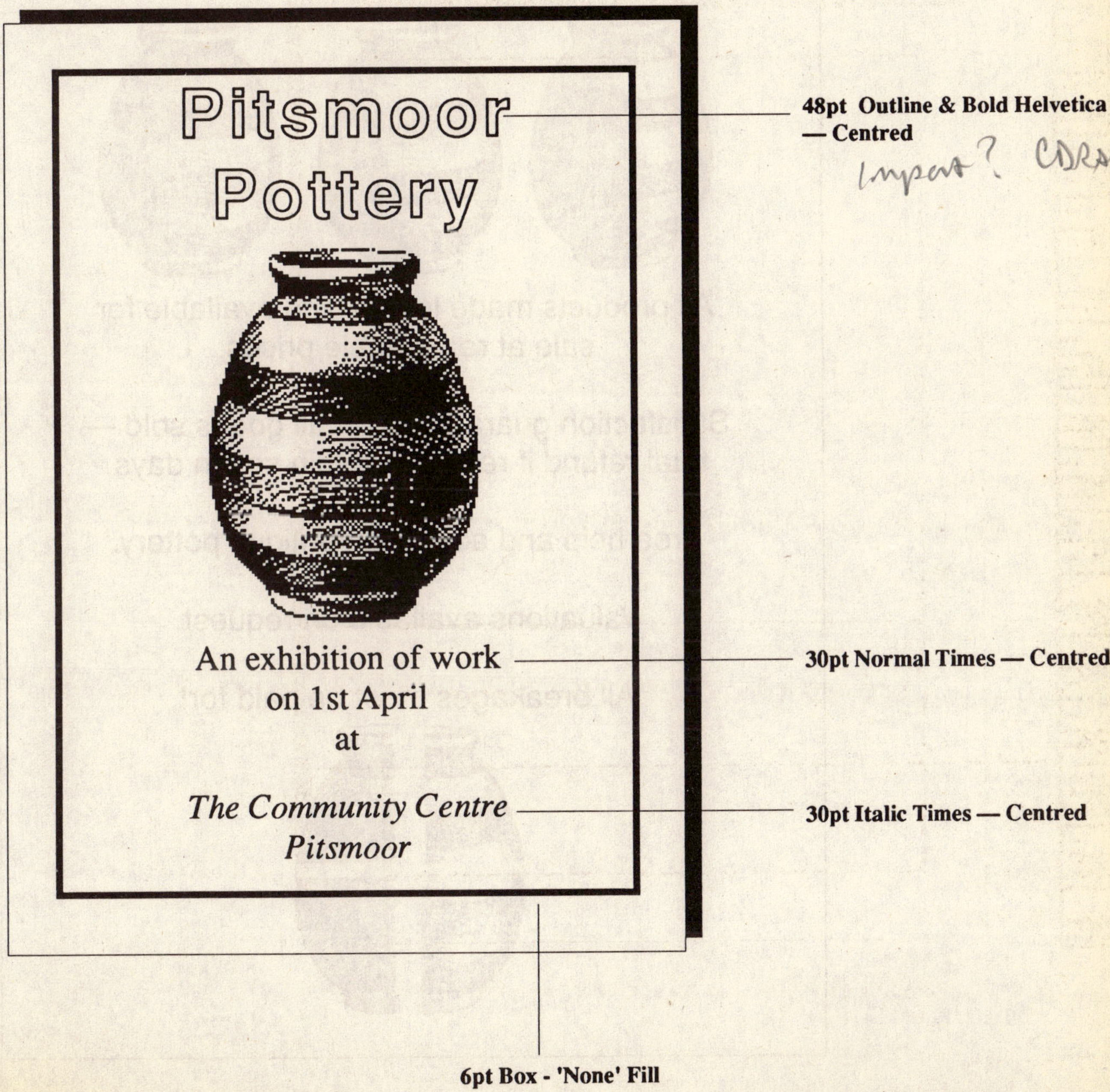
Pitsmoor
Pottery
An exhibition of work
on 1st April
at
The Community Centre
Pitsmoor
48pt Outline & Bold Helvetica — Centred
30pt Normal Times — Centred
30pt Italic Times — Centred
6pt Box - 'None' Fill

Back

All products made locally and available for sale at reasonable prices.

Satisfaction guaranteed on all goods sold — total refund if returned within seven days.

Free help and advice on antique pottery.

Valuations available on request.

All breakages must be paid for!

Guides

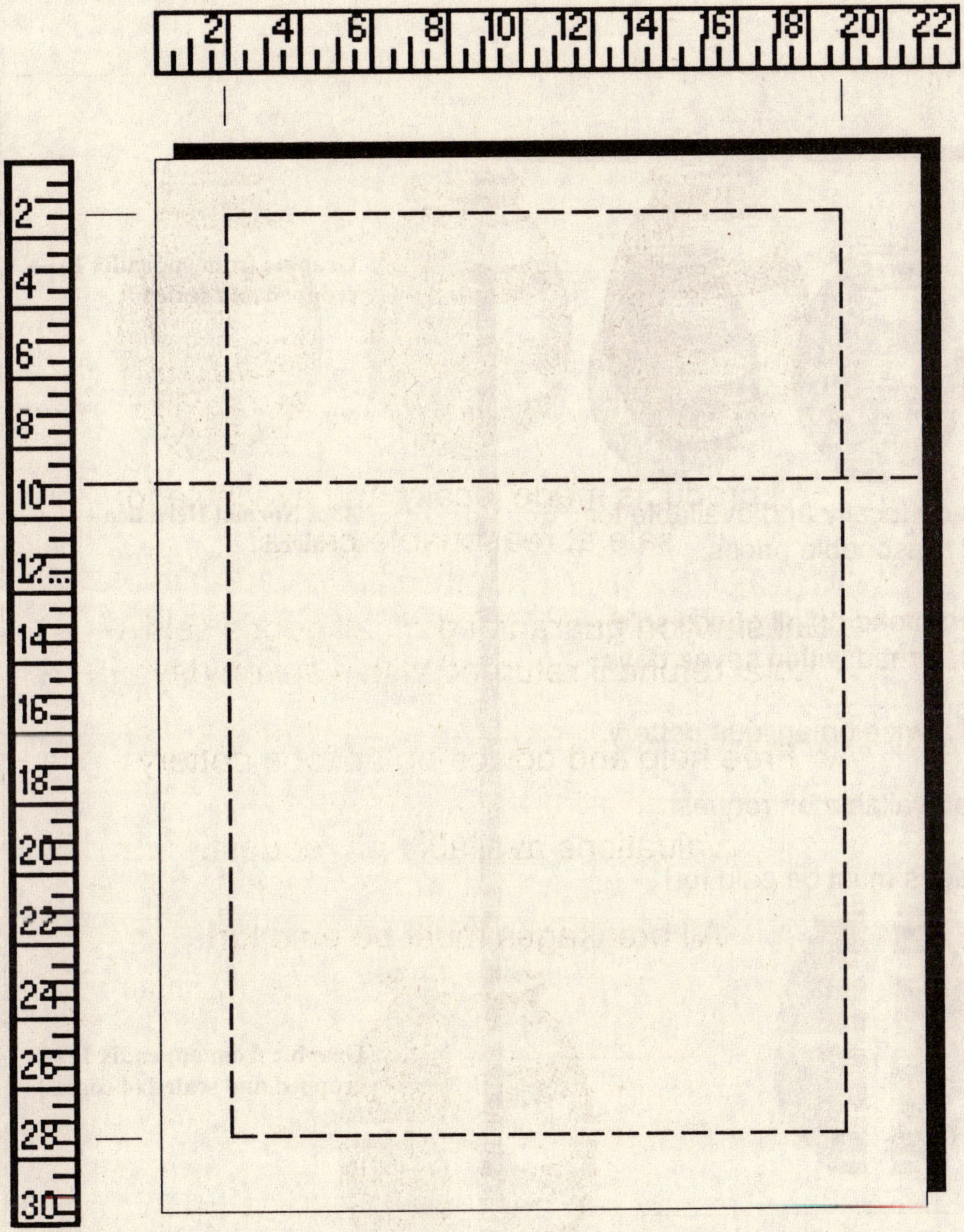

Elements

Graphic from appendix 1e — cropped and scaled

All products made locally and available for sale at reasonable prices.

48pt Normal Helvetica — Centred

Satisfaction guaranteed on all goods sold — total refund if returned within seven days.

Free help and advice on antique pottery.

Valuations available on request.

All breakages must be paid for!

Graphic from appendix 1e — cropped and scaled (4 copies)

Section 3

- pre–defined styles
- advanced techniques
- creating a table of contents
- creating a simple index

Introduction to section 3

By now you should have covered the basics of desk top publishing using PageMaker. In section 3 we will go through some methods of speeding up your word using pre–defined styles and also take a look at some advanced desk top publishing techniques. The last two chapters in this section deal with PageMaker's facilities to automatically generate a table of contents and an index.
We will be covering the techniques mentioned above and also completing the 'D.T.P. News' document in the following chapters:

Chapter 1 — Pre–defined styles

Leading on from the 'Working with paragraphs' chapter in the last section, in this chapter we will see how using pre–defined styles or 'style sheets' can speed up our desk top publishing.

Chapter 2 — Advanced techniques

Demonstrates some of the advanced techniques of desk top publishing and shows how some interesting 'effects' are made.

Chapter 3 — Creating a table of contents

PageMaker's facility to automatically create a table of contents for your publication can be a useful and time saving addition to your knowledge. This chapter explains how to create such a table.

Chapter 4 — Creating a simple index

Explains how to use PageMaker's index generating function to create a simple index for your document.

Documents created in this section

In this section you will be completing the newsletter you began in the previous section.

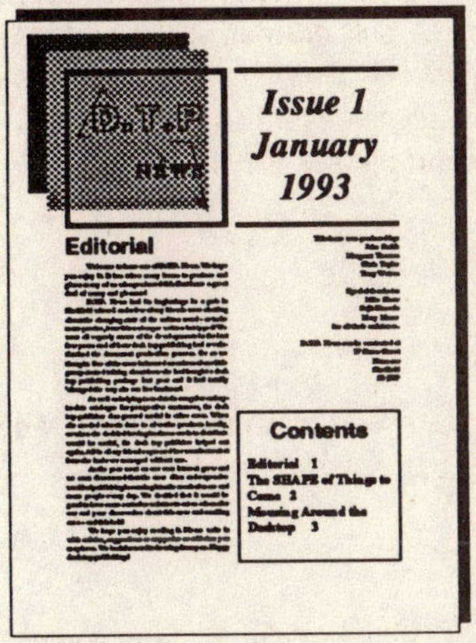

Page 1

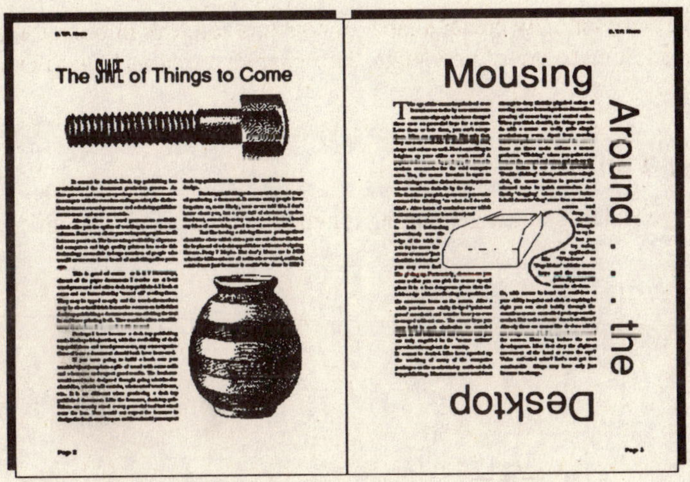

Pages 2 and 3

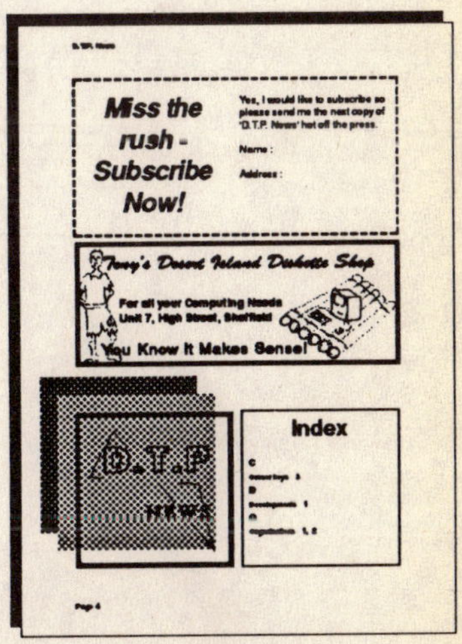

Page 4

Chapter 1

Pre–defined styles

- using pre–defined styles
- adding new styles
- changing an existing style
- removing styles
- working with 'tags'

Introduction to chapter 1

In the last section we used the 'Type specifications', 'Paragraph specifications', 'Indents / tabs' and 'Hyphenation' dialogue boxes to change the attributes of paragraphs of text to a given specification. PageMaker has a further feature — pre–defined styles or 'style sheets' — which allows us to enter specifications for each of these dialogue boxes beforehand and apply them all to a paragraph at the same time. The combined application of these specifications simultaneously gives the paragraph a certain 'style' (hence the term 'style sheets'). The use of style sheets has two main advantages for the desk top publisher. Firstly, once a style sheet has been defined, it can be applied to text as often as desired. This both saves time and helps give documents a consistency. The second advantage of using style sheets is that any changes made to the style sheet is automatically applied to all the text in a document which is in that style (You should note that the term 'style sheets' is different from the 'Type styles' option in the [Type] menu — 'Type styles' refers to whether a piece of text is in bold, italic, etc. while 'style sheets' coves all attributes of a piece of text, including 'Type style').

Activity 1

Using pre–defined styles

Objectives

1. To use a pre–defined style

Introduction

PageMaker has a number of pre–defined styles 'built in'. These are 'Body text', 'Caption', 'Headline', 'Subhead 1', and 'Subhead 2'. In this activity you will be using some of these to format your text.

Guided activity

1. If necessary, **restart PageMaker and open the document you have been creating.**

Figure 1.1

2. **Select the 'Style palette' option from the [Window] menu.**
   A box containing the different pre–defined styles available appears somewhere in the PageMaker window (figure 1.1) — this can be moved in the same way as the toolbox.

3. **Move to page 1 of your sample document and highlight the heading 'Editorial' at the beginning of your first story.**

4. With the word 'Editorial' highlighted, **move the pointer over the word 'Headline' in the style palette (you may need to use the style palettes scroll bars if the word 'Headline' is not in view). Click the mouse button here to select this style.**
   The word 'Editorial' takes on the style 'Headline'.

5. **Check what attributes the word 'Editorial' now has** — with the word still highlighted look at the values set for 'Font', 'Size', 'Leading', etc. in the [Type] menu.

6. **Highlight the first paragraph under the heading 'Editorial' and select the style 'Body text'.**
   The paragraph takes on the style assigned to it — 'Body text'.

7. Again, **check the attributes of the text in the [Type] menu.**

8. We do not have to highlight all of a paragraph to assign a style to it.
Using the text tool, **place the cursor somewhere in the second paragraph after the heading. Select 'Body text' from the style palette.**
The paragraph changes to the 'Body text' style.

9. **Place the cursor within the headline 'Editorial'.**
The 'Headline' style in the style palette becomes highlighted showing this is the style the selected text is in. This is a useful way of checking which style is assigned to a particular piece of text.

Independent activity

1. Change the remaining text in the story to 'Body text' (its best to start from the last paragraph and work up) except for the heading 'Editorial' which should be in the 'Subhead 1' style. The text should increase in size (since body text is 12pt) causing the text block to increase in length or have an arrow in the bottom handle when selected (or both). Don't worry about this.

Activity 2

Adding new styles

Objectives

1. To add a new style to the style palette

Introduction

Having ready made styles is useful but as you progress from one document to another you will probably want to make your own styles. This activity goes through the process of adding new styles to the style palette.

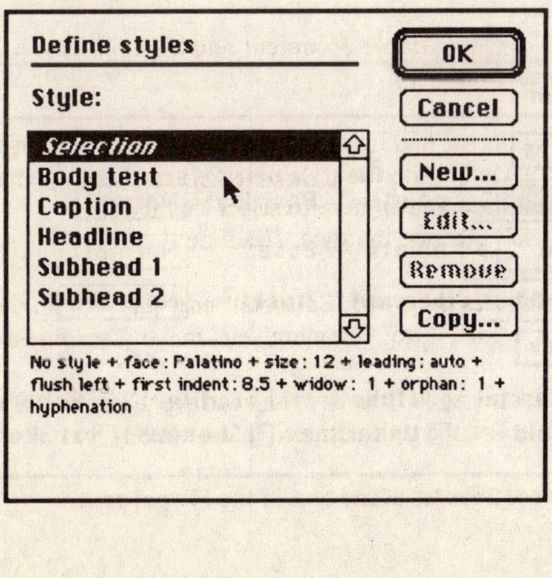

Figure 2.1

Guided activity

1. **Select the 'Define styles' option from the [Type] menu.**
   A dialogue box appears (figure 2.1).

2. When we define a new style it can be based on a previously defined style. This means that the attributes are initially set to those of the style it is based on. Let's define a new style for the body of our stories in 'DTP News' — we can base it on 'Body text'.
   Move the pointer over the 'Body text' option in the box at the left–hand side of the dialogue box and click the mouse button to select it.
   The 'Body text' option becomes highlighted to show it has been selected.

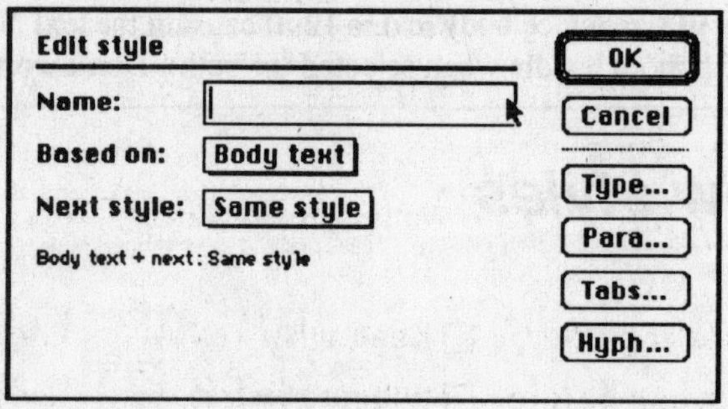

Figure 2.2

3. **Click over the 'New' box to tell PageMaker you want to create a new style sheet based on 'Body text'.**
   A second dialogue box entitled 'Edit style' appears over the first one (figure 2.2).

4. We need to give this new style a name — since it is for use with the 'DTP News' document call this style 'DTP Body' — **type this in the 'Name' box** (do not press ENTER).

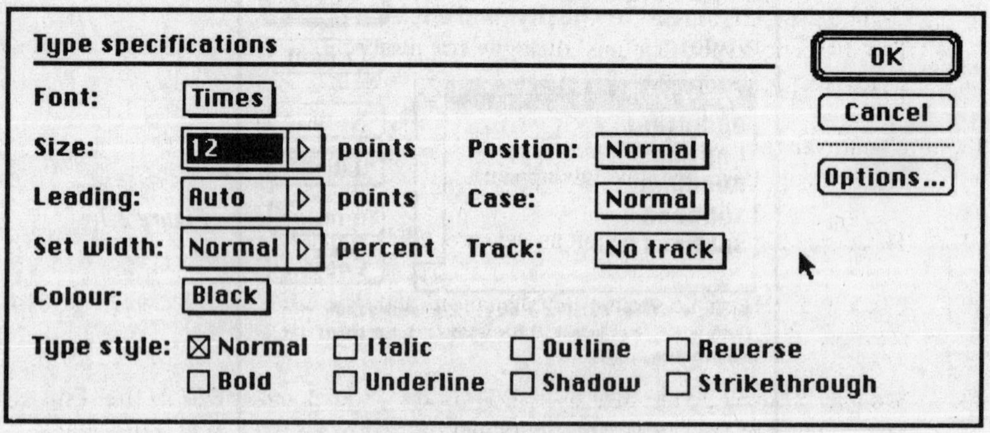

Figure 2.3

5. **Click over the 'Type' box.**
   A third dialogue box appears (figure 2.3). You may recognise this from previous section — it is the 'Type specifications' dialogue box.

6. What you are now looking at are the 'Type specifications' for the style we based 'DTP Body' on — 'Body text'. **Change the 'Size' to 10pt text.**

7. **Click on the 'OK'** to tell PageMaker you have finished with the 'Type specifications' dialogue box.
   This dialogue box disappears and the previous one, 'Edit style' is in view again.

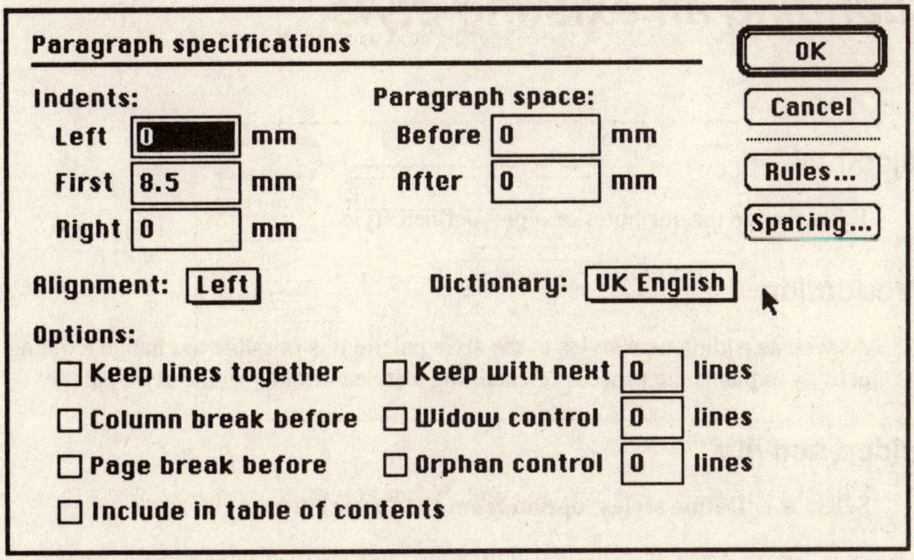

Figure 2.4

8. **Click over the 'Para' box.**
   Another dialogue box appears (figure 2.4), the 'Paragraph specifications' dialogue box, for you to specify details concerning the paragraph.

9. The paragraph specifications are currently the same as the 'Body text' style specifications — **change the 'Alignment' to 'Justify' and click over 'OK'.**
   The 'Paragraph specifications' dialogue box disappears and the previous dialogue box, 'Edit styles' reappears.

10. **Click over the 'Tabs' box.**
    The 'Indent / tabs' dialogue box appears.

11. These specifications can be left as they are. **Click on 'OK'.**

12. **Click over 'Hyph'** to see the 'Hyphenation' dialogue box and click over 'OK' to accept these settings.

13. We have now set up our new style 'DTP Body' — **click over 'OK' in the 'Edit styles' dialogue box. When the 'Define styles' dialogue box reappears click over 'OK' again.**
    PageMaker should now return you to the main window. The style palette has an additional option available — 'DTP Body'.

Independent activity

1. Change the paragraphs in the first story, currently in 'Body text', to the new 'DTP Body' style.
2. Add an additional style — 'DTP Head' — which is based on 'Headline' but in the 'Helvetica' font. Change the heading 'Editorial' to this new style.

Activity 3

Changing an existing style

Objectives

1. To change the attributes of a pre–defined style

Introduction

As well as adding new styles to the style palette it is possible to change existing styles. This activity explains the process of changing a style currently in the style palette.

Guided activity

1. **Select the 'Define styles' option from the [Type] menu.**
2. When the dialogue box appears, **select the 'DTP Body' style from the box on the left–hand side of the dialogue box.**
3. **Click over the 'Edit' box.**
   The 'Edit styles' dialogue box appears. The style 'Name' is 'DTP Body' — the one you selected.
4. **Click over the 'Type' box and, when the 'Type specifications' dialogue box appears, change the 'Size' to 12pt.**
5. Rather than clicking over 'OK' in all of the dialogue boxes one at a time we will use a short cut. **While holding down the OPTION[PC] key click over 'OK' in the current dialogue box.**
   All of the dialogue boxes on the screen are automatically 'OK`ed' one at a time — returning you to the main PageMaker window. This method of holding down the OPTION[PC] key and clicking over 'OK' in the current dialogue box is a useful technique when handling 'layers' of dialogue boxes.
   The text in the story which is in the 'DTP Body' style should now change automatically to 12pt text. If you had 'DTP Body' text on other pages in the document then this would also change automatically.

PC users should hold down the ALT key instead

Independent activity

1. Change the size of 'DTP Body' back to 10pt.

Activity 4

Removing styles

Objectives

1. To remove a pre–defined style

Introduction

As you create more and more new styles the style palette can become cluttered with redundant styles. This activity explains how to remove unwanted styles from the style palette.

Guided activity

1. **Select the 'Define styles' option in the [Type] menu.**
2. **Select the 'DTP Body' style and click over the 'Remove' box.**
3. **Click over 'OK'.**
   When the main PageMaker window is returned the style 'DTP Body' is no longer available in the style palette. The text which was previously in the 'DTP Body' style has not changed (has the same attributes) but if it is highlighted it shows up as having a style of 'Body text+' in the style palette.

Independent activity

1. When we removed 'DTP Body' the paragraphs that were in this style became paragraphs with a style of 'Body text+' attached to them (since there was no longer a style sheet named 'DTP Body' in the 'style palette' the paragraphs reverted to the style 'DTP Body' was based on — 'Body text'. The '+' indicates that the paragraphs are not exactly like 'Body text' — they were bost text 'plus' some changes). If we added a new style called 'DTP Body' these paragraphs would still be assigned the style 'Body text+'. PageMaker does not remember a style once it has been removed — as far as it is concerned 'DTP Body' never existed. If we wanted to assign the style 'DTP Body' to our paragraphs then we would have to make a new style and assign it to each paragraph all over again.
   Add the style 'DTP Body' as before and assign it to the same paragraphs as before (the paragraphs attributes will not change. The only difference is that they are now in the style 'DTP Body').

Activity 5

Working with 'tags'

Objectives

1. To use tags in word processed files

Introduction

The text in the sample document you entered via a word processor (or the 'Story editor') in section 1 was preceded by '<Body text>'. Whenever PageMaker places text from a file it checks to see if the 'Read tags' option in the 'Place' dialogue box is active. If it is then PageMaker looks for 'tags' in the text. These are indicated by the name of a style (such as 'Body text') surrounded by the '< >' characters. The style specified is then applied to the text as it is brought in. Thus the text that is placed already has a style assigned to it.

This means that there are two ways of assigning a style to text. Firstly, we can assign a style when we are first entering the text on the word processor or story editor (by enclosing the name of the desired style at the start of the paragraph with the '< >' characters surrounding it). Secondly, we can bring the text in 'any old way' and assign it a style once it is in PageMaker. By applying a general style using 'tags' when typing the text it can be placed where we want it to go and will be in roughly the right size, font, etc.. The text can then be 'fine tuned' using the style palette in PageMaker itself.

Independent activity

1. Enter the text shown in appendix 1f ready for placing. Include a tag for the style 'DTP Body' at the beginning of the first paragraph.

End of chapter summary

What I want to do	How I do it
• Assign a style to a paragraph	• Click the cursor inside the paragraph then click over the style name in the style palette
• Add a new style	• Select 'Define styles' from the [Type] menu — select 'New' and change specification dialogue boxes as desired
• Change an existing style	• Select 'Define styles' from the [Type] menu — click over style name and select 'Edit' — change specification dialogue boxes as desired
• Remove a style	• Select 'Define styles' from the [Type] menu — click over style name and select 'Remove'
• Add tags to word processed documents	• Precede paragraph by style name enclosed in '< >'

Trouble-shooting

Problem	Possible reason	Solution
• A file containing tags is placed and does not take on the assigned style — the tags themselves are still present	• Tags are not being read	• Ensure 'Read tags' in 'Place' dialogue box is active when placing file

Chapter 2

Advanced techniques

- rotating text
- moving column guides
- drop capitals
- text wrap
- layers
- selecting multiple–items

Introduction to chapter 2

In this chapter we will look at some advanced techniques of desk top publishing. To demonstrate these we will complete page 3 and most of page 4 of the 'DTP News' document you have been creating.

Activity 1

Rotating text

Objectives

1. To rotate a block of text

Introduction

To create the effect shown on page 3 of the sample document the text 'Around...the' and 'Desktop' has to be rotated. This activity takes you through the processes involved in rotating text in this way. Using rotated text can be a complicated process — work your way slowly through the activity making sure you understand each step.

Guided activity

1. Move to page 3 of the sample document. At the side of the page **type in 'Mousing' in 72pt Normal Helvetica text. Align this text to the right.**

2. We will first make a border of guides to put the text into. This will consist of both horizontal and vertical guides so the first thing to do is to make both the rulers measure in the same quantities. **Select the 'Preferences' option from the [Edit] menu and set the 'Measurement system' to measure in 'Picas'** (the vertical ruler should already be in picas).

3. **Add additional horizontal guides 7p below the top margin and 7p above the bottom margin** (you will find this easier if you move the zero mark on the vertical ruler first to the top margin and then to the bottom margin — if necessary refresh your memory by looking at the 3rd activity in chapter 1 of the previous section).

4. **Add an additional vertical guide 7p from the outside margin** (on the right of the page). Moving the horizontal zero mark to line up with the outside margin will make this easier and probably more accurate.

5. **Pick up the 'Mousing' text and place it so that its right–hand side touches the vertical guide you placed 7p from the outside margin and its top touches the top margin** (figure 1.1).

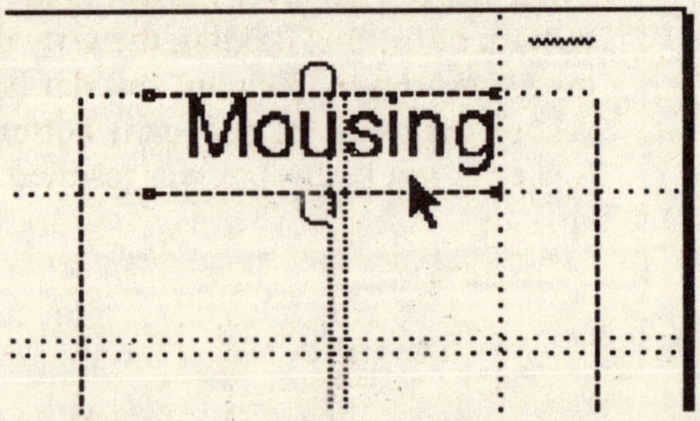

Figure 1.1

6. At the side of the page **type in 'Around . . . the' in 72pt Helvetica text** (ensure there is a space after the word 'Around', in between each dot, and before the word 'the'). **Make this text 'Justified'.**

7. **Select this block of text** with the pointer tool.

8. With the text selected **choose the 'Text rotation' option from the [Element] menu.**
A dialogue box appears for you to tell PageMaker what sort of rotation to apply to this text (figure 1.2).

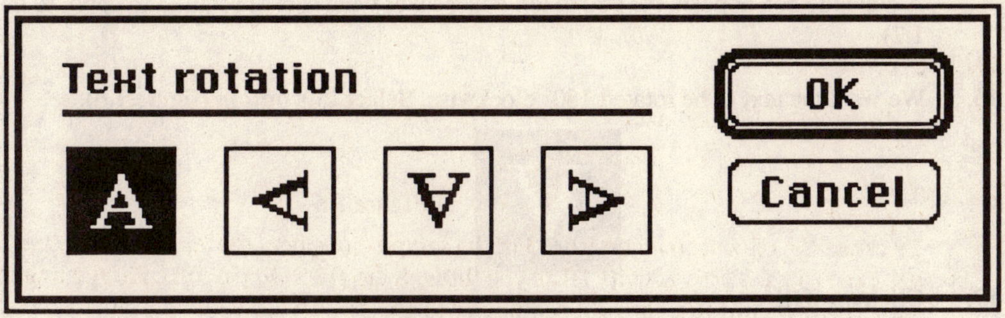

Figure 1.2

9. We want the text to be rotated 90° clockwise. **Select this option** (figure 1.3).

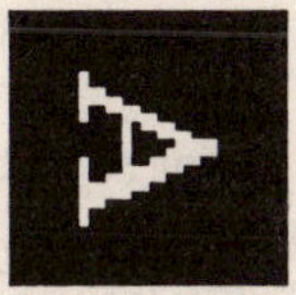

Figure 1.3

10. **Click on 'OK'.**
When the page returns the text in the selected text block has been turned on its side. It no longer has the attributes of a text block, instead it has a dot at each corner and in the middle of each side. When text is rotated it is treated a bit like a graphic.

11. **Pick up this text and place it on the page such that the top of the box containing it touches the guide 7p from the top margin and the right–hand side of the box touches the outside margin** (figure 1.4).

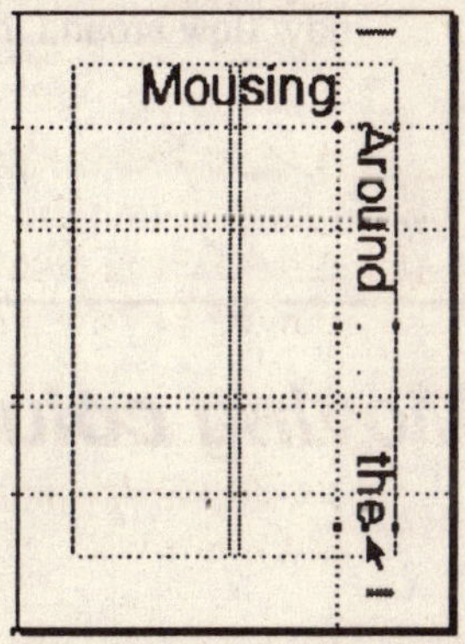

Figure 1.4

12. It is likely that the bottom of the rotated text does not reach as far as the horizontal guide you placed 7p above the bottom margin or goes beyond this guide.
Move the pointer over the dot in the middle of the bottom of the box holding the text. Hold down the mouse button to 'pick up' this dot (just as if it were a graphic you were scaling) **and drag it to rest on the guide 7p above the bottom margin** (figure 1.5).
Since the text in this box was justified it should reduce or expand to fill out the box.

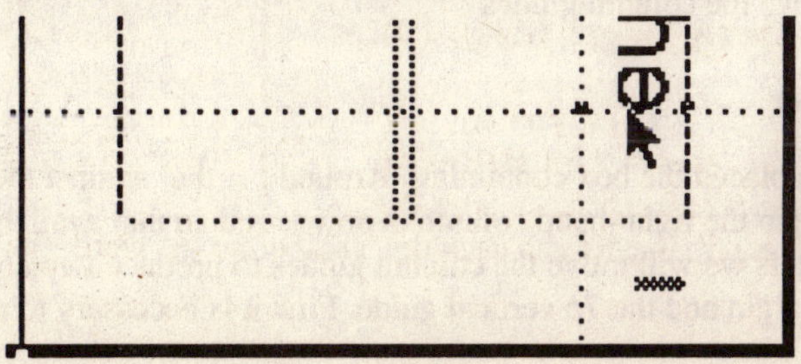

Figure 1.5

13. **At the side of the page type in 'Desktop' in 72pt Helvetica text. Align this text to the left.**

14. **Select this block of text** with the pointer tool.

15. With the text selected **choose the 'Text rotation' option from the [Element] menu.**
A dialogue box appears for you to tell PageMaker what sort of rotation to apply to this text (figure 1.2).

16. We want the text to be rotated 180° clockwise. **Select this option** (figure 1.6).

Figure 1.6

17. **Click on 'OK'.**
When the page returns the text in the selected text block has been turned upside down (180°). It no longer has the attributes of a text block, instead it has a dot at each corner and in the middle of each side.

18. **Pick up this text and place it on the page such that the top of the box containing it touches the guide 7p above the bottom margin and the right–hand side of the box touches the guide you placed 7p from the outside margin** (figure 1.7).
The words 'Mousing Around . . . the Desktop' should now flow around the page.

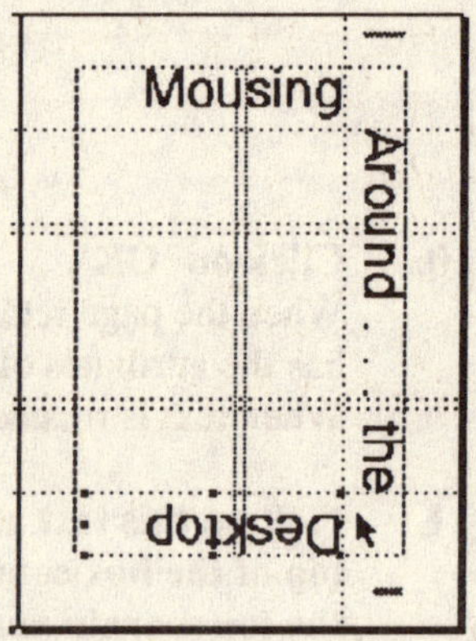

Figure 1.7

Activity 2

Moving column guides

Objectives

1. To re–calculate column width
2. To move the column guides

Introduction

We have placed the box containing 'Around . . . the' against the outside margin. The space available in the right–hand column is now less than that available in the left–hand column. To remedy this we will move the column guides to produce two columns of equal width between the inside margin and the 7p vertical guide. First it is necessary to recalculate how wide these columns will be.

Guided activity

1. **Measure the space between the inside margin and the 7p vertical guide.**
   Move the horizontal zero mark to line up with the inside margin. With the zero mark here, move the pointer so that it touches the guide 7p from the outside margin. The marker on the horizontal ruler which follows the pointer shows 30p — this is the distance available for our two columns (an alternative method of finding this distance would have been to subtract 7p — the distance the guide is from the outside margin — from the distance between the two margins — 18p each plus 1p between them — giving 30p). If we allow 1p for the space between the columns that means we can have two columns of 14.5p each (two 14.5p columns plus 1p in between equals 30p). You may like to convince yourself of all this on paper before continuing.

2. With the 'Lock guides' option inactive, **move the pointer over the column guide on the right–hand side of the first column** (figure 2.1a) **and drag it so that it is 14.5p from the inside margin** (figure 2.1b).
   Being in 'Actual size' will make this considerably easier.

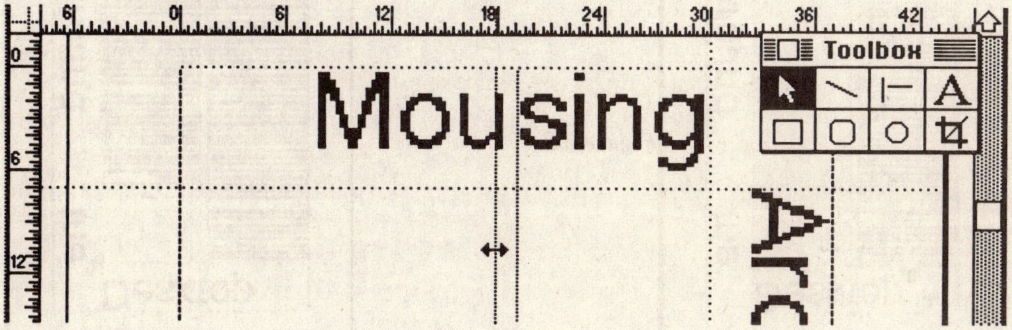

Figure 2.1a

Figure 2.1b

3. We now have two equal columns again — each 14.5p wide. **Lock the guides again.**

Independent activity

1. Place the text for the story (in appendix 1f) which you entered in the previous chapter into the first column. It should start at the guide 7p below the top margin and stop at the guide 7p above the bottom margin.
   In the last chapter you should have assigned a tag to this text to make it into 'DTP Body' style. If this has worked then the text should already be 10pt Times Justified. The paragraphs should also have an indent. For this exercise we do not want this indent so remove it from the paragraphs (try selecting all of the text then choosing the 'Paragraph' option in the [Type] menu). The page should now look like figure 2.2.

3. Continue the story in the second column — starting at the guide 7p below the top margin and continuing as far down the column as it will go (figure 2.3).

Figure 2.2

Figure 2.3

Activity 3

Drop capitals

Objectives

1. To add a drop capital to the text

Introduction

The large letter 'T' at the start of the story in the finished page 3 is called a 'drop capital'. These are often used to add a little interest to the text and also to divide up a story. In this activity we will add this drop capital to the text — be prepared to do a lot of switching between 'Fit in window', 'Actual size' and perhaps even '200% size'!

Guided activity

1. **At the side of the page type in the letter 'T' in 48pt Normal Times text.**
2. **Place an additional vertical guide 2.5p from the inside margin.**
3. **Close the shutter on the text in the first column so that only the top three lines are showing** (figure 3.1).

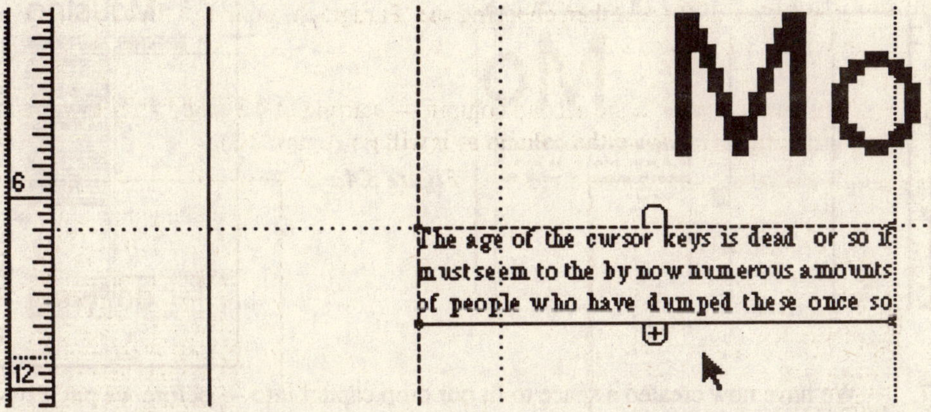

Figure 3.1

4. **Now move the pointer over the dot in the top left–hand corner of this text block and drag it so that it rests over the vertical guide you placed 2.5p from the inside margin** (figure 3.2).

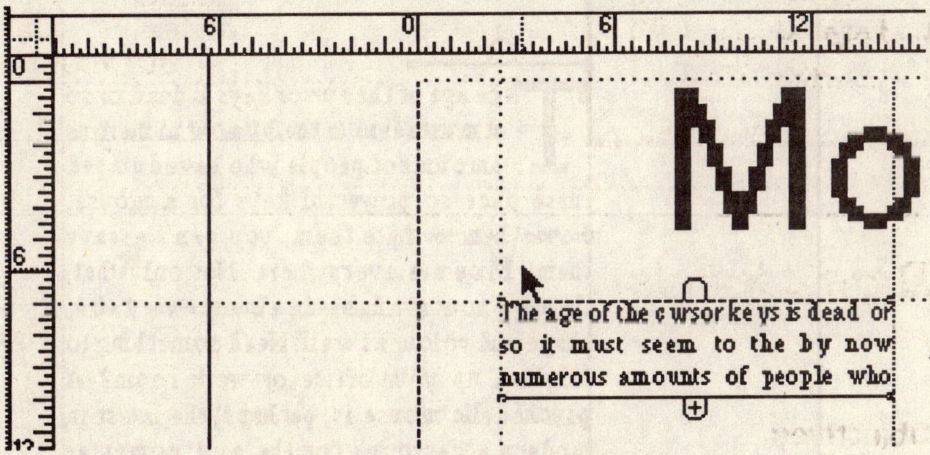

Figure 3.2

5. **With this text block still selected, place an additional horizontal guide so that it lines up with the line at the bottom of this selected text block** (figure 3.3).

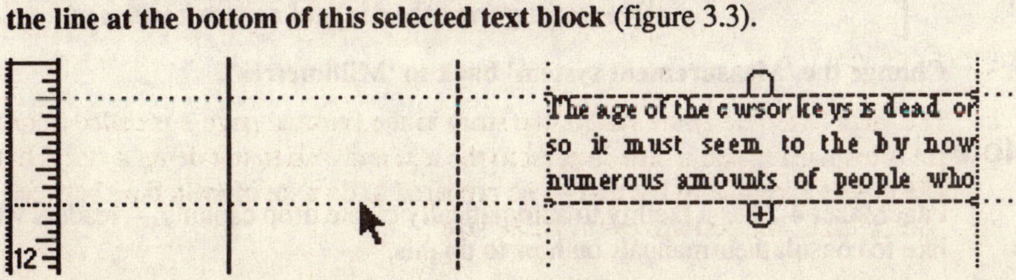

Figure 3.3

6. **Click in the shutter at the bottom of the text block to get some more text. Place this text so that it begins against the inside margin and the top of the text touches the guide you just placed** (figure 3.4a). **Continue the text down to the end of the first column** (figure 3.4b).
By adding a guide to line up with the bottom of the text block holding the top three lines of text we have given ourselves a marker to continue the text from. If we had not done this then the space between line 3 and line 4 of the text in the first column may have differed slightly from the usual space.

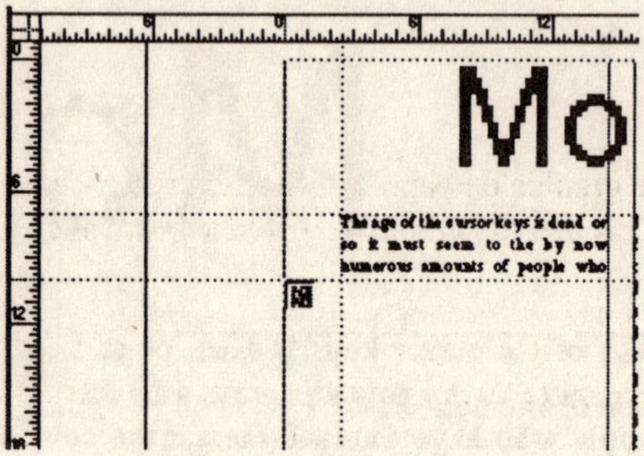

Figure 3.4a

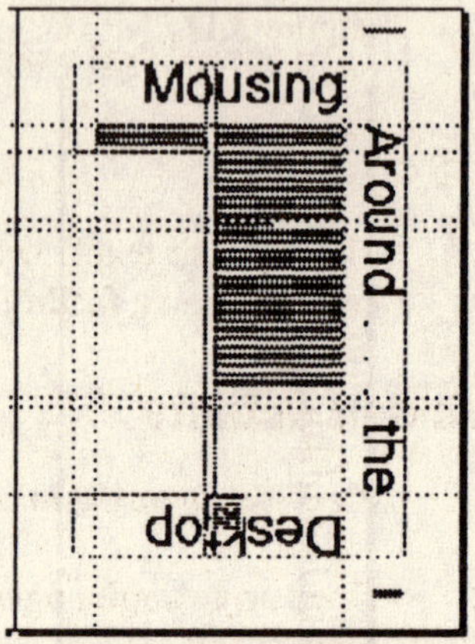

Figure 3.4b

7. We have now created a space to fit our drop capital into — before we put it there **delete the 'T' in the word 'The' at the start of the story.**

8. **Move the large letter 'T' you typed earlier so that it fits into the space created** (figure 3.5).

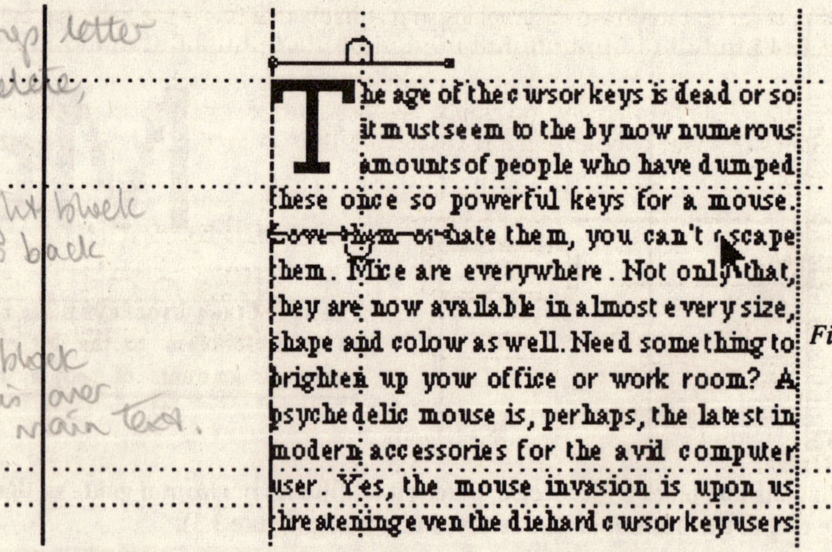

Figure 3.5

9. **Change the 'Measurement system' back to 'Millimetres'.**

Note

PageMaker 4.2 has a facility to automatically create drop capitals — readers with version 4.2 may like to consult their manuals on how to do this.

Activity 4 Text wrap

Objectives

1. To apply 'Text wrap' to a graphic

Introduction

The effect of text flowing around the mouse graphic on page 3 of the finished document was created using a facility called 'text wrap'. This activity explains how to achieve such an effect.

Guided activity

1. **Place the graphic in appendix 1g at the side of the page.**

2. **Crop any rough edges away from it and scale it so that it fits into a space roughly 8cm wide by 4cm tall.**

3. We are going to add a text wrap to this graphic.
With the graphic selected **select the 'Text wrap' option from the [Element] menu.**
A dialogue box appears for you to specify the type of text wrap (figure 4.1). The usual text wrap option is for text to flow over graphics so it is likely that this is the selection currently highlighted (figure 4.2).

4. We want text to flow around the graphic so **click over this icon to select this option** (figure 4.3).
A 'Standoff' value appears in the boxes below. This is how far from the graphic text is not allowed to come.

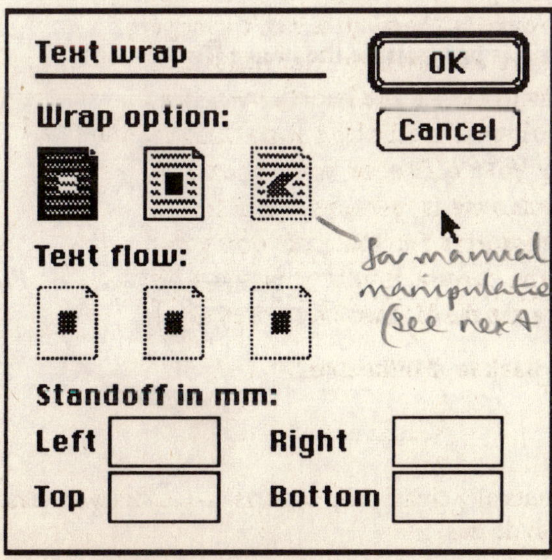

Figure 4.1

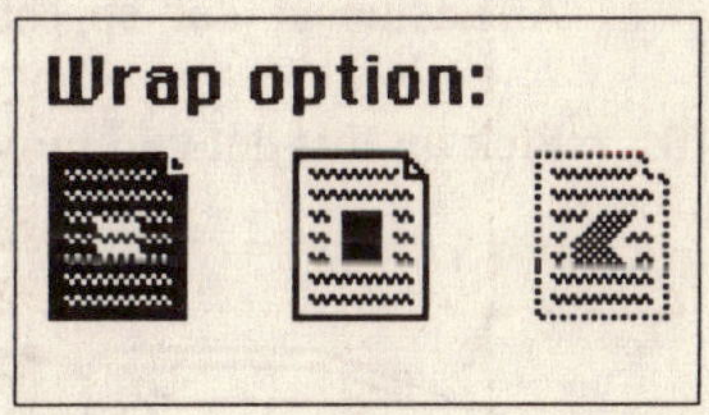

Figure 4.2

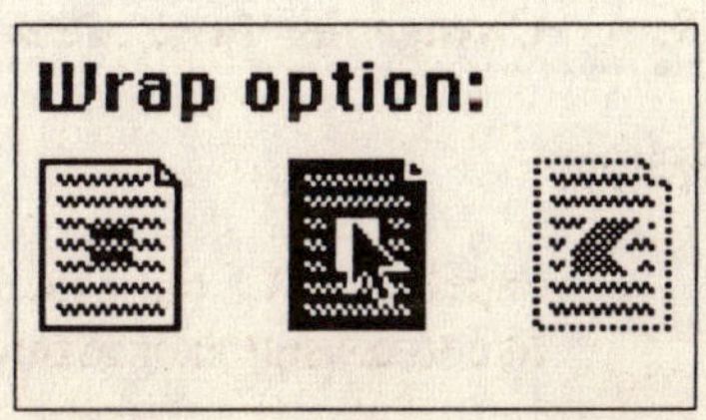

Figure 4.3

5. The type of flow around also needs to be specified. We want the text to flow around the sides of the graphic so **select this icon** (figure 4.4).

Figure 4.4

6. **Click over 'OK'.**
When the page returns the graphic has an additional dotted box around it — this indicates the text wrap.

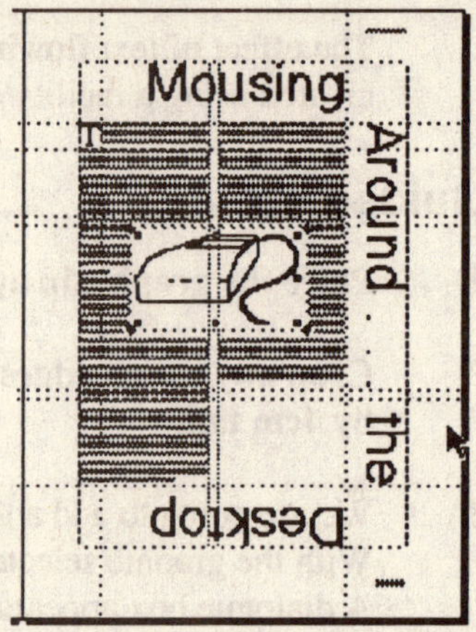

Figure 4.5

7. **Pick up the graphic and move it so that it rests between the two columns, roughly half–way down the page** (if by some misfortune you should drop the graphic by accident, before reaching this location, the text wrap on the graphic may cause all sorts of things to happen — its not nearly as bad as it looks — simply pick up the graphic again and place it at the side of the page before you attempt the procedure once more).
The text flows around the dotted 'text wrap' square surrounding the graphic (figure 4.5).

8. **Move the graphic to the side of the page again and zoom in on it.**

9. We can change the shape of the text wrap box around the graphic so that the text will flow more smoothly along its shape.
Click anywhere along the dotted line which is the text wrap box.
An additional 'dot' appears (figure 4.6a).

10. **Pick up this dot and move it so that it is just outside the image** (figure 4.6b).

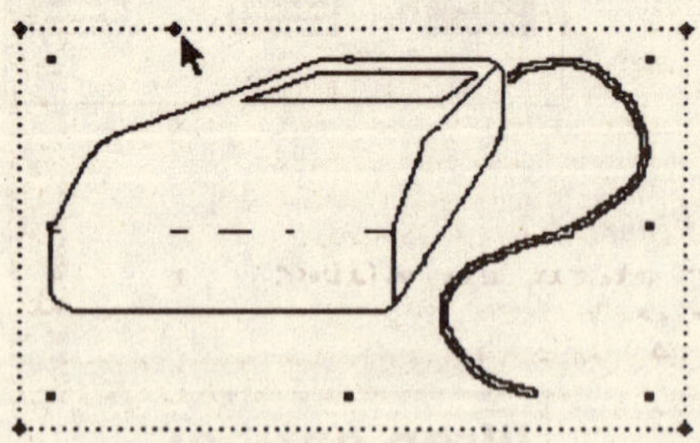

Figure 4.6a

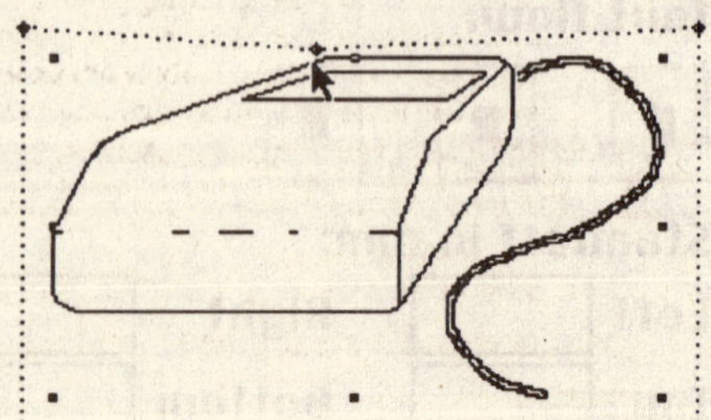

Figure 4.6b

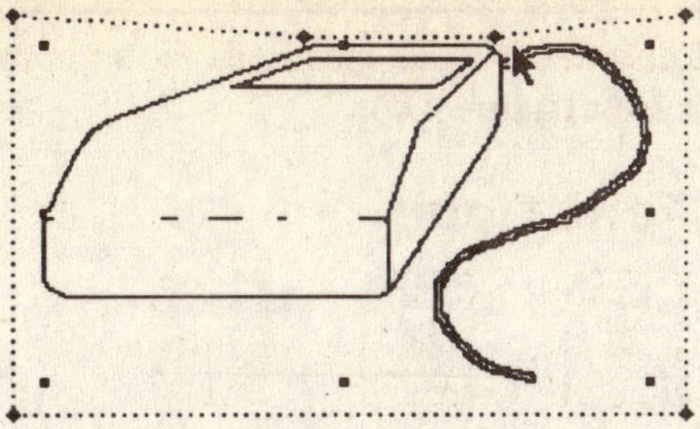

Figure 4.6c

11. **Click another dot and move this also** (figure 4.6c).

12. **Continue right around the graphic until the dotted line follows its contours smoothly as shown in figure 4.7.**

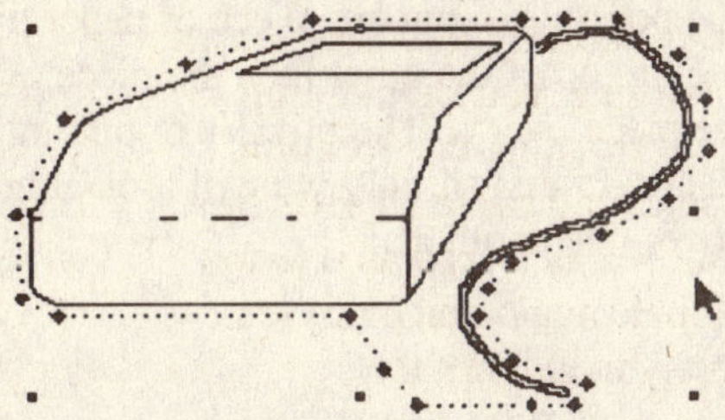

Figure 4.7

13. **Move the graphic onto the page to the same position as before.**
This time text flows around the graphics contours as outlined by the dotted text wrap line (figure 4.8).

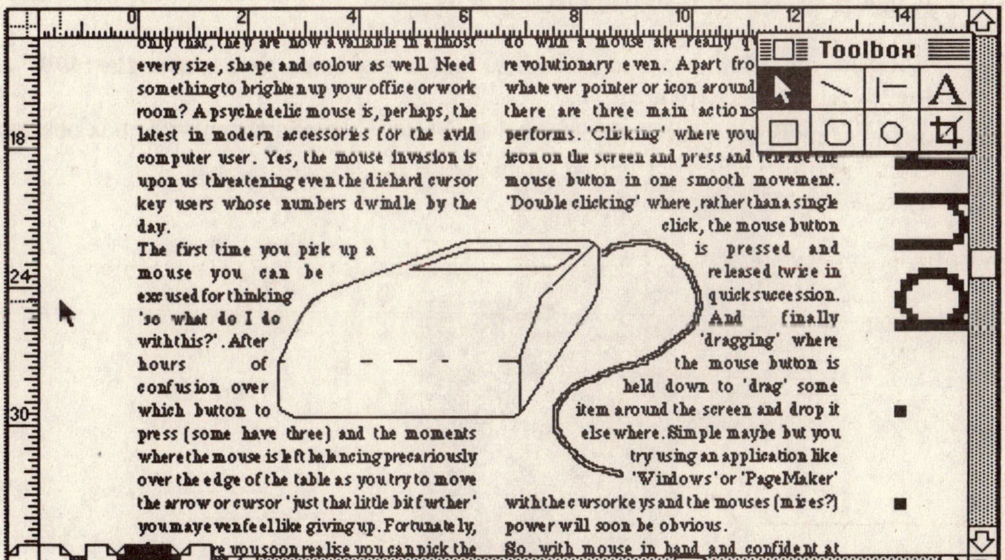

Figure 4.8

14. The text in the second column probably does not reach the bottom margin exactly. With a little patience and a steady hand you can still scale the graphic though, so that it takes up less or more space.
Click to select the graphic and scale it until the text is lined up at the bottom of the second column.

Activity 5 Layers

Objectives

1. To 'layer' elements on a page

Introduction

If you were laying out a page manually, sticking pieces of paper containing text and graphics onto a blank page, it would be possible to put one piece of paper over another. Obviously, if two pieces of paper were placed one on top of the other then the piece of paper on the bottom would have its contents obscured by the piece over it. The process of putting one item over another can have a similar effect in PageMaker. In this activity we will look at how to create an interesting effect by putting layers of items over one another.

Guided activity

1. At the side of the page **draw a box roughly 4cm by 4cm. Give it a 'Fill' of '40%'.**

2. At the side of the page, away from the box you just drew, **draw another box of roughly the same proportions. Give this second box a 'Fill' of '80%'.**

3. **'Pick up' the '80%' box and move it so that one of its corners is over the '40%' box. Drop the '80%' box here** (figure 5.1).
The '80%' box has the dots indicating it is selected. It overlaps the '40%' box obscuring a portion of it — just as if the box were a physical object.

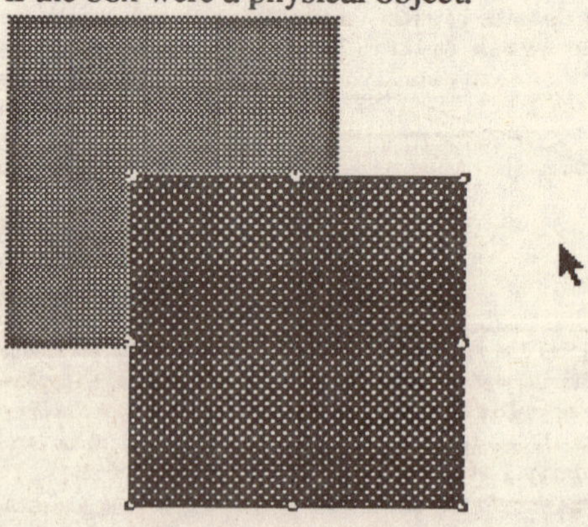

Figure 5.1

4. The '80%' box is now in front of the '40%' box causing a portion of the '40%' box to be obscured.
With the '80%' box still selected, **choose the 'Send to back' option from the [Element] menu.**
The '80%' box changes from being on top of the '40%' box to being behind it. 'Send to back' has caused the selected item (the '80%' box) to be sent to the back of the page. The '80%' box is still selected.

5. With the '80%' box still selected, **choose the 'Bring to front' option from the [Element] menu.** The '80%' box is brought to the front once again, causing it to obscure a portion of the '40%' box once more.

6. **'Cut' both boxes from the desktop.**

7. **Move to page 1 of the 'DTP News' document.**

8. At the side of the page **draw a box 18p by 18p and give it a 'Fill' of '40%'.**

9. **Pick up this box and hold it over the graphic 'DTP News' in the top left–hand side of the page** — do not release the mouse button yet.

10. **Move the box up about 2p and left about 2p and drop the box here** (figure 5.2).

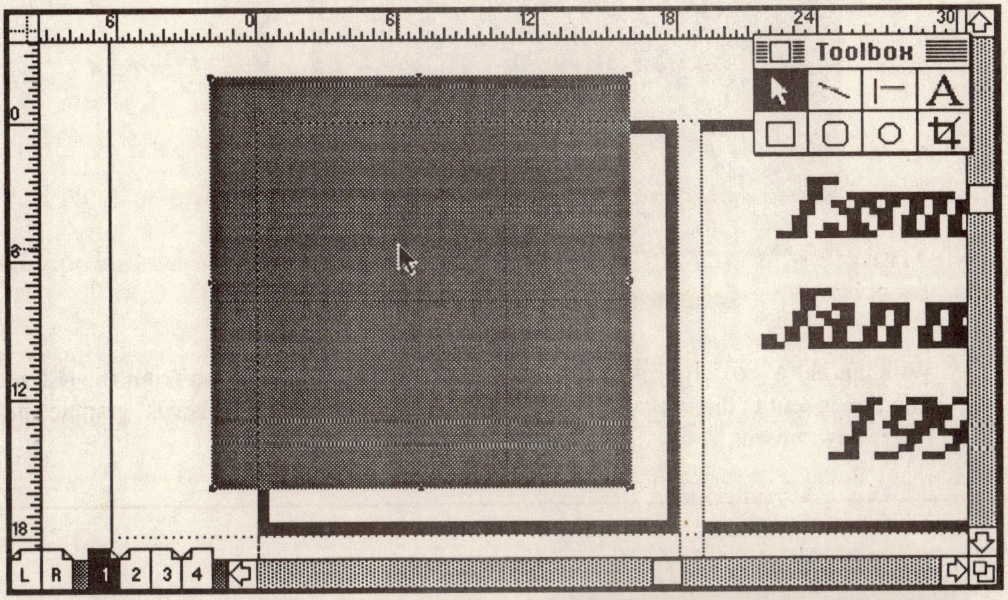

Figure 5.2

11. **With the box still selected, choose the 'Send to back' option from the [Element] menu.** The box goes behind the 'DTP News' graphic. The 'DTP News' graphic may be transparent (depending on how it was prepared) allowing you to see parts of the box through it (figure 5.3) or it may be solid.

Figure 5.3

12. At the side of the page **draw another box 18p by 18p and give it a 'Fill' of '80%'.**

13. **Move the '80%' box over the 'DTP News' graphic as before** — again, don't release the mouse button yet.

14. **Move this box up about 4p and left about 4p and drop the box here** (figure 5.4).

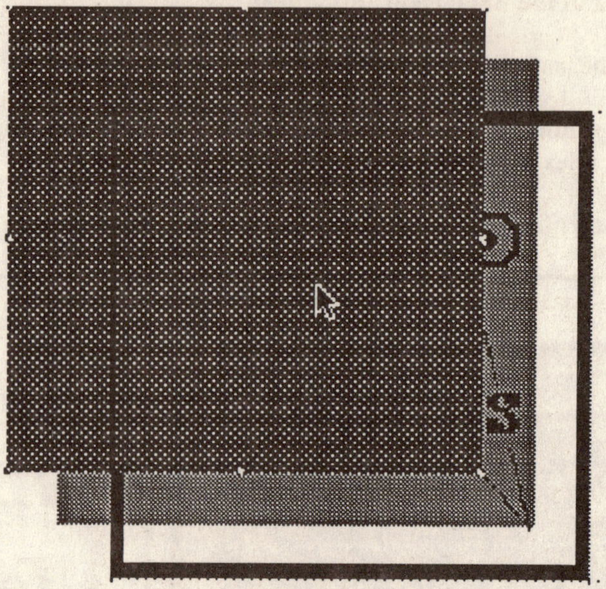

Figure 5.4

15. With the '80%' box still selected, **choose the 'Send to back' option from the [Element] menu.** The box is sent to the back creating a layered effect with the 'DTP News' graphic and the two boxes now present.

Activity 6

Selecting multiple–items

Objectives

1. To select more than one item

Introduction

In this activity we are going to copy the 'DTP News' graphic and the two boxes 'behind' it onto page 4 of the document. To do this it would be useful if we could have more than one item selected simultaneously. Since there are three items involved here we will attempt to select all of them in one go and copy them all to page 4 at the same time. For this activity it is recommended that you use the 'Actual size' view.

Guided activity

1. **Click over the 'DTP News' graphic to select it.**
   The graphic takes on the appearence of a selected graphic.

2. **Move the pointer over a portion of the '40%' box which is to the left or above the 'DTP News' graphic** (figure 6.1). **With the pointer located here hold down the SHIFT key and click the mouse button.**
   The '40%' box becomes selected. The 'DTP News' graphic is still selected also. By holding down the SHIFT key while selecting an item anything that was already selected remains in this state.

Figure 6.1

3. **Move the pointer over a portion of the '80%' box which is to the left or above the '40%' box. With the pointer located here, hold down the SHIFT key and click the mouse button.**
   The '80%' box becomes selected. The 'DTP News' graphic and the '40%' box remain in their selected state.

4. All three of the items we wish to copy are now selected.
   Select the 'Copy' option from the [Edit] menu.
   PageMaker has made a copy of the selected items.

5. **Move to page 4 of the document and select 'Paste' from the [Edit] menu.**
   The three items that were copied appear somewhere in the Pagemaker window. All three are still selected.

6. **Move the pointer to the middle of the 'DTP News' graphic** (you must be very careful at this stage — an accidental click of the mouse button will de–select all three of the items) **and hold down the mouse button.**
   All three items have been picked up.

7. **Move the items (which should move with the pointer) so that the 'DTP News' graphic fits into the grid box at the bottom left–hand side of the page. Drop them here** (figure 6.2).

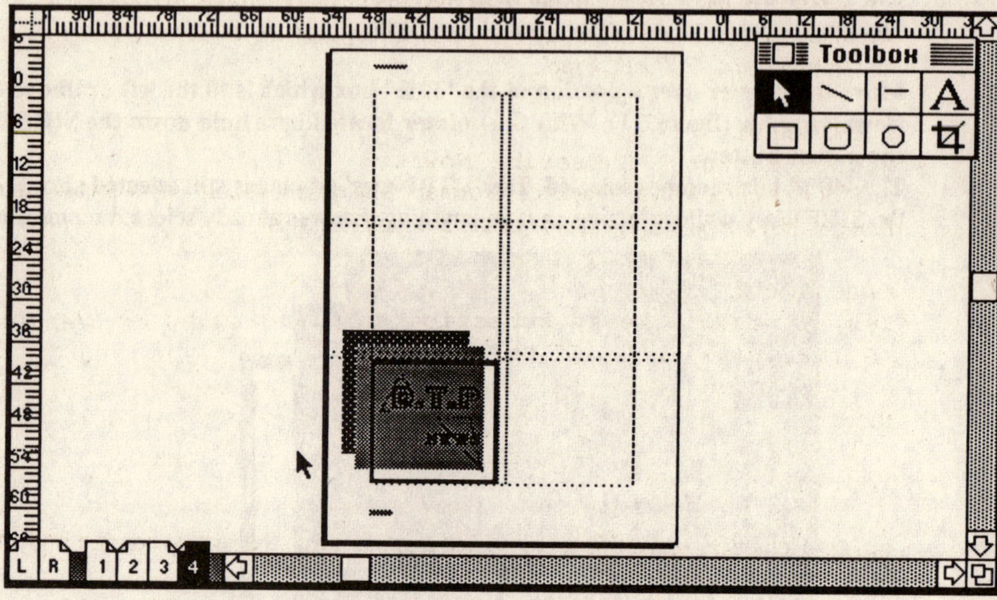

Figure 6.2

8. **Click away from the selected items to de–select them.**
The three items are no longer selected.

Independent activity

1. Before starting the next chapter let's complete some more of page 4:
   • Add a box to the page stretching from the outside margin to the inside margin. The box should be 18p high and rest between the top margin and the guide 18p from the top margin. Give the box a dotted line and a 'Fill' of 'None'.

   • Add the text...
   `Miss the rush - Subscribe Now!`
   in 36pt Helvetica with a 'Track' of 'Normal'. Make the text bold italics and centred. Put this in the first column on the left–hand side of the box you just drew.

   • Add the text...
   ```
   Yes, I would like to subscribe so please send me the next copy of
   'D.T.P. News' hot off the press.

   Name :

   Address :
   ```
   in 14pt Helvetica. Make this text justified and put it into the second column in the right–hand side of the box you drew.

   • Add the graphic in appendix 1h to the page. Crop and scale it so it fits between the inside and outside margins. The top of the graphic should touch the guide 19p from the top margin and the bottom of the graphic should be approximately 33p below the top margin.

   • Add a box to the page following the guides made by the bottom right–hand 'grid box'. Give this box a 2p 'Line' and a 'Fill' of 'None'.

End of chapter summary

What I want to do	How I do it
• Rotate a block of text	• Select block of text with pointer tool and choose 'Text rotation' option from [Element] menu
• Move position of column guides	• Ensure 'Lock guides' is inactive and drag column guide to new position with pointer
• Make text wrap around a graphic	• Select graphic and choose 'Text wrap' from [Element] menu — shape of dotted box around graphic (which is the text wrap box) can be changed by clicking on it and dragging dot which appears to new position
• Bring item in a group of overlapping items to the front of the page	• Select item and choose 'Bring to front' from [Element] menu
• Put item in a group of overlapping items to the back of the page	• Select item and choose 'Send to back' from [Element] menu

Trouble–shooting

Problem	Possible reason	Solution
• When rotating text there is a space inside the text block before the words themselves	• There is a paragraph indent present	• Rotate text back to normal, highlight and choose 'Paragraph' from [Type] menu — if any indents present make them zero before rotating again
• Cannot select a particular item from group of items	• Too many items over one another for easy selection	• Click away from items and try selection again at '400% size' — if this not successful, click on top item and 'Send to back' until required item in view

Chapter 3

Creating a table of contents

• including items in a table of contents
• creating a table of contents

Introduction to chapter 3

PageMaker has the ability to automatically create a table of contents for your publications. This chapter goes through the process of selecting items for inclusion in a table of contents and creating the table from these selections.

Activity 1

Including items in a table of contents

Objectives

1. To include an item in the table of contents

Introduction

This activity goes through the process of selecting an item for inclusion in the table of contents.

Guided activity

1. **Place the cursor within the heading 'Editorial' on page 1 of your sample document.**

2. **Select the 'Paragraph' option from the [Type] menu.**
   At the bottom of the 'Paragraph specifications' dialogue box is the option to 'Include in table of contents'.

3. If the 'Include in table of contents' option is not active then **click in the box to make it active.**
   You have just selected this paragraph (the headline 'Editorial') for inclusion in the table of contents. The box next to 'Include in table of contents' should now have a cross in it.

4. **Click over 'OK' in the 'Paragraph specifications' dialogue box.**

Independent activity

1. Ensure the other headings in the document are selected for inclusion in the table of contents.

Note

Some style sheets are automatically selected for inclusion in the table of contents (the style 'Headline' for example).

Activity 2

Creating a table of contents

Objectives

1. To create a table of contents

Introduction

Once all the appropriate items have been selected for inclusion in the table of contents the next step is to create it. This activity goes through the process of creating the table of contents.

Guided activity

1. **Move to page 1 of your document.**

2. **Select the 'Create TOC' option from the [Options] menu.**
   The 'Create table of contents' dialogue box appears (figure 2.1).
   At the top of this dialogue box is the 'Title' of the contents page — we will leave this as 'Contents'.
   Since this is the first table of contents you are creating the option to 'Replace existing table of contents' is not available.
   PageMaker can join several documents together to form a larger publication (which it refers to as a 'book'). Since this document is not part of a larger publication the option to 'Include book publications' is also not available.

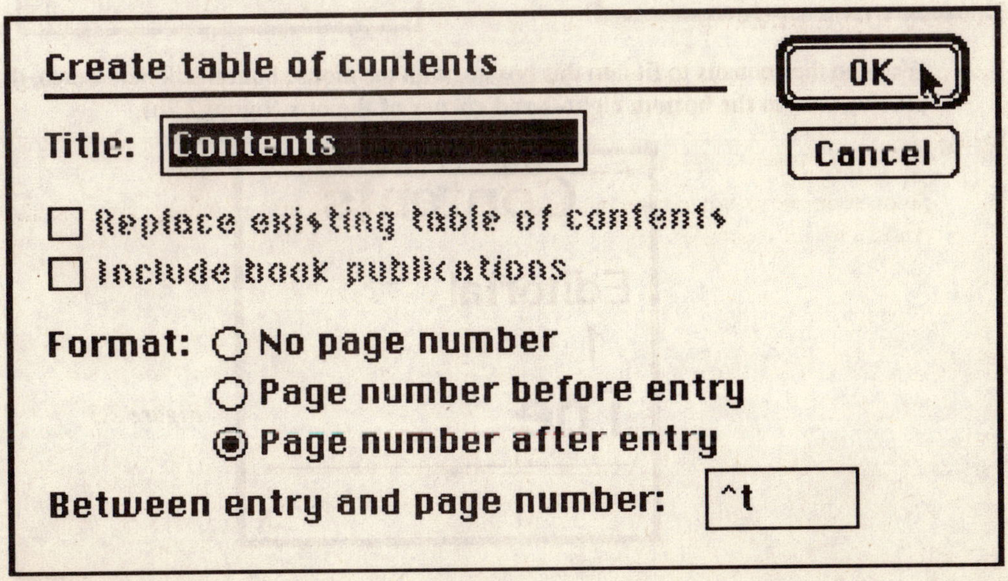

Figure 2.1

3. From the list of 'Formats' available, **ensure the 'Page number after entry' option is active** — this will cause the page numbers to come after the heading in the contents table.

4. The box for 'Between entry and page number' specifies what will come between the entry in the list of contents and the page number. The special code in the box stands for a 'tab space', i.e.
Editorial 1
A complete list of the different codes available should be included in your PageMaker manual.
Leave the 'Between entry and page number' code as '^t'.

5. **Click in the 'OK' box.**
PageMaker pauses for a moment as it goes through your document creating a table of contents. When it has finished your pointer has changed to the text placing icon. PageMaker is now holding your table of contents ready to be placed anywhere in your document.
There is also an additional style in the style palette, 'TOC title'. We will look at this in a moment.

6. **Move the text placing icon to the top left–hand corner of the box at the bottom of the second column and hold down the mouse button** (figure 2.2a).

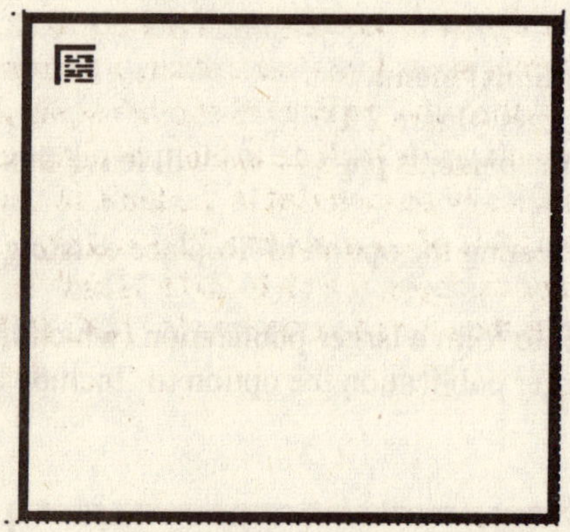

Figure 2.2a

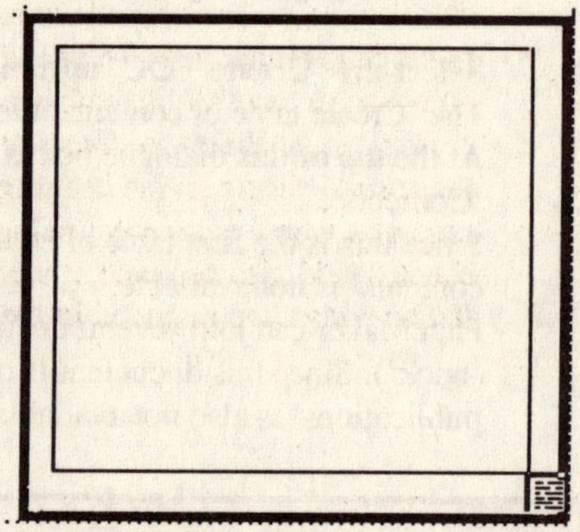

Figure 2.2b

7. We want the contents to fit into this box so, with the mouse button still held down, **drag the text placing icon to the bottom right–hand corner of the box** (figure 2.2b).

Figure 2.3

8. **Release the mouse button here.**
The table of contents should be placed in the box you just specified.
The entries for each heading have the same attributes as the original heading (figure 2.3). In this instance this is not how we want them (not least because they won't fit into the box). Let's change all the entries into the 'Subhead 1' style.

9. **Place the cursor anywhere in the first entry, 'Editorial', and select the style 'Subhead 1'.**
The entry changes to the style 'Subhead 1'.

10. **Repeat the process for the remaining entries.**

11. The entry for 'Mousing around the Desktop' only has the word 'Mousing'. This is because the paragraph we selected for inclusion in the table of contents only contained this word.
Edit this entry so it reads 'Mousing Around the Desktop'.

Note

The sample document you are using has been designed to demonstrate different desk top publishing techniques. The headings are in different sizes, fonts, etc.. In large documents it is common to have all the headings in one style, all the sub–headings in another style, and so on. By creating style sheets for these headings and activating the 'Include in table of contents' option in these style sheets all the headings would automatically be included in the table of contents. In the case of a whole style sheet being included in the table of contents an additional style for that style sheet would also be made at content creation. For example, if a style 'DTP Head' was used for all the headings and included in the table of contents then the additional style 'TOC DTP Head'

End of chapter summary

What I want to do	How I do it
• Include a heading in the table of contents	• Place cursor in heading and select 'Paragraph' from [Type] menu — ensure option to 'Include in table of contents' is active
• Create a table of contents	• Select 'Create TOC' from [Options] menu — place table of contents onto page using text placing icon

Trouble–shooting

Problem	Possible reason	Solution
• Items appear in table of contents that were not knowingly selected	• Using styles automatically included in table of contents	• Check 'Paragraph' specifications for unexpected heading — if 'Include in table of contents' option active then make inactive and try again

Chapter 4

Creating a simple index

• creating an index entry
• creating an index

Introduction to chapter 4

PageMaker has the ability to create an index with varying degrees of complexity for your publications. In this chapter we will look at how to create a simple index for the sample document you have been creating (this is a little artificial since a document of this size and nature is unlikely to include an index in reality). PageMaker does not intuitively know which information we want in an index, we have to specify this. Neither does it know which topics we want. For example, in the sample document we may wish to include a topic called 'Organisations' in our index. This would be used to refer to the organisations mentioned throughout the document so may include the address of 'DTP News' on page 1 and the 'Association of Good Taste' on page 2. Our index entry for this would look like:

O
Organisations 1, 2

The word 'Organisations' is the 'topic' and makes references to pages '1' and '2' of the document.

Activity 1

Creating an index entry

Objectives

1. To create an index entry

Introduction

In this activity we will look at how to add an item to the index we are creating.

Guided activity

1. Using the text tool, **place the cursor somewhere within the address of 'DTP News' included in the second column of the first page.**

2. With the cursor located here, **select the 'Index entry' option from the [Options] menu.** A 'Create index entry' dialogue box appears.

3. The first box under the word 'Topic' is used to hold the topic of the word the cursor is currently placed in.
Type 'Organisations' in the box (figure 1.1).

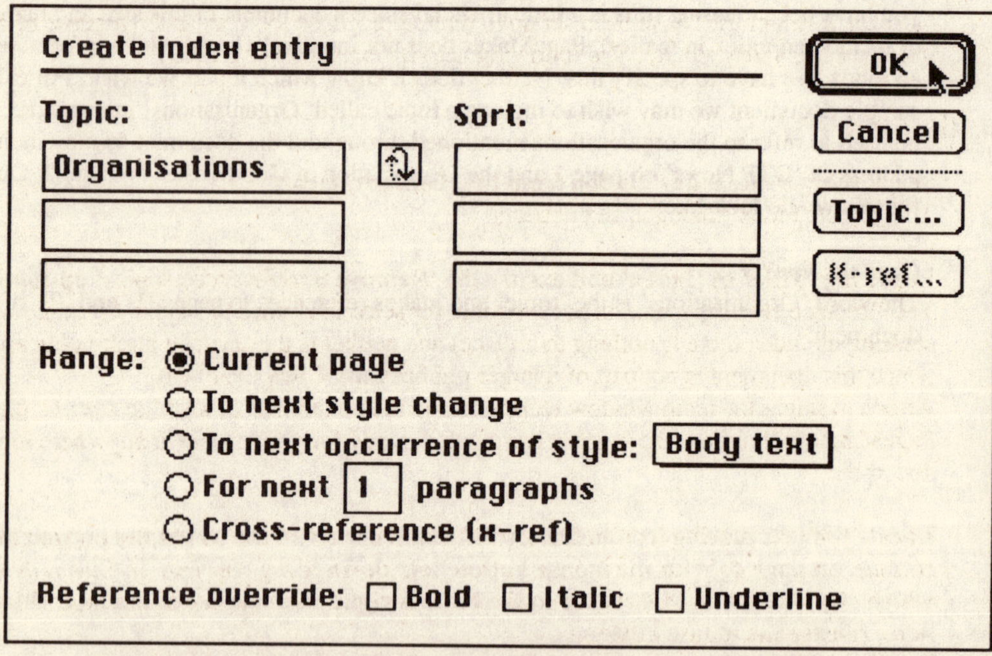

Figure 1.1

4. This particular reference starts and ends on a single page (i.e. it doesn't continue onto page 2). **Ensure the 'Range' is set to 'Current page' then click over 'OK'.**
You have now set up a new topic entitled 'Organisations'. This topic already has one reference - to the page holding the address of 'DTP News'.

5. **Move to page 2 and place the cursor within the words 'Association of Good Taste' in the last paragraph of the story.**

6. **Select the 'Index entry' option again and type in the topic 'Organisations' as before. Ensure the 'Range' is set to 'Current page' then click over 'OK'.**
The topic 'Organisations' now has two references - page 1 and page 2.

Independent activity

1. Go through the sample document and add index entries for the word 'cursor' in the first paragraph of the story on page 3 (use the topic name 'Cursor keys' for this entry) and the word 'developments' in the editorial on page 1 (under the topic 'Developments').

Activity 2

Creating an index

Objectives

1. To create an index for the specified index entries

Introduction

Now the index entries have been set up in their appropriate topic areas the process of creating the index itself is fairly simple. The following activity explains this process.

Guided activity

1. **Select the 'Create index' option from the [Options] menu.**
The 'Create index' dialogue box appears.

2. **Leave the 'Title' as 'Index' and ensure the 'Remove unreferenced topics' option is active.**
The 'Replace existing index' is not available for selection (since this is the first time we are creating an index there is nothing to replace) and neither is the 'Include book publications' option (since this document is not part of a larger publication). **Click over 'OK'.**
After a moment the main window reappears and the pointer has changed to the text placing icon. PageMaker is 'holding' the index it has created, ready for you to place it anywhere in your document.

3. **Locate the text placing icon in the top left-hand corner of the box at the bottom of the second column on page 4. With the mouse button held down 'drag' the icon so that it draws a box which stretches from this corner to the bottom right-hand corner of the box. With the icon here, release the mouse button.**
The 'index' PageMaker has created fills as much of this box as it can.
There are also some additional entries in the Style palette, 'Index level 1', 'Index section' and 'Index title'. These refer to the styles assigned to the topics, the letters denoting each section, and the title of the index respectively. They can be used in the same way as the 'TOC' styles.

End of chapter summary

What I want to do	How I do it
• Add an index entry	• Place cursor in area to index and select 'Index entry' from the [Options] menu
• Create an index	• Select 'Create index' from the [Options] menu — place index using text placing icon

Trouble–shooting

Index creation can become a complicated process depending on what type of index you are creating — it is suggested that you consult your PageMaker manuals if specific problems arise with index creation.

Additional Exercises

- booklet for talk on desk top publishing

Project

Booklet for Talk on Desk Top Publishing

Page 1

Desk Top Publishing and 'The Person in the Street'

A talk by Professor C Package

Pages 2 & 3

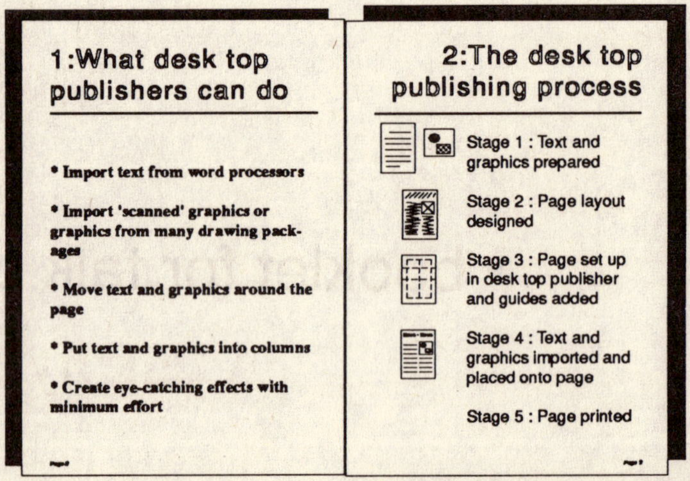
1:What desk top publishers can do

- Import text from word processors
- Import 'scanned' graphics or graphics from many drawing packages
- Move text and graphics around the page
- Put text and graphics into columns
- Create eye-catching effects with minimum effort

2:The desk top publishing process

Stage 1 : Text and graphics prepared

Stage 2 : Page layout designed

Stage 3 : Page set up in desk top publisher and guides added

Stage 4 : Text and graphics imported and placed onto page

Stage 5 : Page printed

Page 4

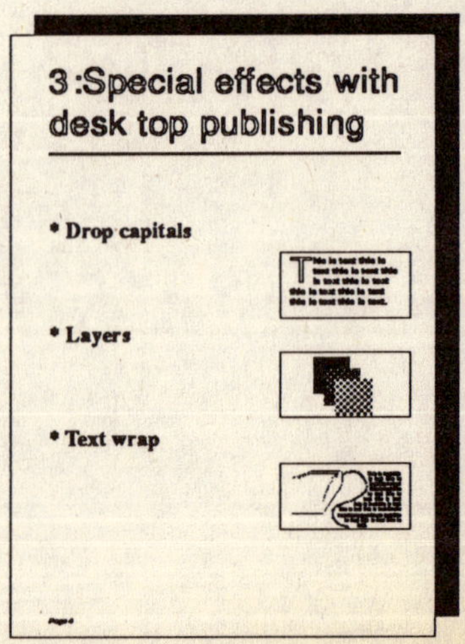
3:Special effects with desk top publishing

- Drop capitals
- Layers
- Text wrap

Page 1

Desk Top Publishing and 'The Person in the Street'

A talk by Professor C Package

Guides

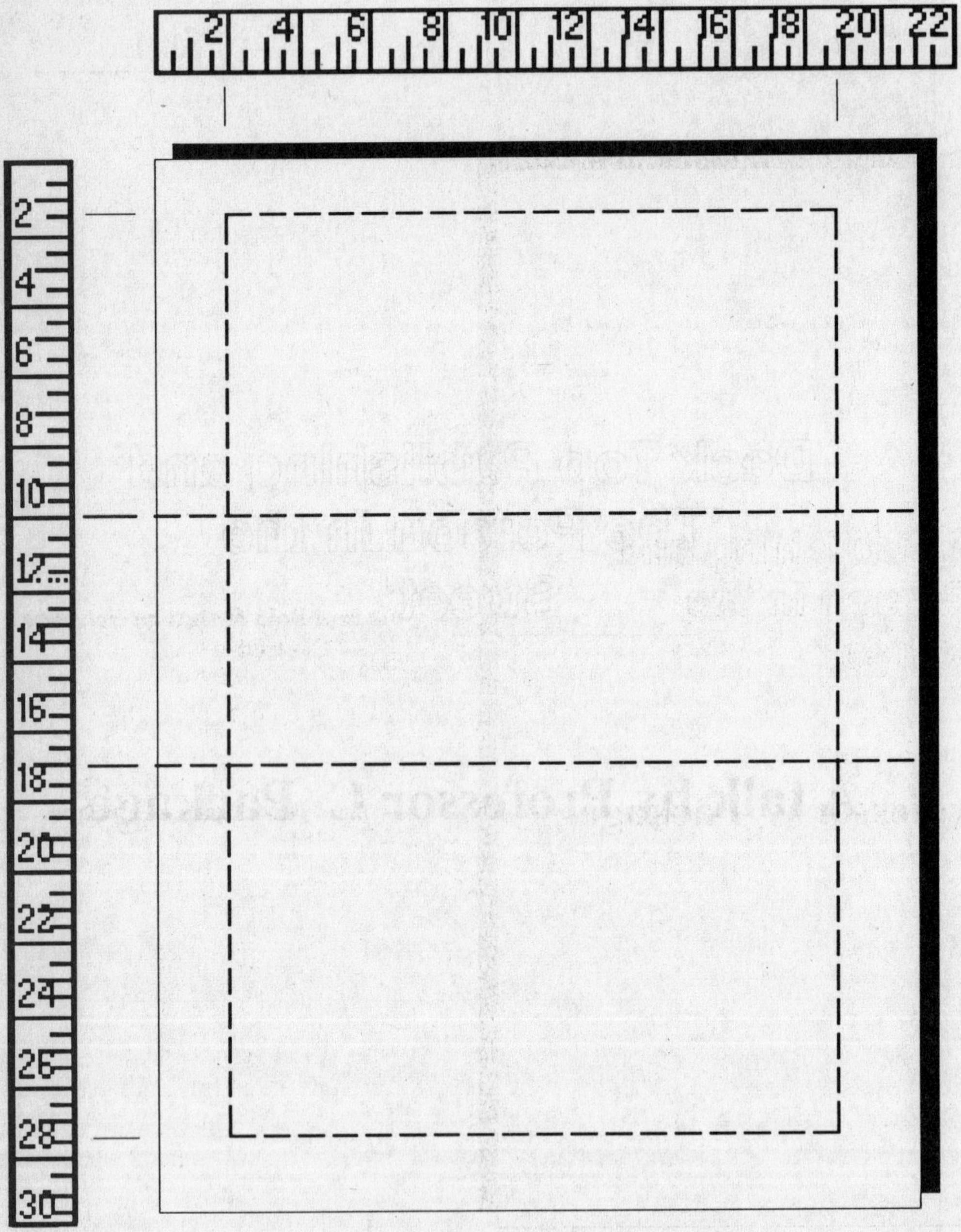

Elements

Desk Top Publishing and 'The Person in the Street'

36pt Bold & Outline Helvetica — Centred

A talk by Professor C Package

36pt Bold Times — Centred

Page 2

1:What desk top publishers can do

*** Import text from word processors**

*** Import 'scanned' graphics or graphics from many drawing packages**

*** Move text and graphics around the page**

*** Put text and graphics into columns**

*** Create eye-catching effects with minimum effort**

Page 2

Guides

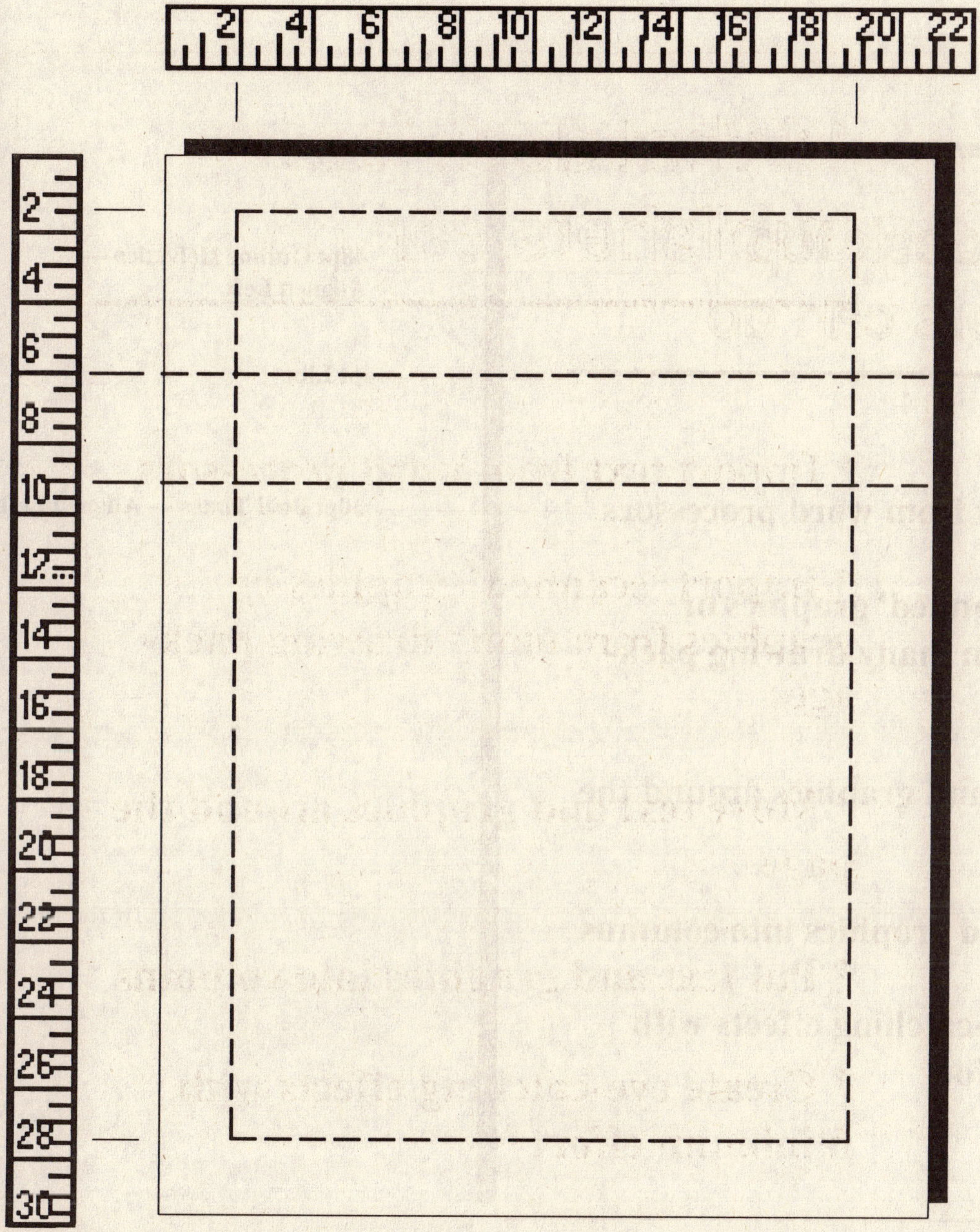

Elements

1:What desk top publishers can do

48pt Outline Helvetica — Aligned Left

4pt Line

* Import text from word processors

30pt Bold Times — Aligned Left

* Import 'scanned' graphics or graphics from many drawing packages

* Move text and graphics around the page

* Put text and graphics into columns

* Create eye-catching effects with minimum effort

Page 2

Page 3

2:The desk top publishing process

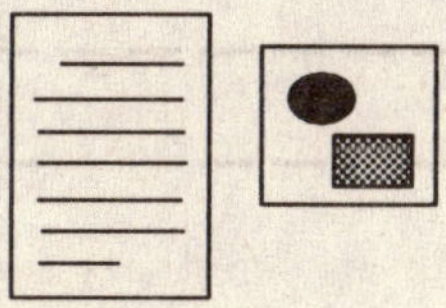

Stage 1 : Text and graphics prepared

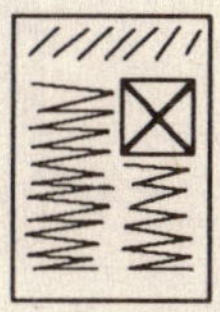

Stage 2 : Page layout designed

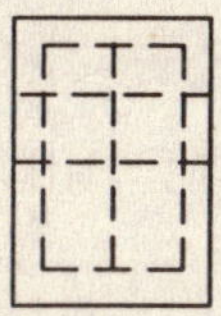

Stage 3 : Page set up in desk top publisher and guides added

Stage 4 : Text and graphics imported and placed onto page

Stage 5 : Page printed

Page 3

Guides

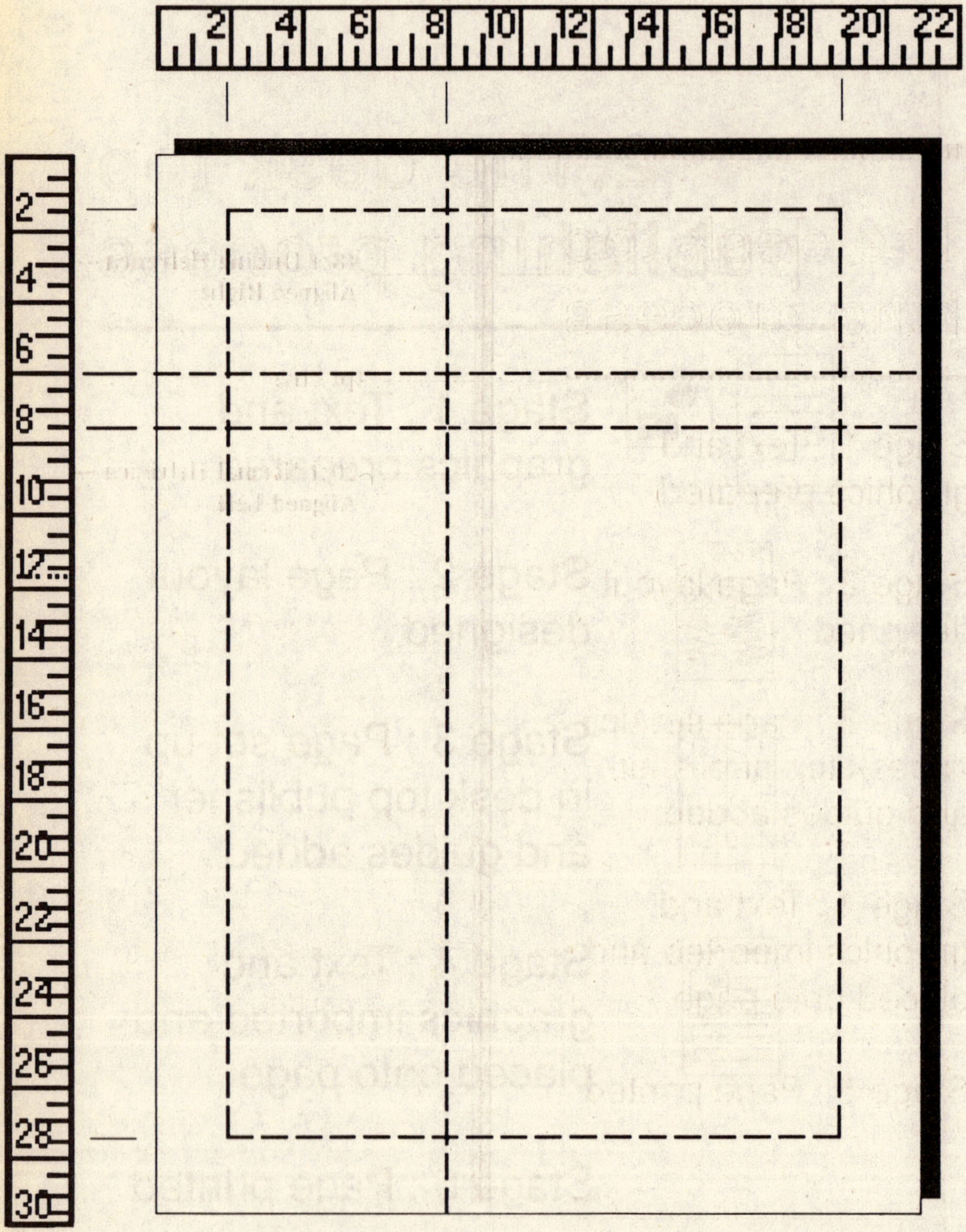

Elements

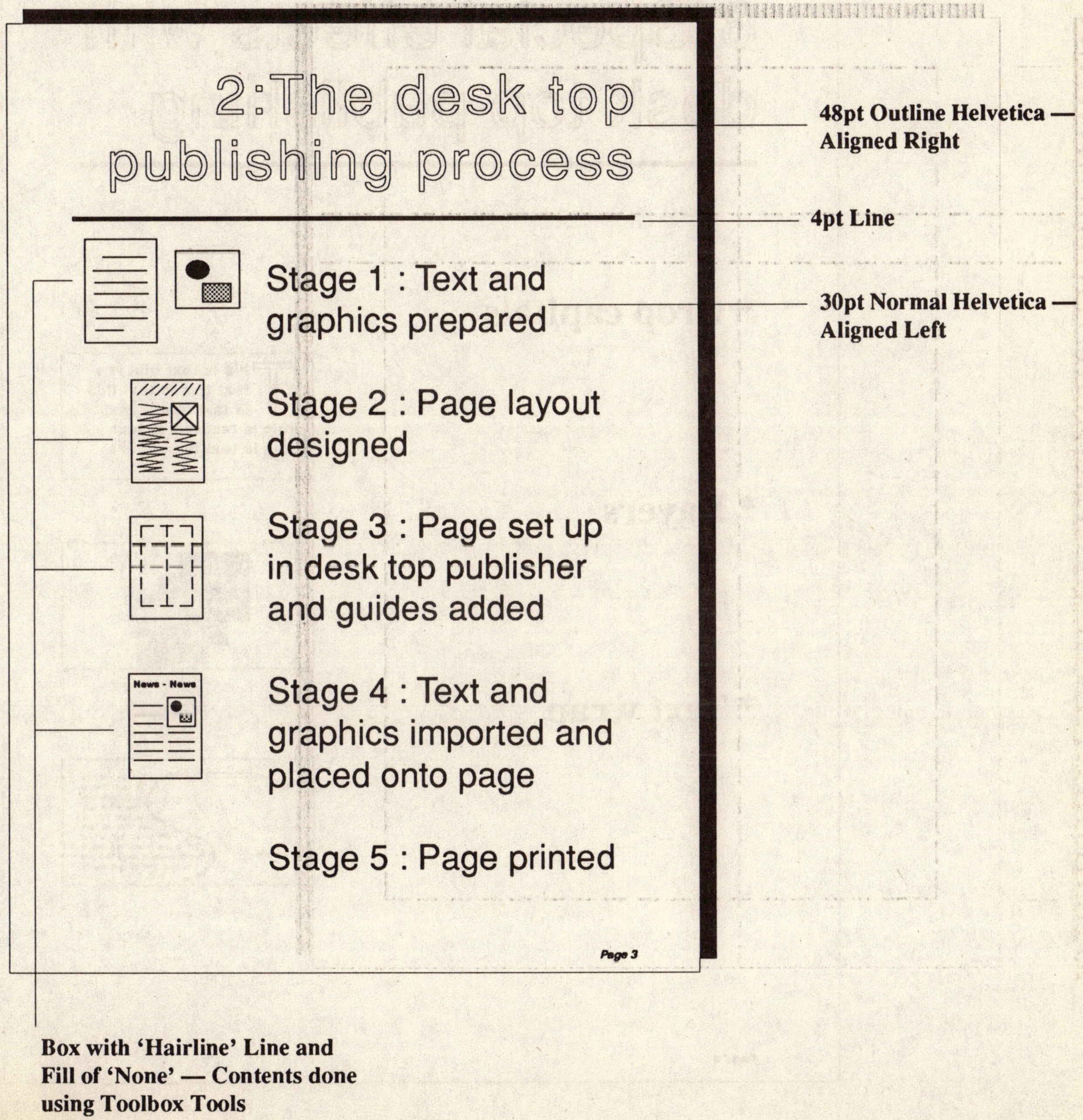
2:The desk top publishing process
Stage 1 : Text and graphics prepared
Stage 2 : Page layout designed
Stage 3 : Page set up in desk top publisher and guides added
Stage 4 : Text and graphics imported and placed onto page
Stage 5 : Page printed
Page 3
48pt Outline Helvetica — Aligned Right
4pt Line
30pt Normal Helvetica — Aligned Left
Box with 'Hairline' Line and Fill of 'None' — Contents done using Toolbox Tools

Page 4

3 :Special effects with desk top publishing

*** Drop capitals**

This is text this is text this is text this is text this is text this is text this is text this is text.

*** Layers**

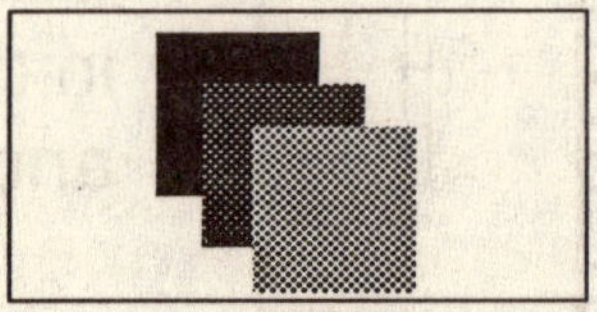

*** Text wrap**

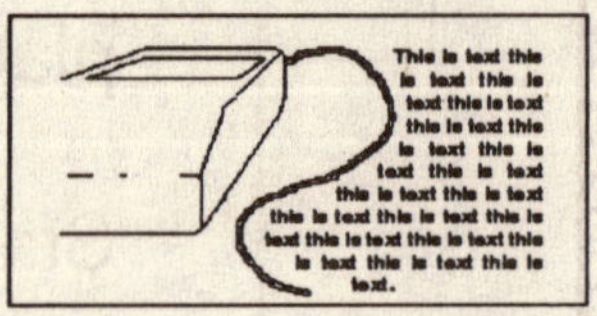

Page 4

Guides

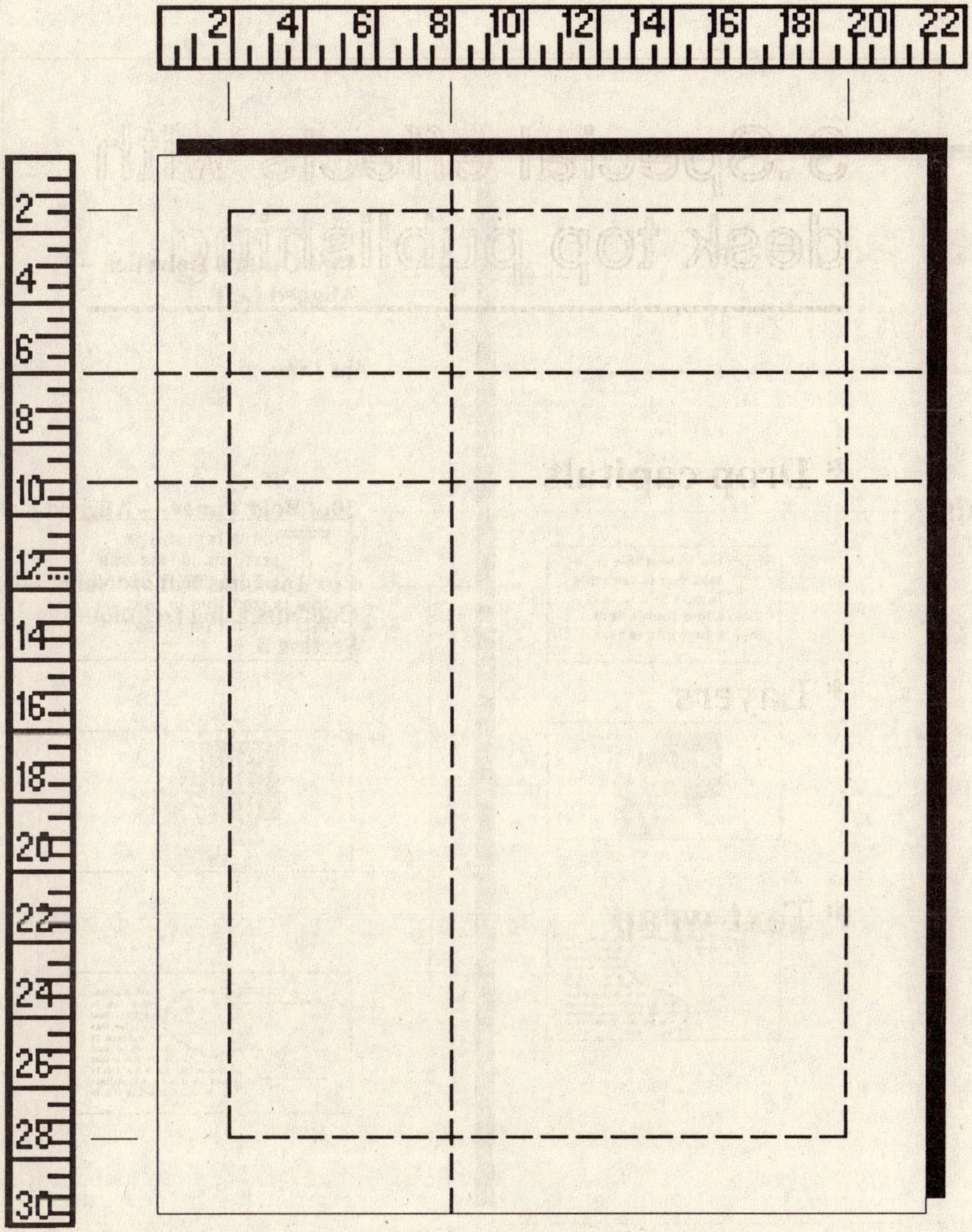

Elements

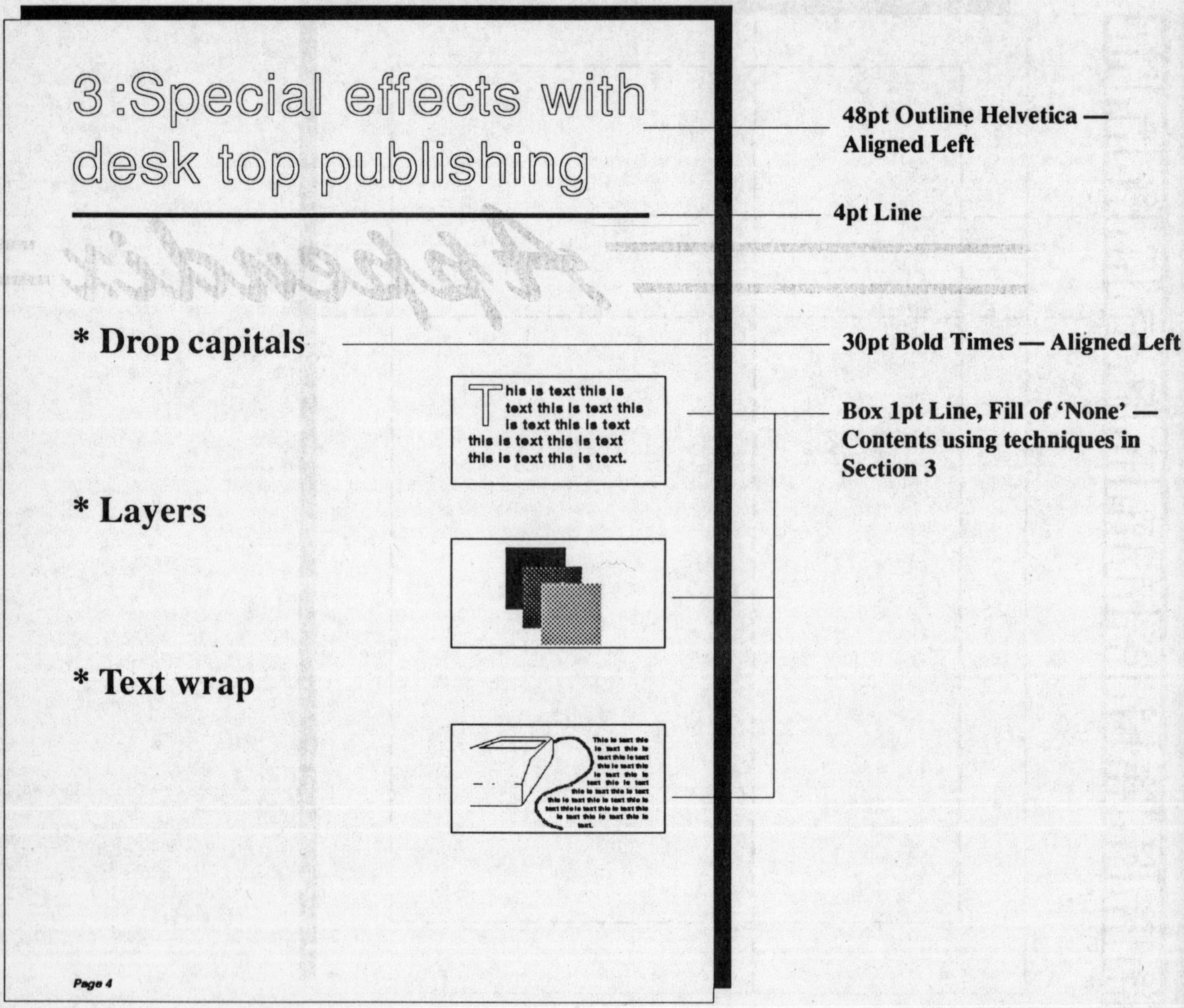
3 :Special effects with desk top publishing
* Drop capitals
This is text this is text this is text this is text this is text this is text this is text this is text.
* Layers
* Text wrap
Page 4
48pt Outline Helvetica — Aligned Left
4pt Line
30pt Bold Times — Aligned Left
Box 1pt Line, Fill of 'None' — Contents using techniques in Section 3

Appendix

Appendix 1a

Appendix 1b

Editorial

Welcome to issue one of D.T.P. News. We hope you enjoy it. It has taken many hours to produce and given many of us who produced this first issue a great deal of worry and pleasure!

D.T.P. News had its beginnings in a pub in Sheffield where I and a few of my friends were chatting about the changing state of the written word - or to be more precise, how it is no longer written but typed! We were all vaguely aware of the developments in the last few years and of how desk top publishing had revolutionised the document production process. Or so we thought. One of the more informed members of our little group started talking about how she had bought a desk top publishing package last year and it had totally 'changed the way she ran her business'.

As well as helping to maintain a regular and up-to-date catalogue for prospective customers, the desk top publisher also proved useful in other areas. When she needed adverts done to advertise products locally, or when she decided having business cards to distribute would be useful, the desk top publisher helped out again. All in all my friend expressed her wonderment at how she had ever managed without one.

As the year went on our own interest grew and we soon discovered that the once alien and expensive world of publishing is coming into the reach of more and more people every day. We decided that it would be good to have some sort of newsletter to act as a focus for our and your discoveries about this new and exciting area - and this is it!

We hope you enjoy reading it. Please write in with articles, suggestions or any praise or criticism you may have. We look forward to hearing from you. Happy desk top publishing!

Appendix 1c

It cannot be denied. Desk top publishing has revolutionised the document production process. As time goes on and computer package manufacturers seek to compete with the ever demanding market, the distinction between a word processor and a desk top publisher seems more and more uncertain.

Already there are word processors available which offer you the option of working in more than one column. Some even allow you to import graphics to fit between your text. The increasing availability of powerful computers and high quality printers has made this technology accessible to large numbers of people who would never even have heard of such things five years ago.

This is good of course, or is it? Nowadays, almost all the paper documents I receive are at least word processed and often desk top published. I look at some and are immediately 'turned off' reading them. They may be typed neatly and the words themselves may be clear but I think it must be a common belief that desk top publishing a document means sticking the text in and laser printing it all. The result is often a terrible mess that is less than comfortable to read.

Perhaps I have become a desk top publishing snob. Perhaps it is just that, with the availability of desk top publishers and word processors, my own expectations of how a document should look have increased.

If you were going to build a book case you wouldn't just jump into a pile of wood with some nails and a hammer and expect good results. The bookcase would need to be designed thought going what its size should be, what it will contain, what sort of wood to use, etc.. It is no different when producing a desk top published document. Like the hammer, desk top publishers are merely a tool, a very powerful tool, but a tool none the less. You would not expect the hammer to design the book case for you, neither should you expect desk top publishers to remove the need for document design.

Desk top publishing a document is the final stage of producing a document. It seems many people have forgotten or, more likely, were never told this. I don't know about you, but a page full of shadowed, underlined text, covered in many varied shaded boxes, is not my idea of something good to read over breakfast.

Just like having a driving licence perhaps there should be an 'Association of Good Taste' law which states you are not allowed behind the keyboard of a desk top publisher without a designing licence. Petty? Maybe. But don't blame me in 2010 when the billboards are all written in reversed, outlined, rotated text - just because it couldn't be done in 2019!

Appendix 1d

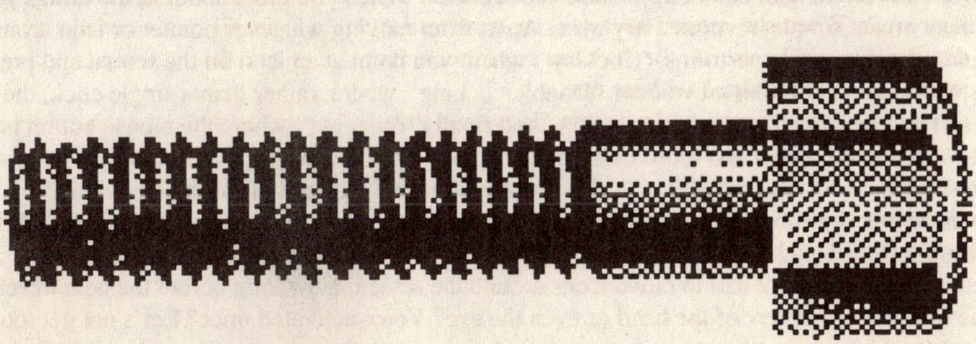

Appendix 1e

Appendix 1f

he age of the cursor keys is dead or so it must seem to the by now numerous amounts of people who have dumped these once so powerful keys for a mouse. Love them or hate them, you can't escape them. Mice are everywhere. Not only that, they are now available in almost every size, shape and colour as well. Need something to brighten up your office or work room? A psychedelic mouse is, perhaps, the latest in modern accessories for the avid computer user. Yes, the mouse invasion is upon us threatening even the diehard cursor key users whose numbers dwindle by the day.

The first time you pick up a mouse you can be excused for thinking 'so what do I do with this?' After hours of confusion over which button to press (some have three) and the moments where the mouse is left balancing precariously over the edge of the table as you try to move the arrow or cursor 'just that little bit further' you may even feel like giving up. Fortunately, chances are you soon realise you can pick the mouse up and place it in a less dangerous place than the tables edge without effecting the position of the numerous icons on the screen. After a while you become a fully fledged 'point and press' merchant and wonder how you ever managed without one. The cursor keys you once held in such admiration are scowled upon as old fashioned and tedious and you are truly engulfed in the 'mouse culture' prevalent throughout the country.

It cannot be denied. Mice have speeded up the working of many of the computer packages on the market today not least desk top publishing. Most mouse users would not attempt to deny that the physical action of moving a mouse is much preferred to endless pressing of cursor keys and control codes. When you think about it, the things you can do with a mouse are really quite simple revolutionary even. Apart from moving whatever pointer or icon around the screen there are three main actions a mouse performs. 'Clicking' where you point at an icon on the screen and press and release the mouse button in one smooth movement. 'Double clicking' where, rather than a single click, the mouse button is pressed and released twice in quick succession. And finally 'dragging' where the mouse button is held down to 'drag' some item around the screen and drop it elsewhere. Simple maybe but you try using an application like 'Windows' or 'PageMaker' with the cursor keys and the mouses (mices?) power will soon be obvious.

So, with mouse in hand and confident at your ability to point and click at anything in sight you can stroll boldly through the countless mouse controlled packages on the market. But wait a minute does it end here? Already there are mouse like devices which use a large control ball to move icons around the screen. How long before the next development. Mice that obey the slightest movement of the hand or even the eye? Voice activated mice? Let's not get too comfortable things may have only just become to change.

Appendix 1g

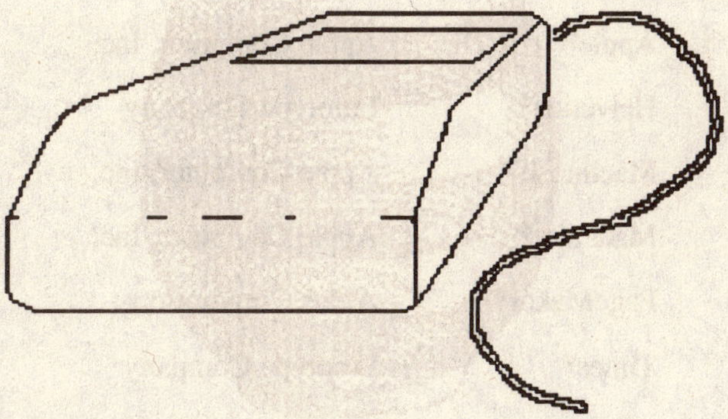

Appendix 1h

Appendix 2 — Trademarks

Apple®	Apple Computer, Inc.
Helvetica®	Linotype Company
Macintosh®	Apple Computer, Inc.
MacPaint®	Apple Computer, Inc.
PageMaker®	Aldus Corporation
Times®	Linotype Company

Spelling = Click (using text tool) where sp. check sd start.
From Edit, select spelling = replace, add, ignore options
Select 'All stories' for whole text.
NB Prompts are given

Index

A

Abandoning documents 49
'Actual size' option 35
Adding boxes 64–65
Adding graphics 99–102
Adding lines 62
Adding styles 139–142
Adding to table of contents 166
Additional guides 17–19, 89–90
'Align centre' option 57
'Alignment' option 57
ASCII import filter 33
'Autoflow' option 32

B

Body text 138, 143
'Bold' option 53
Box drawing tool 95
'Bring to front' option 159

C

Centring text 56–57
Changing boxes 65–66
Changing styles 142–143
Changing text 45–48, 58–59, 108–110
Clip art 98
'Close' option 49
'Close story' option 29
Colour palette 15
Column guides 150–152
'Column guides' option 16–17, 88
'Copy' option 91, 161
Create index dialogue box 173
'Create index entry dialogue box 172
'Create index' option 173
'Create TOC' option 167
Creating an index 173
Cropping graphics 99–102
Cropping tool 100
Cursor 12, 46
'Cut' option 37
Cutting text blocks 37

D

'Define styles' option 140, 142, 143
Discarding a story 29
Double–sided pages 12, 84
Drawing packages 98
Drop capitals 152–163

E

'Edit story' option 29
Edit styles dialogue box 140
Entering text 27, 52–53
'Exit' option 22
'Export' option 29

F

Facing pages 12, 84
'Fill' option 64, 95, 158
First indent 121
'Fit in window' option 35
Flowing text 38–40
'Font' option 109
Footers 91–93

G

Graphic placing icon 100
Greeked text 34
'Guides' option 14

H

Handles 34
Headers 91–93
Hiding master page items 95
Hyphenation dialogue box 122–123, 141
'Hyphenation' option 123

I

Importing graphics 98
Importing text 28, 33
Indents 120
Indents / tabs dialogue box 121–122, 141
Index entries 172–173
'Index entry' option 172

Inside margins 84
'Italic' option 119

J

'Justify' option 118

L

Layers 158–163
Leading 110–111
'Leading' option 111
Leaving PageMaker 22
'Line' option 64, 95
Line spacing 110–111
'LM' marker 94
'Lock guides' option 19, 41

M

MacPaint 98
Master pages 87–88
Measurement system 18
Menus 6–8
Moving column guides 150–152
Moving graphics 103–105
Moving guides 41
Moving lines 63–64
Moving text blocks 42, 54–56
Multiple–items 160–163
Multiple-page documents 84

N

'New' option 11
'None' option 64, 95
Number of columns 16
Number of pages 12

O

Obtaining graphics 98
'Open' option 23, 24
Opening documents 23–24, 24–25
Orientation 12
'Other' option 52, 113
Outside margins 84
Overlapping items 158–163

P

Page dimensions 11
Page grids 87, 90
Page icons 88
Page numbers 93–94
Page setup dialogue box 6, 11, 84
Page size 7, 11
Page views 35–36
Paintbrush 98
'Paper' option 95
'Paragraph' option 120, 166
Paragraph specifications dialogue box 120–121, 141
'Paste' option 91, 161
'PB' marker 93
Picas 84
Place dialogue box 32
'Place' option 32, 100
Pre–prepared graphics 98
Pre-defined styles 138–139
Preferences dialogue box 18, 84
'Print' option 67
Printing documents 66–67

Q

'Quit' option 22

R

Reading tags 33
Recompose publication 11
Removing guides 92
Removing styles 143
Removing text blocks 37
Repeating guides 87–88
'RM' marker 94
Rotating text 148–150
Ruler indicator 18
'Rulers' option 17

S

'Save as' option 20, 21
Save publication dialogue box 20
Saving a document 19–20, 21–22
Scaling graphics 103–105
Scanners 98
Scroll bars 14, 35
Scroll box 35
'Select all' option 46
Selected text blocks 34
Selecting multiple–items 160–163

'Send to back' option 158
'Set width' option 112
Shortcuts 49
'Size' option 47, 52
Smart quotes 67
'Snap to guides' option 19, 33
Space between columns 16
Special effects 113–115
Square corner box tool 64
Standoff 155
Start page number 12
Stories 39
Story editor 28–29
Stretching lines 63–64
Style palette 15, 138
Style sheets 137, 166

T

Tags 144
Target printer 11
Text block length 43
Text blocks 31, 54, 108–110
'Text rotation' option 149
Text tool 12, 46, 52
Text wrap 155–163
'Text wrap' option 155
Toolbox 14, 46
'Track' option 112
Tracking 111–113
Type specifications dialogue box 118–120, 141
'Type specs' option 119
'Type style' option 53

V

Vertical ruler 18

W

Width of text 111–113, 113–115
Word processors 28

Z

'Zero lock' option 89
Zero mark setter 90
Zero marker 90